W9-CSW-769

open water diver
MANUAL
ENGLISH

PADI
padi.com

Student Diver

Address

City, State/Province

Telephone

Instructor   Date

PADI Open Water Diver Manual

© PADI 2016

No part of this product may be reproduced, sold or distributed in any form without the written permission of the publisher.
® indicates a trademark is registered in the U.S. and certain other countries.

Published by PADI
30151 Tomas
Rancho Santa Margarita, CA 92688-2125 USA

ISBN 978-1-878663-16-0

Printed in Canada

Product No. 79180 (Rev. 04/17) Version 3.02

introduction

section one

introdu

ction

By the end of this section, I should be able to answer these questions:

1. What does certification in this course mean? Why is training important in scuba diving?

2. What are the three basic parts of the PADI Open Water Diver course? What is the purpose of each part?

3. What general schedule will my instructor follow in conducting my PADI Open Water Diver course?

4. What are the requirements for taking the course and for earning my certification?

The PADI Open Water Diver Course

Your first time on scuba feels amazing. For most divers, that first breath underwater is unforgettable, opening the door to a different world. What you will feel and see are unique; there is no experience like diving.

Only you can say why scuba interests you. Looking for adventure? Diving is one of the world's most adventurous activities. Love nature? No other environment approaches the abundance and diversity of a pristine coral reef, or the intriguing life in a lake or flooded quarry. Does discovery drive you? Even at frequently visited dive sites you'll see things most people never see and go where most people never go.

Scuba delivers adrenaline and intensity, or serenity and peace. You can take on rewarding challenges that require training, planning, equipment and focus, or you can drift relaxed through some of the world's most tranquil and beautiful settings. There's always something new to see, somewhere new to explore and some new way to enjoy it. You can't outgrow diving.

Training and Certification as a PADI Open Water Diver

During the PADI Open Water Diver course, you'll learn what you need to know to explore the underwater world using scuba. Most people find it a rewarding challenge that's not overly difficult. Training is important because:

- It enables diving to be rewarding and meaningful, so you can get out of it what you want.

- There are potential hazards to avoid, reduce and/or manage.

- Like any adventure sport, diving has risks that you must accept.

Certification shows that you met the course requirements. Dive centers and resorts require proof of certification before they will rent scuba equipment or fill scuba cylinders. As a PADI Open Water Diver, you will be trained to a maximum depth of 18 metres/60 feet (or the actual depth you reached,

5. What do "performance-based learning" and "student-centered learning" mean? How do they relate to taking PADI courses?

6. How can I learn most effectively during Knowledge Development and the Confined Water and Open Water Dives? How does getting my PADI Dive Center or Resort to help me with my equipment help me learn to dive and enjoy diving better?

7. What are 11 reasons to dive?

8. What are five things I can do before the end of the course to help me continue to enjoy and be involved with diving after certification?

9. Why should I seek an orientation, supervision and/or additional training when diving in a new dive environment?

if shallower). You'll also be qualified to dive in conditions as good as, or better than, those in which you trained, within the no stop limits of your dive computer or tables (you'll learn about these limits in Sections Four and Five). As a PADI Scuba Diver, you may dive under PADI Instructor or PADI Divemaster supervision as deep as 12 metres/40 feet.

Course Overview

The PADI Open Water Diver course has three parts: Knowledge Development, Confined Water Dives and Open Water Dives.

Knowledge Development covers the principles, concepts and terms that you need to know for safety and so you can enjoy diving. Short exercises, quizzes and knowledge reviews help you assess and confirm learning as you go.

During the Confined Water Dives, you learn and practice scuba skills in a pool or water with pool-like conditions under direct instructor supervision. You also practice applying what you learn in Knowledge Development. You'll enjoy making one or more *minidives*, which take you through the same steps you follow when you make Open Water Dives.

You make Open Water Dives with your instructor at sites suited to beginning divers. You practice, apply and demonstrate what you learn in Knowledge Development and the Confined Water Dives.

The five Knowledge Development sections correspond with the five Confined Water Dives. You complete four Open Water Dives

PADI OPEN WATER DIVER AND SCUBA DIVER CERTIFICATION

The PADI Open Water Diver certification is the world's most popular and recognized scuba credential. It is a full, entry level certification you earn by successfully completing the entire course. It qualifies you to:

- Dive without instructor supervisions while applying the knowledge and skills you learn in this course, within the limits of your training and experience.
- Obtain air fills, scuba equipment and other dive services.
- Plan, conduct and log open water dives when equipped properly and accompanied by a buddy in conditions in which you have training and/ or experience.
- Continue your diver training in the PADI Advanced Open Water Diver course, and/or in PADI Specialty courses.

You can earn the PADI Scuba Diver certification by completing only a portion of the Open Water Diver course (Knowledge Development Sections 1-3, Confined Water Dives 1-3, and Open Water Dives 1-2). It qualifies you to:

- Dive under the inwater supervision of a PADI Instructor or PADI Divemaster within the limits of your training and experience.
- Obtain air fills, scuba equipment and other services for use while diving under supervision.
- Plan, conduct and log open water dives with assistance when equipped properly and accompanied in the water by a certified professional in conditions in which you have training and/or experience.

Download the PADI App (iOS or Android) for access to your dive log, your PADI credentials in the form of eCards, and other benefits.

ABOUT PADI AND YOUR PADI INSTRUCTOR, DIVE CENTER OR RESORT

PADI is the Professional Association of Diving Instructors, the world's largest diver training organization. PADI Worldwide establishes training programs, materials and standards, monitors their quality, certifies instructors, and provides support services for PADI Members.

Your PADI Instructor is a professional who is qualified to conduct PADI training. To reach this leadership position, your instructor has successfully completed a series of required courses, including the comprehensive Instructor Development Course, followed by independent tests in the two-day Instructor Examination. PADI Dive Centers and Resorts are professional operations dedicated to meeting your diving needs. Visit your dive operation online and in person for help choosing and servicing gear, dive travel and staying plugged into the diving lifestyle.

The worldwide PADI Regional Headquarters (Offices) constantly monitor for individuals misrepresenting themselves as authorized to teach PADI courses. You can verify that the individual conducting your program is an authorized PADI Instructor.

When you take your PADI Open Water Diver course through an authorized PADI Dive Center or Resort (see the Dive Shop Locator at padi.com), it's highly likely your instructor is an authorized PADI Instructor. But, if you doubt it for some reason, ask to see your instructor's certification card. Check the photo and note the instructor number. For further verification, you may call your local PADI Regional Headquarters, or you can verify that the individual is authorized to conduct the PADI program you're taking with Pro Chek at padi.com. You can also find consumer alerts there.

If at any time you have questions about the instructor conducting your program, please contact the local PADI Regional Headquarters using the information at padi.com.

PADI'S FOUR E PHILOSOPHY

Equipment, Education, Experience, Environment

The diving lifestyle requires four elements: equipment, education, experience and environment – the "Four Es."

You need **equipment,** because diving is a technical activity. You need **education** (PADI training) to learn to dive and to progress into the underwater activities that interest you. Diving is an **experience,** so you need opportunities for local diving and dive travel. Without a healthy aquatic **environment,** the underwater world loses much of its interest and appeal.

Your local PADI Dive Center or Resort keeps you plugged into the Four Es. The professionals there bring equipment, education, experience and environment under one roof. As life and travels take you from one place to the next, use the Dive Shop Locator on padi.com to connect to PADI Dive Center or Resorts around the globe. Those are the best places to get all your diving needs.

WATCH FOR THIS SYMBOL

As you read the Open Water Diver Manual, you'll notice this symbol. It alerts you to important safety information. Pay close attention when you see this symbol and consult your instructor if you do not understand the material.

(two for PADI Scuba Divers) over at least two days (one for PADI Scuba Divers). Your instructor has scheduling flexibility that still accommodates an appropriate instructional sequence.

Course Requirements

To scuba dive, you need a mature attitude, good judgment and the self-discipline to follow the guidelines and principles required for safe diving. There are also some minimum age, swimming skill and fitness requirements.

Age

Prior to the start of the course, you must be at least 10 years old. Local regulations may specify a higher minimum age. Note that 10-14 years olds earn a PADI Junior Diver certification that carries a few restrictions. After certification, 10-11 years old must dive with a parent/guardian or PADI Professional to a maximum depth of 12 metres/40 feet, and 12-14 year olds must dive with an adult certified diver.

Basic Swimming Skills

To be a scuba diver, you need adequate swimming skills. Prior to your second open water dive, you will demonstrate that you can float or tread water without aids for 10 minutes, and prior to certification, that you can swim 200 metres/yards with no aids, or 300 metres/yards with mask, fins and snorkel.

Medical Fitness

You don't need to be an athlete to dive, but you do need good physical health. A few medical conditions can be hazardous while diving. Also, like any active recreation, diving can be physically demanding, so individuals who may be predisposed to heart attack or cardiovascular disease need to exercise caution. As a prudent precaution, before any inwater training, you'll complete a Medical Statement that screens for conditions that a physician should evaluate. For your safety, answer *all* questions *honestly* and *completely*.

- If you answer "yes" to any condition, a physician must approve you for diving by completing and signing the statement prior to any inwater training.

During the Confined Water Dives, you learn and practice scuba skills in a pool or water with pool-like conditions under direct instructor supervision.

You make open water dives at sites suited to beginning divers. You practice, apply and demonstrate what you learn in Knowledge Development and Confined Water Dives.

The Medical Statement screens for conditions that should be evaluated by a physician. For your safety, answer *all* questions *honestly* and *completely*.

- In some areas, local law requires a medical exam and a physician's signature in *all* cases.

- If you don't yet have a medical form, you can download it from padi.com.

Getting the Most Out of the PADI Open Water Diver Course

The PADI Open Water Diver course is designed to be an enjoyable, rewarding learning experience. Understanding how to prepare for each session and how to approach your dives helps you get the most out of it.

Performance-Based and Student-Centered Learning

PADI courses apply *performance-based learning,* which means you progress and attain certification by demonstrating that you meet specific learning objectives. *Student-centered learning* means that the course, materials and your instructor address how you learn most effectively.

You pay for the training, but you earn the certification. Meeting these objectives is what's important – not how long it takes. It only matters that you can perform your

As the world's largest diver training organization, PADI Professionals are the most culturally and ethnically diverse recreational dive professionals in the entire dive community. At this writing, more than 136,000 PADI Instructors, Assistant Instructors and Divemasters teach diving and offer dive services in more than 183 countries and territories. You can find PADI diver materials in more than 24 languages.

Today, virtually anyone can find a PADI Instructor nearby who speaks the same language. The PADI organization also reaches all corners of the world with two of diving's most popular websites, padi.com and ScubaEarth®.

Globally, more than **20 million** PADI certifications have been issued. Wherever you go diving, you can be confident that the local dive community will recognize your diver credentials – even if "PADI" is the only word you can speak in the local language.

scuba skills correctly and reliably – that's performance-based learning. It does not matter whether it takes one try or 10 to master each. You must meet certification requirements, but your instructor realizes that how you learn may differ from how others learn. So, the course pace matches what you need to become a capable and confident diver – that's student-centered learning.

If you approach learning as discussed here, you'll learn better, faster and enjoy the process more.

Knowledge Development

1. **Flip through what you're going to read.** Scan the manual quickly, generally noting headings, topics, pictures and so on. Focus on what you're going to read immediately (like a section) more thoroughly.

   Why it's important: You learn best by linking new information with existing mental "structures." Reviewing ahead helps establish these mental "structures" giving your brain new places to "attach" what you're learning.

2. **Read the learning objectives for each subsection, then read the subsection.** Look for the answers to each question; when you find an answer, highlight it or note it on a pad.

   Why it's important: Knowing what you need to learn makes your reading active instead of passive. This focuses you, because you're seeking the information you need. Actually writing speeds learning more than simply noting mentally, because you immediately engage with the information. It also helps you review more quickly later.

3. **Answer the exercise questions at the end of each subsection.** These are not tests, and the answers are right there. They're simple and quick. Actually mark the answer (multiple choice letter, True or False, etc.), then check how you did. If you missed one, review the material until you understand. If you still don't get it, be sure to ask your instructor.

   Why it's important: Immediately answering questions confirms learning, and helps transfer what you're learning to your long-term memory. It also confirms that you're learning as you go, which is important because misunderstanding something can create learning difficulties later.

4. **Watch the video.** After you've read an entire section, watch the corresponding section of the PADI *Open Water Diver Video*. The video reinforces the concepts you've learned. It also shows the details for some of the skills you'll practice. If you prefer to watch the video, then read the manual, that's fine. Choose the way that best suits you.

Why it's important: Video and the written word have different strengths when you're learning something, and people have different learning styles. Video is a more efficient teaching medium for some topics, written is more efficient for others, and they overlap. This repetition helps transfer what you're learning to long-term memory.

5. **Answer the knowledge reviews at the end of each section.** If you don't know something, review the information and then answer. If you still don't understand, ask your instructor. Your instructor will go over your knowledge reviews, to check that you understand the material.

    Why it's important: The knowledge reviews help confirm and reinforce how concepts interconnect, and help you retain what you're learning. They also let you both make sure you understand foundational concepts before moving on.

6. **Complete the assigned independent study before each session.** Your instructor will let you know what to complete, by when, so you can schedule the time you need and take it seriously. If you need a different schedule, let your instructor know so you can come up with one that works together.

    Why it's important: Your independent study establishes the foundation for subsequent learning in review sessions with your instructor, confined water dives and open water dives. **Failure to complete the assigned independent study can create *significant* delays. Your instructor may have to cancel and reschedule sessions until you complete the assignment.** Let your instructor know if you need a different schedule. If something comes up that keeps you from completing a section, if possible, contact your instructor before your next meeting.

Complete the assigned independent study before each session. Your instructor will let you know what to complete, by when, so you can schedule the time you need.

7. **Get your instructor's help.** When you meet, your instructor will review your knowledge review(s). Discuss any areas in which you had difficulties and ask questions. Your instructor will help you apply what you're learning to your needs and local diving.

    Why it's important: The better you communicate your personal interests and characteristics the more your instructor can help.

8. **Complete the section quiz and final exam.** You will complete a quiz for each of the first four sections, and a comprehensive final exam after Section Five. Before each, take a moment to review each section and your notes.

    Why it's important: You must demonstrate mastery of the knowledge development material with a score of 75 percent or higher on each quiz/exam, and review any missed items until you understand them. If you score less than 75 percent, you'll take a make-up quiz or exam after you've had a chance to go over what you missed.

Confined Water Dives

Arrive for your confined water dives with your personal equipment adjusted and ready (the pros at your PADI Dive Center or Resort will help you with this). As much as possible, treat the confined water dives as practice open water dives. Do what you would on an open water dive, and avoid doing things you can't do in open water. Also, there are no arbitrary skills in this course. Everything you learn has a real-world purpose in diving. If you don't know why you would do something, ask.

- If you wear contact lenses, let your instructor know. Do without them if you can, but wear them if you need them to read gauges, etc.

- Pay attention to your instructor's skill demonstrations and note the emphasized details.

- Develop good habits. This is important because *what you do by habit is what you tend to do when dealing with a problem.*

- Be in good health. It's your responsibility to postpone diving if you don't feel well, or are ill or injured, until you're back to normal health.

Tell your instructor how you feel. Your instructor can only be certain that you're *comfortable* and *confident* with your skills if you say so.

Importantly, tell your instructor how you *feel* about your *comfort* and *confidence* with your skills. Your instructor can tell if you can perform a skill properly, but can only be certain that you're comfortable and confident if you say so. Your instructor will ask you to assess your confidence with your skills – don't hesitate to speak privately if you feel you can be more open that way. It's normal to be a bit nervous when you start, but you should be gaining confidence. Even if you can perform every skill competently, if you want more experience before moving on, *tell your instructor* so you can schedule more time. Similarly, be clear if you don't feel well or if there is anything else that might interfere with learning effectively or diving safely. Your instructor's goal is to help you become a diver – clear, honest two-way communication is part of the process.

Open Water Dives

Your open water dives bring everything together. By the time you go on your first open water scuba dive, you'll have mastered the basic skills you need. Your instructor continues to develop, assess and refine your abilities with you during these four dives at a local site suitable for beginning divers. You'll learn a lot – but you'll also have a lot of fun. Get the most out of these dives by:

- Listening to your instructor's recommendations about how to prepare.

- Asking your physician or pharmacist about seasickness medication if you're prone to seasickness and will be diving from a boat.

- Arriving adequately rested and fed. Diving is a physical activity, so be physically ready to focus on the experience and what you're doing.

- Paying close attention to the predive briefings, doing your part in planning each dive, and speaking up if you don't understand something.

- Logging your dives (eLog or paper) to track your diving progress and experiences.

Get Your PADI Dive Center or Resort's Help Choosing Your Equipment

Diving is a technical activity – it is impossible without equipment. You will learn a lot about equipment, but there are hundreds of features and options, as well as new models and improvements, introduced regularly. It is impossible for a course to include all of these. The professionals at your PADI Dive Center or Resort can help you sort through the choices and get the best gear for you, your budget and the types of diving you want to enjoy. They also keep up on the latest improvements, changes and newest options.

Proper fit is important for the best equipment function and comfort. Being comfortable makes diving more enjoyable, and speeds learning by eliminating distractions. Professional guidance is the best way to get a proper, comfortable fit. You have to try on most pieces of equipment to get the right fit and the place to do this is your local PADI Dive Center or Resort.

Ideally, learn to dive in your own gear. Equipment you choose with professional guidance usually has the best possible fit, and the most comfort. Your instructor will teach you how to tailor and refine your equipment to your personal preferences. This adds significantly both to your experience during the course, and to enjoying diving as a certified PADI Open Water Diver.

Getting the Most Out of Being a Diver

During this course, you are becoming something new – a scuba diver. It's important to think *now* about how to continue in diving after the course. You already have reasons to dive, or you wouldn't be here. However, different reasons motivate people to take up diving. Some common ones include:

- **Adventuring and exploring.** Diving is one of the most accessible "adventure" sports, open to people with a wide age range, different physical characteristics and varied interests.

1 *Your open water dives* bring together and continue to develop your abilities. You'll learn a lot – but you'll also have a lot of fun.

2 *Ideally, learn to dive in your own gear.* The professionals at your PADI Dive Center or Resort are the best way to sort through the choices you have.

- **Enjoying and observing nature.** The underwater world has far more natural abundance and diversity than the terrestrial world.

LEADING-EDGE EDUCATION

What does it take to create a diver training program? It requires applying established instructional system design theory, educational psychology and cognitive psychology to create valid, state-of-the-art courses and materials. Apparently, mainstream bodies in higher education agree: Organizations in international governments and education recognize the instructional quality of PADI training. The American Council on Education's College Credit Recommendation Service (ACE Credit) independently evaluated PADI courses, and recommends many of them for college credit. Similar authoritative bodies in Australia, Canada, England, Wales, Northern Ireland, Japan and New Zealand have recognized PADI courses for academic credit, or for educational credit for competency that transfers to other fields. These acknowledgments corroborate the educational validity of PADI courses, and the PADI organization's ability to meet its educational goals. As a diver training organization, PADI is unique in having received such a broad range of academic recognition internationally.

In addition, PADI courses *exceed* all the minimum ISO (International Standards Organization) and World Recreational Scuba Training Council (WRSTC) standards for entry-level scuba diver training.

Visit the course credits page on padi.com for current academic credit availability, links and to download applications.

A PHILOSOPHY OF ACCESS

Performance-Based and Student-Centered Learning

Learning to dive means meeting specific performance requirements. The techniques presented here are popular ways of meeting these performance requirements, but in most cases, they're not the *only* methods. PADI's approach uses instructional design to apply student-centered learning to performance-based training, which makes diving accessible to people with a broad range of physical and intellectual capabilities.

Through their design, PADI courses accommodate these differences by allowing students to apply their strengths to offset physical and/or intellectual challenges. This makes diving accessible to a wide range of people *without* compromising safe diving practices, confidence or comfort.

For example, in a given situation most divers might enter the water by stepping in, but an individual with limited leg use may not have that option. But, there are other entry techniques that work just as well. Such an individual might enter the water by rolling in backwards.

If a suggested technique doesn't work because of your personal situation, ask your instructor to help you adapt the technique, or develop a new one, to meet the requirement some other way.

Because the PADI organization has global experience training literally millions of divers from all walks of life, a Training Consultant at one of the PADI Regional Headquarters can recommend alternative techniques for your situation.

If for some reason a personal challenge makes it impossible for you to earn full certification, diving is likely still open to you. Many individuals in this situation can still continue to dive with direct professional supervision.

PADI courses accommodate individual differences by allowing people to meet performance requirements by creatively adapting techniques so that personal strengths offset weaknesses.

- **Spending time doing something wonderful with friends and/or family.** Diving allows people with different interests, skill levels and experience to enjoy themselves together.

- **Getting out on the water as well as under it.** Boating, beaches, lakes and resorts add to diving.

- **Taking photos and videos.** The underwater world presents unique challenges and opportunities for image makers to enjoy.

- **Investigating sunken ships.** Many divers find themselves attracted to shipwrecks, submerged artifacts and other historical remnants they can visit underwater.

- **Taking on new personal challenges.** Each dive activity, environment and technology offers something new to learn and master.

- **Becoming familiar with new technologies.** Dive gear integrates different types of equipment, each fascinating in its evolution.

- **Making new friends.** Connecting with the dive community, online and where you live, bonds you with dive buddies around the world.

- **Making a difference in environmental conservation.** The global dive community has become a unified voice speaking to business and government about conserving the oceans we all rely on.

- **Enjoying a world that differs markedly from the world above the surface.** Diving lets you visit the Earth's final frontier, "inner space." This is especially appealing to some people with physical limitations; underwater, they move freely.

Transitioning from *learning* to dive to *being* a diver means getting into the diving lifestyle. You're most likely to stay involved if you do one or *more* of the following things *before* you complete this course:

1. Join and participate in your local dive center's dive club and/or social events, and log onto ScubaEarth®. Diving is a social activity;

You already have reasons why you want to dive, or you wouldn't be here. However, different reasons motivate different people to take up diving; some of these may become important to you as you engage in the diving lifestyle and gain experience.

Throughout the course, you'll see both metric and imperial measurements. Use the system you prefer, or both, but be aware that sometimes the referenced figures are not exactly equal.

The reason is that divers use "round" numbers for many purposes, so the preferred figure in each system may differ slightly. For example, a general reserve air supply pressure is 50 bar/500 psi. Fifty bar actually equals 750 psi, but 50 bar/500 psi are easy figures to reference on an air gauge, so those are what divers commonly use.

getting to know other divers opens opportunities to dive, and these groups welcome newcomers with open arms.

2. Enroll in a PADI course such as underwater photography, wreck diving, etc. (enroll now, but successfully complete your PADI Open Water Diver certification before taking most specialty diver courses). These courses are a great way to go diving while having adventures, learning new skills and getting to know other divers. PADI Specialty Diver courses usually involve one or two days of open water diving learning a new activity. The PADI Advanced Open Water Diver course lets you try specialties with your instructor. It was designed specifically for PADI Open Water Divers; you qualify to take it immediately. Visit padi.com or talk to your instructor about the many courses available.

    You can begin a few courses, such as PADI Dry Suit Diver and PADI Enriched Air Diver, during your PADI Open Water Diver course. This gets you involved in the next steps immediately.

3. Sign up for a dive trip that involves travel, and/or plan a local dive. See your professional dive center or resort about dive travel and dive holidays – having a pro guide your first dives is a fun approach.

4. Invest in your first scuba equipment – regulator, BCD, dive computer and/or wet suit or dry suit – as soon as you can. Divers who have their own gear dive more and enjoy diving more.

5. Take part in a local environmental project or event. Ask your dive operator (PADI Dive Center or Resort) about their involvement with Project AWARE, or visit projectaware.org.

Your Local PADI Dive Center or Resort

Your PADI Dive Center or Resort plays an important role in your involvement with diving because it brings everything into one place. The professionals there connect you with other divers, can recommend and book dive travel, guide equipment choices and provide service for it, and offer the PADI courses you'll want as you gain experience and expand your interests.

If you have questions, need advice, want to try something new or just want to hang with other divers, your local dive operator is the best place to start. You'll find that by developing a relationship with your local PADI professionals, you gain more than some skilled service providers. You make new friends who want to help you get out of diving what you got into it for.

Your PADI Dive Center or Resort plays an important role in your involvement with diving because it brings everything into one place.

A World of Diving

You can enjoy diving around the world in many different environments. This course teaches you the foundational skills of diving in a local environment using appropriate techniques. However, different environments may require different techniques and gear. For example, cool environments may call for diving in a dry suit – so you'd want training in the PADI Dry Suit Diver course.

When you dive in a new environment or at an unfamiliar dive site, get a local orientation, guided dive and/or additional training – which is most appropriate depends upon how different the new site is from those with which you're familiar. Doing this:

- Helps you find the best local diving.

- Helps you enjoy diving by assuring you are comfortable, avoid problems and know what to look for that's interesting, special or unique – especially when you're new to diving.

- Helps ensure you have the right equipment.

- Informs you about local hazards of which you may not be aware.

- Teaches you any special techniques you need.

When visiting a new dive site/environment, check with your local PADI Dive Center, Resort or Professional for recommendations on the orientation/supervision/training that's appropriate. PADI Discover Local Diving is designed specifically for orienting you as a certified diver to a new location.

Exercise I-1

1. As a newly certified PADI Open Water Diver, I will be trained to dive with a buddy as deep as

   _____.

   ☐ a. 10 metres/30 feet

   ☐ b. 18 metres/60 feet

   ☐ c. 30 metres/100 feet

   ☐ d. 40 metres/130 feet

2. Certain medical conditions can be hazardous while diving, so it is important to answer all questions on the Medical Statement honestly and completely.

   ☐ True

   ☐ False

3. PADI courses are performance-based. This means that to be certified, I must

   ☐ a. meet specific performance requirements.

   ☐ b. spend a given number of hours in training.

   ☐ c. simply pay for the course.

4. Failure to complete assigned independent study can create significant delays, and my instructor may have to cancel and reschedule sessions until I complete the assignment.

   ☐ True

   ☐ False

5. When diving in a new dive environment, two benefits of seeking an orientation, supervision and/or additional training are that it helps me avoid problems and that it helps me enjoy the dive more.

   ☐ True

   ☐ False

How did you do?

1. b. 2. True. 3. a. 4. True. 5. True

section

The experience of diving is exciting because you feel new sensations. These result from underwater properties that differ from what you're used to in the terrestrial world.

LEARNING OBJECTIVES

By the end of this section, I should be able to answer these questions:

1. What is the relationship between my depth in water and the pressure?

2. What is the pressure change for each 10 metres/33 feet of depth change?

3. What is the relationship between pressure, and the volume and density of air?

4. If I take a volume of air from one depth to another depth, how much will the volume and density change?

Being a Diver I

Even in confined water, the experience of diving is exciting, because you feel new sensations. This is because the underwater world differs in several ways from the terrestrial world to which you're accustomed. We'll look at:

- How water creates pressure and how you adjust for it.
- Why and how you can float, sink or be almost weightless in water.
- How seeing, hearing and moving differ in water.
- Why water absorbs heat and how you stay warm.

Each of these directly affects your safety and enjoyment as a diver.

Water Pressure and Air Volume Effects

Depth and Pressure

Right now, you are under pressure exerted by the air in the atmosphere that surrounds you. It's actually the *weight* of the air. At sea level the pressure is fairly uniform, and expressed as one *bar* (metric) or one *atmosphere* (imperial – abbreviated *ata*).

Underwater, you're under more pressure because water also has weight, which combines with the atmosphere's weight (pressure). Because water is much denser and heavier than air, 10 metres/33 feet exerts the same pressure as the whole atmosphere.

Therefore, the pressure increases by one bar/ata for each 10 metres/33 feet you descend (go down). Likewise, it decreases one bar/atmosphere for every 10 metres/33 feet you ascend (come up). So:

Depth	Pressure
0m/0ft	1 bar/ata
10m/33ft	2 bar/ata
20m/66ft	3 bar/ata
30m/99ft	4 bar/ata
40m/132ft	5 bar/ata

- At 0 metres/feet (sea level), the total pressure is 1 bar/ata.
- At 10 metres/33 feet, the total pressure is 2 bar/ata – one of air plus one of water.
- At 20 metres/66 feet, the total pressure is 3 bar/ata.
- At 30 metres/99 feet, the total pressure is 4 bar/ata.

Pressure and Air Volume and Density

Water can't be compressed so its volume and density don't change with pressure changes. And, since your body tissues are mostly made of water, you don't feel pressure changes on most of your body while diving.

But, pressure changes do change the volume and density of air (or any other gas). As the pressure increases – as you go deeper – a gas volume decreases because the gas molecules get compressed. The gas density increases because all the molecules are there, but they're packed into a smaller area.

This is one of the most important principles you learn, because as a diver, it affects all the air spaces in, or in contact with, your body. These include your ears, sinuses, lungs, mask and, when using one, a dry suit. You'll also learn that this principle affects controlling your buoyancy, how long your air supply lasts and some important safety rules.

Air volume and density change proportionately with pressure. This means if you go from the surface to 10 metres/33 feet, you double the pressure to 2 bar/ata (1 air plus 1 water), a given air volume halves, and its density doubles. If you go to 20 metres/66 feet, the pressure is 3 bar/ata (1 air plus

2 water). An air volume would be one-third the surface volume, and the density would triple.

Depth	Pressure	Air Volume	Air Density
0m/0ft	1 bar/ata	1	x 1
10m/33ft	2 bar/ata	1/2	x 2
20m/66ft	3 bar/ata	1/3	x 3
30m/99ft	4 bar/ata	1/4	x 4
40m/132ft	5 bar/ata	1/5	x 5

Pressure-Volume-Density Relationship

Example:

- You start your descent with a balloon filled with 3 litres of air.
- At 10 metres/33 feet, its volume decreases to 1.5 litres; the density will be doubled.
- At 20 metres/66 feet, its volume decreases to 1 litre; the density will be tripled.
- The relationship is the same with any measurement system (gallons, cubic feet, etc.) of air or any other gas.

Depth	Pressure	Air Volume	Air Density	
0m/0ft	1 bar/ata	1	x 1	
10m/33ft	2 bar/ata	1/2	x 2	
20m/66ft	3 bar/ata	1/3	x 3	
30m/99ft	4 bar/ata	1/4	x 4	
40m/132ft	5 bar/ata	1/5	x 5	

This predictable relationship between pressure and air (gas) volume and density exists with every depth change whether descending or ascending. For example, suppose you have 1 litre of air at 30 metres/99 feet. What would the volume and density be at the surface?

- The pressure at 30 metres/99 feet is 4 bar/ata (3 of water plus 1 of air).
- The pressure at the surface is 1 bar/ata, so the pressure is 1/4th the pressure at 30 metres/99 feet.
- One litre of air brought to the surface from 30 metres/99 feet will expand to 4 litres at the surface. The air density would be 1/4th the density at 30 metres/ 99 feet.

Depth	Pressure	Air Volume	Air Density	
0m/0ft	1 bar/ata	1	x 1	
10m/33ft	2 bar/ata	1/2	x 2	
20m/66ft	3 bar/ata	1/3	x 3	
30m/99ft	4 bar/ata	1/4	x 4	
40m/132ft	5 bar/ata	1/5	x 5	

Now suppose you fill a balloon completely and seal it at 10 metres/33 feet. What happens as you ascend? The balloon expands, growing larger until it stretches past its failure point and bursts. To prevent this, you'd leave the balloon unsealed and vent some of the expanding air as you ascend.

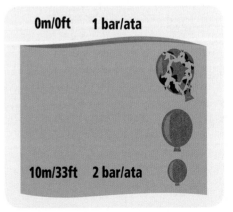

0m/0ft   1 bar/ata

10m/33ft   2 bar/ata

1. As you descend in water the pressure
   - ☐ a. increases.
   - ☐ b. decreases.
   - ☐ c. does not change.

2. A depth change of 10 metres/33 feet causes a pressure change of _____.
   - ☐ a. 1 bar/ata
   - ☐ b. 2 bar/ata
   - ☐ c. 3 bar/ata
   - ☐ d. 4 bar/ata

3. If you take 6 litres of air from the surface to 20 metres/66 feet, the volume will be _____ litres.
   - ☐ a. 1
   - ☐ b. 2
   - ☐ c. 3
   - ☐ d. 4

4. The density of the air in the previous question would be _____ the density at the surface.
   - ☐ a. one-third
   - ☐ b. one-half
   - ☐ c. three times
   - ☐ d. four times

5. A balloon fully inflated and sealed at 10 metres/33 feet, would probably _____ during ascent to the surface.
   - ☐ a. shrink (become smaller)
   - ☐ b. burst

How did you do?
1. a. 2. a. 3. b. 4. c. 5. b.

LEARNING OBJECTIVES

By the end of this section, I should be able to answer these questions:

1. What three major body air spaces does increasing pressure affect as I descend?

2. What is a "squeeze"?

3. What is "equalization" and how do I equalize as I descend?

4. How often should I equalize?

5. What should I do if I can't equalize? What can happen if I don't or can't equalize and keep descending?

6. Why should I equalize gently?

7. Why does congestion from a cold or allergy temporarily keep me from diving? Why should I never dive with earplugs?

8. What other body air spaces are affected by increasing pressure? How do I equalize them?

The Effects of Increasing Pressure on Body Air Spaces

Although *most* of your body is made of water and doesn't feel increasing pressure, increasing pressure *does* affect *air* spaces in and in contact with your body. This is because the pressure compresses the air in the space. As the air volume decreases, water pressure pushes in on body tissues surrounding the space, and you feel it. The three major body air spaces affected are:

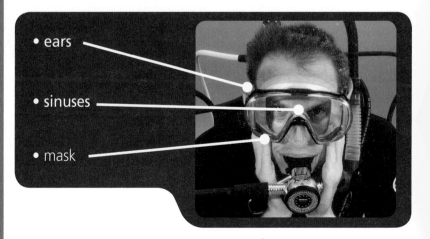

- ears
- sinuses
- mask

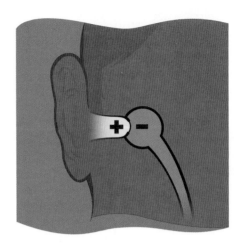

Discomfort in the ears as you descend is from an ear squeeze. It is caused by pressure pushing your eardrum and surrounding tissues inward.

If you don't adjust for increasing pressure compressing a body air space, you can get a squeeze. A squeeze causes discomfort and, if not corrected, can cause injury by pressure imbalance that pushes tissues into an air space. This happens because there is greater pressure outside the air space than inside it.

Discomfort in the ears as you descend is from an ear squeeze. It is caused by pressure pushing your eardrum and surrounding tissues inward. A pulling or sucking sensation on your face is from a mask squeeze. Discomfort in your cheeks, central forehead and along the nose is from a sinus squeeze. Other squeezes are possible, but not common.

Equalization

You can easily prevent squeezes. Do this by adding air to the air spaces as you descend. This keeps their pressure equal with the outside pressure, so they stay at their normal volume. This is called *equalization*.

To equalize your ears and sinuses, pinch your nose and blow gently against it. This sends air from your throat into your ears and sinuses. Some people find that wiggling their jaws side-to-side and swallowing also works.

To equalize your mask, blow air into it through your nose as you descend. This is why you can't use goggles for scuba diving – they don't enclose your nose, so you can't equalize them.

Equalize every metre/few feet, *before* you feel discomfort. If you wait until you feel discomfort, equalization may be difficult or impossible. When you equalize as often as you should, you don't feel discomfort or pain.

⚠️ If you can't equalize, ***stop your descent*** immediately. **Signal your buddy(ies) or instructor** – *they have no way of knowing you have an equalization problem unless you tell them.* Signal "problem" and point to your ear (you'll learn these and other hand signals later in this section).

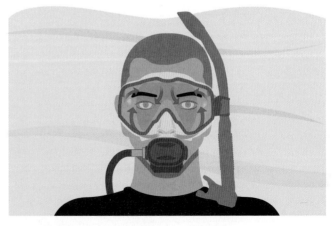

To equalize your mask, blow air into it through your nose.

- Ascend slightly until the discomfort passes and try again. Be patient. After you equalize, descend more slowly, equalizing more frequently.

- If you still can't equalize, stop the dive.

⚠ **Continuing to descend with unequalized air spaces can lead to serious injuries.** Ear injuries include fluid accumulating in the middle ear, and eardrum rupture. Eardrum rupture underwater can cause severe vertigo (dizziness and loss of balance), and requires medical treatment.

An unequalized mask can cause bruising around your eyes. While it's usually not serious and clears with time, its appearance is dramatic and may be alarming.

A physician should check serious squeezes to avoid long-term injury and complications.

⚠ Equalize *gently.* **Never attempt a forceful and/or extended equalization. A forceful, extended equalization can cause serious permanent injuries to your ears and hearing.**

- Use short, frequent, gentle equalizations.

- If short, frequent, gentle equalizations don't work, stop your descent, signal your buddy(ies)/instructor, ascend until the discomfort passes and try again.

With practice, equalizing becomes easier for most people.

Never dive with a cold or allergy. They can cause congestion that might block normal air flow and may make equalization of body air passages difficult or impossible. Using cold medications is not recommended. They can wear off during a dive, and can cause equalization problems as you ascend (more about this shortly). Wait until you're well.

You never use earplugs while diving. They create air spaces that you can't equalize (the exceptions are special ear protectors made

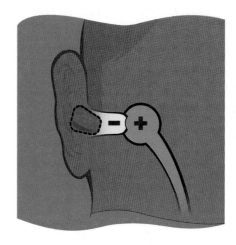

You never use earplugs while diving because they create air spaces that you can't equalize.

specifically for diving). Similarly, a wet suit hood that seals too tightly against an ear can act like an earplug. If so, pull the hood away from your ear momentarily.

Increasing pressure may affect other body air spaces as you descend. It's very rare, but an air space can develop in filled teeth and cause discomfort. If it happens, stop your

If you can't equalize, stop your descent immediately. Signal your buddy(ies) or instructor – they have no way of knowing you have an equalization problem unless you tell them.

descent because you can't equalize this air space. See your dentist to correct the air space; regular dental checkups help avoid this problem.

A *dry suit* holds a layer of air around your body during the dive. Increasing pressure compresses this air, but you learn to equalize this space in the PADI Dry Suit Diver course. If you will use a dry suit during this course, your instructor will show you how to equalize it.

Your lungs are a large air space, but scuba provides air at the surrounding pressure. So, you don't need to do anything special to equalize your lungs *other than to breathe normally and continuously*. When skin diving (breath-hold diving), your lungs compress as you descend, but they are designed to do this. The only possible concerns are if you were to descend after exhaling completely, or if you were to breath-hold dive, *very* deep (60 metres/200 feet or more). These are unlikely for most divers.

Exercise 1-2

1. As I descend, increasing pressure affects my (choose all that apply):
   - ☐ a. mask.
   - ☐ b. ears.
   - ☐ c. sinuses.
   - ☐ d. skin.

2. A squeeze is caused by
   - ☐ a. wearing my wet suit or other gear too tightly.
   - ☐ b. a pressure imbalance between the surrounding pressure and an air space.

3. Equalization is the process of
   - ☐ a. adding air to an air space.
   - ☐ b. removing air from an air space.
   - ☐ c. reducing the surrounding pressure.
   - ☐ d. increasing the surrounding pressure.

4. I should equalize
   - ☐ a. when I feel pain or discomfort.
   - ☐ b. only if I can't tolerate the pain or discomfort.
   - ☐ c. before I feel pain or discomfort.
   - ☐ d. when I reach the bottom.

5. I'm descending and discover I can't equalize. The first thing I would do is
   - ☐ a. equalize more forcefully.
   - ☐ b. stop my descent and signal my buddy/the instructor.
   - ☐ c. slow my descent and see if the problem corrects itself.

6. I equalize gently because an extended, forceful equalization can cause permanent damage to my ears and hearing.
   - ☐ True
   - ☐ False

7. On a day I plan to go diving, I wake up with my sinuses blocked due to a cold or allergy. I should
   - ☐ a. take an approved decongestant so I will be able to equalize.
   - ☐ b. plan to take a lot longer as I descend.
   - ☐ c. cancel the dive until I'm well.

8. When scuba diving, normal breathing keeps your lungs equalized to the surrounding pressure.
   - ☐ True
   - ☐ False

How did you do?
1. a, b, c. 2. b. 3. a. 4. c. 5. b. 6. True. 7. c. 8. True.

LEARNING OBJECTIVES

By the end of this section, I should be able to answer these questions:

1. What is the most important rule in scuba diving?

2. What can happen if I don't follow the most important rule in scuba diving?

3. What is a "reverse block"?

4. What should I do if I feel discomfort in my ears, sinuses, stomach, intestines or teeth while ascending?

The Effects of Decreasing Pressure on Body Air Spaces

As you learned, as pressure decreases during ascent, air expands, and the air you added to a body air space increases in volume. This expanding air must exit body air spaces. Normally, this happens naturally in your ears, mask and sinuses, so you do not need to do anything to equalize them as you ascend.

The Most Important Rule in Scuba Diving

Expanding air in your *lungs* is most important. Because scuba supplies air at the surrounding pressure, your lungs are at normal volume at depth. When ascending, the air in your lungs expands, but this is not a problem when you breathe normally. Your lungs stay at their normal volume because you release expanding air with each exhalation.

⚠ **If during ascent you were to hold your breath, blocking your airway, your lungs would over expand. They would be much like a balloon filled and sealed at depth, which expanding air would burst during ascent.**

⚠ **Expanding air can cause serious lung overexpansion (lung rupture) injuries.** For this reason, **the most important rule in scuba diving is to breathe continuously and never, ever hold your breath.** Even slight pressure changes – as little as a metre/2-3 feet – can cause these injuries if you were to ascend holding a full breath.

Lung overexpansion injuries are difficult to treat and can cause paralysis and death by forcing air into the bloodstream and chest cavities. Treatment usually requires recompression (being put back under pressure) in a chamber as soon as possible. However, diving commonly takes place several hours (or more) from a recompression chamber.

While very serious, lung overexpansion injuries are among the easiest to avoid. Breathe at all times and never hold your breath.

This rule is so important, that any time your regulator is not in your mouth you exhale a slow, steady bubble stream so you aren't holding your breath. Also, do not dive with lung congestion, which can trap air in the lungs and cause overexpansion injuries.

The most important rule in scuba diving is to breathe continuously and never, ever hold your breath. If you were to hold your breath, expanding air can cause serious lung overexpansion injuries.

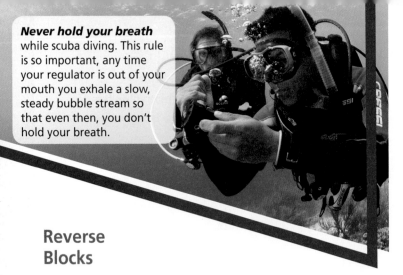

Never hold your breath while scuba diving. This rule is so important, any time your regulator is out of your mouth you exhale a slow, steady bubble stream so that even then, you don't hold your breath.

Reverse Blocks

Although body air spaces usually cause no problems during ascent, in some instances you can have a *reverse block.* A reverse block (also called a *reverse squeeze*) results when expanding air becomes trapped in a body air space.

Reverse blocks can result from using a decongestant to dive with a cold or allergy. During the dive, the decongestant can wear off and the congestion can trap air in the ears and/or sinuses. (Again, don't dive with cold/allergy congestion, even with medications.)

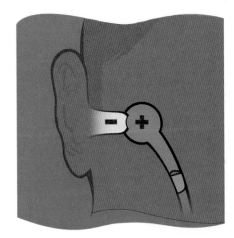

Reverse blocks can result from using a decongestant to dive with a cold or allergy. During the dive, the decongestant wears off, then congestion traps air in the ears and/or sinuses.

Gas forming in the stomach/intestines during a dive can cause discomfort on ascent if it doesn't pass. You prevent this by avoiding gas-producing foods prior to diving, and not swallowing air while diving.

Earlier, you learned that a tooth squeeze is rare, but possible. A reverse tooth squeeze is also rare, but can result if air seeps into secondary erosion under a filling during a dive and can't exit fast enough as you ascend. Again, see your dentist if you ever experience such a problem.

If you feel discomfort in any air space during ascent, immediately slow or stop your ascent. Descend a metre/few feet to reduce the discomfort and give the trapped air time to work its way out. Ascend more slowly, giving the expanding gas time to exit. If you have severe or frequent reverse blocks, see a physician knowledgeable in dive medicine.

Exercise 1-3

1. The most important rule in scuba diving is to
   - ☐ a. always dive with a buddy.
   - ☐ b. breathe continuously and never hold your breath.
   - ☐ c. check your air supply every five minutes.

2. Failure to follow the most important rule in scuba diving can cause severe lung overexpansion injuries, which can result in paralysis or death.
   - ☐ True
   - ☐ False

3. During ascent I feel discomfort in my ears. I should
   - ☐ a. continue my ascent at a slightly faster rate.
   - ☐ b. stop, descend slightly and allow trapped air to work its way out.
   - ☐ c. use a decongestant before my next dive.
   - ☐ d. equalize by blowing gently against blocked nostrils.

   How did you do?
   1. b. 2. True. 3. b.

By the end of this section, I should be able to answer these questions:

1. How does depth affect how long my air supply lasts?

2. What's the most efficient way to breathe dense air underwater?

3. How do I breathe to reduce anxiety when under stress?

4. What are my four breathing rules as a scuba diver?

Breathing Underwater

You've already learned that pressure increases with depth, and decreases an air volume while increasing its density. Because scuba provides air at the surrounding pressure, as you go deeper each breath takes more air from your scuba cylinder. Therefore, the deeper you are, the faster you use your air.

Depth	Pressure	Air Volume	Air Density
0m/0ft	1 bar/ata	1	x 1
10m/33ft	2 bar/ata	1/2	x 2
20m/66ft	3 bar/ata	1/3	x 3
30m/99ft	4 bar/ata	1/4	x 4
40m/132ft	5 bar/ata	1/5	x 5

How fast you use your air follows the pressure/volume relationship you learned earlier.

How fast you use your air follows the pressure/volume relationship you just learned.

- Your air supply lasts ½ as long at 10 metres/33 feet (2 bar/ata) than at the surface (1 bar/ata).

- Your air supply lasts 1/3 as long at 20 metres/66 feet (3 bar/ata) than at the surface (1 bar/ata), ¼ at 30 metres/99 feet and so on.

Your breathing rate also affects how long your air supply lasts; you use your air faster when swimming than while stationary.

Pressure reduces an air volume by compressing the molecules closer together. This means that the air gets denser as you go deeper; denser air is harder to breathe than air at normal surface pressure. The deeper you are, the more energy you use to breathe. Additionally, breathing faster uses significantly more energy (at the surface or at any depth) – it takes about four times the energy to breathe twice as fast. So, the deeper you are, the more effort and energy you spend if you breathe fast.

Therefore, take *slow, deep* breaths. Breathing slowly and deeply is the most efficient way to breathe while scuba diving. Pace yourself and dive relaxed. To make your air last, save energy and don't over exert. Avoid getting winded or out of breath underwater. We'll look more at this in Section Two.

Slow, deep breathing also helps you handle stress and anxiety. When an emergency or a perceived threat causes anxiety, your body responds by increasing breathing. But, the process works both ways to some extent – if you decrease and control your breathing, you help control and manage anxiety. This helps you deal with problems based on your training instead of emotion.

If you're faced with a problem while diving, stop what you're doing, then reduce anxiety by maintaining or restoring slow, deep breathing as you handle it.

Let's summarize the four breathing rules you've learned to follow as a scuba diver.

1. Breathe *continuously* and *never*, ever, hold your breath.

2. Breathe *slowly* and *deeply*.

3. Do not allow yourself to get winded or out of breath.

4. If faced with a problem, stop, then reduce anxiety by maintaining or restoring s*low, deep* breathing.

If you're faced with a problem while diving, stop what you're doing, then reduce anxiety by maintaining or restoring slow, deep breathing as you handle it.

Exercise 1-4

1. My buddy and I descend to 12 metres/40 feet. I would expect to use my air _____ at 6 metres/20 feet.
   - ☐ a. slower than
   - ☐ b. at the same rate as
   - ☐ c. faster than

2. The most efficient way to breathe dense air underwater is to breathe
   - ☐ a. shallowly and slowly.
   - ☐ b. shallowly and rapidly.
   - ☐ c. deeply and slowly.
   - ☐ d. deeply and rapidly.

3. My body responds to anxiety with increased breathing, but slow breathing helps reduce anxiety.
   - ☐ True
   - ☐ False

4. Which of the following are among the breathing rules I follow as a diver? (Choose all that apply):
   - ☐ a. Breathe continuously and never, ever, hold my breath.
   - ☐ b. Breathe slowly and deeply.
   - ☐ c. Do not allow myself to get winded or out-of-breath.
   - ☐ d. If faced with a problem, stop, then maintain or restore slow, deep breathing.

How did you do?
1. c. 2. c. 3. True. 4. a, b, c, d.

Buoyancy and Controlling Buoyancy

Buoyancy is one of the properties that make diving special. Buoyancy cancels the pull of gravity, allowing you to "fly" and feel "weightless." Unless you're an astronaut, there's no other way to experience this for more than a few short seconds. Understanding the basic principles will help you learn to control and enjoy buoyancy as a diver.

Buoyancy is an upward force acting on an object in water, which is why you feel "lighter" in water. This force is caused by the water displaced (pushed aside) by the object, and is equal to the weight of the water displaced. There are three types of buoyancy:

- If an object weighs less than the water it displaces, it floats. This is *positive* buoyancy.

- If an object weighs more than the water it displaces, it sinks. This is *negative* buoyancy.

- If an object weighs the same as the water it displaces, it neither floats nor sinks. This is *neutral* buoyancy.

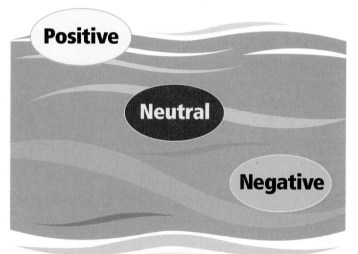

An object that floats is positively buoyant. An object that sinks is negatively buoyant. An object that neither sinks nor floats is neutrally buoyant.

Salt water has dissolved minerals (salt) in it, so a given volume weighs more than fresh water. Because salt water weighs more, it causes more buoyancy – more upward force. All else being the same, you have more buoyancy when diving in the ocean than when diving in fresh water.

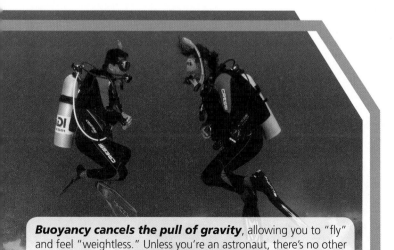

Buoyancy cancels the pull of gravity, allowing you to "fly" and feel "weightless." Unless you're an astronaut, there's no other way to experience this for more than a few short seconds.

You'll learn to use two pieces of equipment to control your buoyancy: your *weight system* and your BCD *(Buoyancy Control Device)*. Because they're central to your skill as a diver, many divers make their BCD and weight system two of their initial equipment investments.

Your weight system holds just enough lead weight to offset your positive buoyancy. You need this because most people float, and some of your gear – like a wet suit – also floats.

Use just enough weight to allow you to descend, but you *shouldn't* sink rapidly.

How much weight you need depends upon your gear, your physical characteristics and whether you're diving in fresh or salt water. You will learn more about weight systems and how much weight to use shortly.

To actually change your buoyancy during a dive, you use your BCD. Inflating and deflating it increases and decreases your volume – how much water you displace. This adjusts your buoyancy so you can be positively, negatively or neutrally buoyant when you want. This is one of the key dive

Inhaling increases your volume, displacement and buoyancy. Exhaling decreases your volume, displacement and buoyancy.

skills you'll master, and you'll begin learning to use your BCD during your first confined water dive.

You use your BCD frequently because your buoyancy tends to change when you change depth. Some pieces of scuba equipment – particularly wet suits – have gas spaces. Just like body air spaces, these spaces compress as pressure increases and expand as pressure decreases.

When you descend, their volume decreases, which reduces the water displaced. This reduces your buoyancy (makes you more negatively buoyant). You offset this by adding air to your BCD (if diving with a dry suit, you may add air to the suit).

When you ascend, it works the other way. The gas volume in your gear re-expands and your buoyancy increases. The air you added to your BCD (or dry suit) also expands and further increases your buoyancy. To control your buoyancy, as you ascend you vent (release) the air you added on the way down.

Your weight system holds just enough lead to offset your positive buoyancy. You inflate and deflate your BCD to change your buoyancy during a dive.

You'll notice that your breathing affects your buoyancy. When you inhale, your chest expands, increasing your volume, displacement and buoyancy. When you exhale, you contract your chest, decreasing your volume, displacement and buoyancy. While the change isn't large, with practice, you'll learn to use breathing to fine-tune buoyancy *without* holding your breath.

It is important to master buoyancy control because it affects almost everything you do in and underwater.

It deserves focus and attention as you practice in confined water and on your open water dives. Buoyancy control allows you to:

- Descend and ascend at a slow, controlled rate.
- Stop a descent or ascent and maintain your depth with little effort.
- Float comfortably on the surface.
- Save energy and avoid harming sensitive aquatic organisms by swimming neutrally buoyant and controlling your movements.
- Maintain the underwater visibility by helping you not stir up the bottom.
- *Enjoy* one of the sensations unique to diving – "weightlessness."

Buoyancy control is central to almost everything you do underwater, so it deserves focus and attention as you practice in confined water and on your open water dives.

Exercise 1-5

1. Buoyancy is a force that pushes an object in water upward.
   - ☐ True
   - ☐ False

2. My sunglasses case falls out of my pocket into the water, but fortunately, it floats so I retrieve it. I would say my sunglasses case is _____ buoyant.
   - ☐ a. positively
   - ☐ b. negatively
   - ☐ c. neutrally

3. Salt water causes more buoyancy than fresh water because it is less dense and weighs less.
   - ☐ True
   - ☐ False

4. To control my buoyancy, normally I will use my weight system and my
   - ☐ a. fins.
   - ☐ b. scuba cylinder.
   - ☐ c. wet suit.
   - ☐ d. BCD.

5. When I descend, my buoyancy tends to _____. When I ascend, it tends to _____.
   - ☐ a. increase, increase
   - ☐ b. increase, decrease
   - ☐ c. decrease, increase
   - ☐ d. decrease, decrease

6. Underwater, when I inhale, my buoyancy
   - ☐ a. decreases slightly.
   - ☐ b. increases slightly.
   - ☐ c. doesn't change.

7. It is important to master buoyancy control because it affects almost everything I do in and underwater.
   - ☐ True
   - ☐ False

How did you do?
1. True. 2. a. 3. False. Salt water causes more buoyancy because it is more dense and weighs more; buoyancy results from the weight of the water displaced. 4. d. 5. c. 6. b. 7. True

The Buddy System

In recreational diving, you don't dive alone, but use the buddy system. The buddy system is diving with another diver or divers in a team that provides shared assistance and safety benefits. It is so integral to recreational diving that your training includes the buddy system from the start. You and your buddy:

- Plan your dives together.

- Help each other gear up and check each other's equipment.

- Remind each other of dive time and depth limits.

- Assist each other if there's a problem.

- Assist each other with what each wants to do on the dive.

The buddy system is diving with another diver or divers in a team that provides shared assistance and safety benefits. It is so integral to recreational diving that your training includes the buddy system from the start.

The dive community established and continues to prioritize the buddy system because it has three overall benefits.

1. Practicality – you assist each other before, during and after the dive.

2. Safety – you help each other prevent problems, and you assist each other if there is an emergency.

3. Fun – diving is a social activity; it's rewarding and fun to have someone to share underwater adventures.

Exercise 1-6

1. In recreational diving, the buddy system means diving with another diver or divers in a team that provides assistance and safety benefits.
   ☐ True
   ☐ False

2. Overall benefits of the buddy system include (choose all that apply):
   ☐ a. practicality
   ☐ b. safety
   ☐ c. fun

   How did you do?
   1. True. 2. a, b, c.

37

Becoming a diver involves learning to use and apply dive technology. Learning about scuba gear and how to choose what's right for you is essential.

LEARNING OBJECTIVES

By the end of this section, I should be able to answer these questions:

1. What are the three most important considerations in choosing scuba equipment?

2. What are four secondary considerations when choosing scuba equipment?

3. How do I generally care for scuba equipment?

Equipment I

Manufacturers continually evolve different equipment types and styles that improve performance and accommodate different types of diving, sizing, dive environments and personal preferences.

The best way to sort through the different makes and models is to get professional help – it's part of what dive professionals do. Your local PADI dive shop can provide the best information on the types and options available, making it the best place to get guidance on your equipment decisions and investments.

This course covers the purpose for each piece of gear, as well as basic considerations related to fitting, selection, use and care. But, with new models and options constantly becoming available, see your dive operator or instructor for more specific information related to individual brands and models.

It's important to keep up with current options and innovations. The gear you invest in will usually last many years. But, you may trade up sooner because something new accommodates what you want, better. Staying connected to the dive community through your local PADI Dive Center, Resort or Instructor, the PADI Diving Society, ScubaEarth® and other online dive communities, dive magazines and publications, with friends who dive, and so on, will generally help you keep up with the latest-and-greatest in scuba technologies.

Choosing and Caring for Scuba Equipment

Let's look at the basic principles that apply to selecting and maintaining almost every piece of scuba gear.

Primary Considerations

The three most important considerations when choosing scuba gear are *suitability, fit* and *comfort*.

Suitability means that the equipment is appropriate for you and the dive. If planning a dive in cool water, your short sleeve wet suit – perfectly suitable for tropical diving – may not be suitable.

Fit means the equipment is sized and adjusted for you. Many pieces of gear will not function, or function poorly, if they don't fit right. Your PADI dive shop and instructor will help you learn to select gear that fits and adjust it.

Comfort means you can wear the item for an hour or more without a significant distraction due to its feel or configuration. Uncomfortable equipment that annoys you can take the fun out of a dive. It can sometimes distract you from safety issues. Be sure your gear fits and is comfortable. To a point, a professional can tell if something fits, but you have to say whether it is or isn't comfortable.

Secondary Considerations

Once your gear is suitable, comfortable and fits, there are four secondary considerations: cost and features, serviceability, color and style, and accessories.

Cost and features – You can choose gear from a price range, with more features on higher-end models.

Serviceability – Consider that some equipment requires annual or biannual professional servicing. Most dive operations service the brands they sell, so getting gear from your PADI dive shop typically covers this.

Color and style – You can choose gear that looks good and is color-coordinated.

One benefit of joining the ScubaEarth® community is that you can record all your equipment in "the cloud." This gives you access to the information anywhere, and ScubaEarth® reminds you when you have service due.

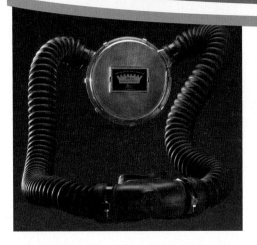  

Manufacturers evolve different equipment styles, such as these regulators from the early 1950s, mid 1970s and today. Your local PADI dive shop can provide the best information on the types and options available, making it the best place to get guidance on your equipment decisions.

Accessories – For each piece of equipment, your PADI Professional can suggest related accessories. A professional at your PADI dive shop may, for example, suggest retainers that hold equipment where it belongs, or an appropriate mask defog so you see clearly. These contribute *significantly* to diving comfort and convenience. Don't neglect useful accessories.

General Care

Different pieces of scuba gear have specific care requirements, but all items have the following steps in common:

1. Inspect your equipment for proper operation, wear and damage before each use. ***Don't dive with anything that isn't in good working order.*** You can take care of some issues, such as replacing a mask or fin strap that looks worn. For major issues, such as a problem with your scuba regulator, you'll usually need to have the equipment professionally serviced.

2. Rinse everything thoroughly in clean, fresh water after use in salt water, chlorinated or fresh water with silt or dirt. Allow it to dry out of the sun before storage in a cool, dry place. This is important for keeping your gear reliable and allowing it to give you many years of service. While divers are not a major cause of invasive species problems, thoroughly cleaning your gear also helps reduce accidentally transferring organisms between environments. Check the web for regional information about accidental organism transfer.

3. Avoid leaving your kit exposed to direct sunlight for extended periods, and cover it between dives. Sunlight tends to bleach out colors and speeds the deterioration of some materials.

4. Some items require periodic professional inspection, overhaul and/or adjustment. Have these items serviced regularly.

5. Follow any maintenance requirements specified by the manufacturer. See the manufacturer's literature and/or website.

Exercise 1-7

1. The three most important considerations in choosing scuba equipment are suitability, fit and _____.
   - ☐ a. cost and features
   - ☐ b. color and style
   - ☐ c. manufacturer
   - ☐ d. comfort

2. Getting the service my gear needs may be a consideration when choosing equipment.
   - ☐ True
   - ☐ False

3. Before each use, I should_____my equipment.
   - ☐ a. inspect
   - ☐ b. wash
   - ☐ c. warm
   - ☐ d. dry

   How did you do?
   1. d. 2. True. 3. a.

Suitability means that the equipment is appropriate for you and the dive. A short wet suit suitable for tropical diving would not be suitable for a dive in cold water.

Fit means the equipment is sized and adjusted for you. Your instructor or dive center staff will help you learn to select gear that fits and how to adjust it.

FROM AN ENTHUSIASTIC DIVER

"The more I learn about dive equipment – check out the *Encyclopedia of Recreational Diving* and the Equipment Specialist course – the more it fascinates me. My dive computers are especially interesting because each generation does more – it's easy to fall in love with the hot new one.

"When I first learned to dive, my instructor advised us to get our own gear because it's more convenient and, long term, cheaper than renting if you're an active diver. He told us that personal equipment is always adjusted for you, tends to be top-of-the-line, that you can pick the gear that exactly fits your needs, and so on.

"But, my instructor didn't tell me that I would *want* to own my own equipment, and I do. You know how your wardrobe is the clothes you like and no matter what you wear, what you're wearing is you? That's how it is with your gear. It doesn't matter which of my suits, regulators and BCDs I choose, it's *me* – my gear is how I dive and part of who I am as a diver."

Rinse your equipment thoroughly in clean, fresh water after use in salt water, chlorinated water or dirty fresh water. Allow it to dry out of the sun before storage in a cool, dry place. ▶

MARK YOUR GEAR

Divers often have identical or similar equipment, so use a gear marker (see your dive operator) to put your initials on yours to reduce confusion and accidental loss. Marking your gear doesn't have to make it ugly, though. Put your initials where you can see them when you're not kitted up, but can't when you are – like *inside* fin pockets.

To check for proper fit, you can place most masks gently against your face and inhale slightly through your nose. They should stay in place with light suction without pushing or twisting to make a seal.

LEARNING OBJECTIVES

By the end of this section, I should be able to answer these questions:

1. Why do I need a mask?

2. Why does my mask need to enclose my nose?

3. What features should I consider when choosing a mask? How do I check the fit?

4. How do I prepare a new mask for diving?

Dive Masks

You need a mask to see clearly underwater. Your eyes must be in air to focus properly, but your mask creates an air space that you have to equalize. This is why your mask *must* enclose your nose – so you can blow air into it. It's also why you never scuba dive with goggles. You can't equalize them, so you would get a squeeze.

You need a good quality mask made specifically for scuba diving. Your PADI Dive Center or Resort will likely have quite a few from which to choose, and can assist

you. To check for proper fit, you can place most masks gently against your face and inhale slightly through your nose. They should stay in place with light suction without pushing or twisting to make a seal.

Among masks that fit, these features are desirable:

- **Low profile –** A mask that sits as close to your face as possible (but still fits) gives you a wider field of view. It also requires less air for clearing of water and equalizing.

Among masks that fit you, features and considerations include a low profile, a wide vision field, silicone color and frame color.

PRESCRIPTION OPTIONS

If you wear glasses or contact lenses, you have a few options and your dive center can make recommendations.

1. Do without. If you have mild near-sightedness, you may find that you really don't need to do anything. Underwater, you can't see as far so your vision may be adequate. If you use reading glasses, you may also be fine without correction because water magnifies what you see.

2. Wear your contact lenses. There's some risk of loss if you flood your mask, but this is rare. Have another set or your glasses waiting at the surface in case. It's a good idea to see your eye care provider for recommendations.

3. Get a prescription mask. Several suppliers will make custom lenses to your prescription and bond them into your mask with special adhesives.

4. "Readers" are often an option. Divers who need reading glasses can get small lenses bonded into the bottom corners of their masks to make it easier to read their gauges.

- **Wide vision field** – Beyond low profile, some masks have special shapes to accommodate more field of view. Some have side windows for peripheral vision.

- **Silicone color** – Some divers like the open "feel" of clear silicone rubber; others like the reduced glare of black.

- **Frame color** – You can usually match the rest of your kit.

A new mask needs some preparation. You *may* need to scrub the interior of the glass with a mask cleaner made for this purpose. This removes protective chemicals that some manufacturers apply. These chemicals increase a mask's tendency to fog. However, this is not true of all masks, so check manufacturer literature for specific recommendations.

Other than that, your main preparation is to adjust the strap. Fit it over the crown of your head, above your ears, with a snug but not overly tight fit. Secure the strap-locking device if it has one. Many masks allow you to put them on slightly loose, then tighten for a perfect fit.

Exercise 1-8

1. I need a mask because
   - ☐ a. I will inhale water without it.
   - ☐ b. my eyes must be in air to focus.

2. My mask encloses my nose so I can
   - ☐ a. equalize the mask.
   - ☐ b. suck the mask into place.

3. From among masks that fit me, I should choose a mask that fits as far away from my face as possible.
   - ☐ True
   - ☐ False

4. I want to adjust my mask so the strap rests
   - ☐ a. below my ears, above the neck.
   - ☐ b. over my ears, below the crown of my head.
   - ☐ c. above my ears, over the crown of my head.

How did you do?
1. b. 2. a. 3. False. Choose a low profile that sits as close to your face as possible. 4. c.

LEARNING OBJECTIVES

By the end of this section, I should be able to answer these questions:

1. Why do I need a snorkel?
2. What features should I consider when choosing a snorkel?
3. How do I prepare my snorkel for diving?

Snorkels

Although scuba equipment supplies air, snorkels are standard equipment for scuba diving for several reasons. At the surface, a snorkel saves your air supply while your face is in the water and makes it easier to breathe when there's chop or splashing waves that could get into your mouth. It also allows you to save air when you look underwater (to adjust your gear or see what's below) or swim with your face in the water (much less tiring than repeatedly lifting your head to breathe). A snorkel is even more important for these purposes if you come up with little air remaining and have a moderately long swim to the boat or shore, or have to wait in the water while other divers exit.

Sometimes you see divers who aren't wearing snorkels. With some types of diving, this is appropriate. Even in these instances, though, many divers will have a collapsible snorkel in their pocket in case they need it.

Get a snorkel made specifically for divers so it has the features you need. Adjust it to fit comfortably in your mouth with the top at the crown of your head. Optional features and considerations include:

Flexible lower portion – Allows the snorkel mouthpiece to drop out of the way when not in use.

Self-drain valve – Makes it easier to blow water out of the snorkel.

Splash guard – Reduces the amount of water that can splash in during use.

Color – You can match your other gear, though some divers like a bright color that's easy to see.

Snorkels are standard equipment because, at the surface, they conserve your air supply when you need to breathe with your face in the water.

You usually invest in your mask and snorkel together, and your PADI Instructor or dive operator can help you select and prepare them. Your snorkel goes on the *left* side (because your regulator is on the right) of the mask strap using its clip, slot or keeper. Adjust it so that with the mouthpiece in, the tip is over the crown of your head. This puts it at the highest point when you're face down in the water. When standing up (out of water) with your mask on and snorkel in, the tip will be *behind* your head when positioned properly.

Adjust your snorkel so that with the mouthpiece in, the tip is over the crown of your head. When standing up (out of water), the tip will be behind your head when positioned properly.

Exercise 1-9

1. Snorkels are standard equipment for scuba diving because they allow me to breathe with my face in the water, or in rough conditions, without wasting my scuba air, especially when I have little scuba air remaining.
   - ☐ True
   - ☐ False

2. Some scuba divers prefer a snorkel with a flexible lower portion so it drops out of the way when not in use.
   - ☐ True
   - ☐ False

3. When my snorkel is in my mouth, the tip should be
   - ☐ a. above my forehead.
   - ☐ b. over the crown of my head.
   - ☐ c. at the base of my skull.

   How did you do?
   1. True. 2. True. 3. b.

Considerations when choosing a snorkel include a:

❶ flexible lower portion,

❷ self-drain valve and

❸ splash guard.

LEARNING OBJECTIVES

By the end of this section, I should be able to answer these questions:

1. Why do I need fins?

2. What are the two basic fin styles?

3. What features should I consider when choosing fins?

4. How do I prepare my fins for diving?

Fins

Fins provide a large surface area for your powerful leg muscles to push against so you move efficiently through water. (See Alternate Propulsion for options for people with leg-related physical challenges.)

There are two basic fin styles: *adjustable strap* and *full-foot*. Adjustable fins are open at the heel and straps hold them in place. You usually wear wet suit boots with adjustable fins, which provide warmth and foot protection when walking on shore or a boat deck.

Full-foot fins enclose the heel and fit like snug shoes or slippers. You usually wear full-foot fins with bare feet or thin fin socks, so they're for warm water use. Full-foot fins have different blade sizes – some are suited to scuba, but others are best for snorkeling only.

Primary considerations in choosing fins are fit and blade size. When selecting adjustable fins, try them while wearing wet suit boots. It helps to wet your feet (or fin socks) when trying on full-foot fins so they slide on easily. Fins should fit comfortably, yet not feel loose. Your instructor or dive center pro can help you.

Blade size is usually proportional to foot pocket size, but different models may offer some choices. The larger and stiffer the blade, the more strength you need, but the more thrust you get. Very small, flexible blades take less muscle, but may be very inefficient. Fins intended exclusively for snorkeling may have blades that are smaller than optimal for scuba diving. The "typical" size blade on most scuba fins that fit you is usually the best all-round size.

Optional features and considerations include:

Material – Different materials affect performance, and make fins heavier or lighter.

There are two basic fin styles: adjustable strap and full-foot. Adjustable fins are open at the heel and straps hold them in place. Full-foot fins enclose the heel and fit like snug shoes or slippers. Considerations when choosing fins are fit and blade size, with options that range from material to strap styles.

ALTERNATE PROPULSION

People with physical challenges that limit leg strength and/or motion often can't swim effectively with fins. One alternative is to wear webbed gloves – hand fins, in effect – which help use the arms for swimming.

DPVs – Diver Propulsion Vehicles (a.k.a. "scooters") are fun ways for any diver to get around. Divers with physical challenges also commonly use these in addition to webbed gloves.

For more information, ask your instructor about the PADI Diver Propulsion Vehicle Diver course, or visit padi.com.

Split fins – Some divers prefer the kicking characteristics of fins that have a split down the blade center.

Vents – Some fins let water pass through in key areas to assist performance.

Quick-release straps – Many adjustable fins have quick release buckles that make them easier to remove.

Spring straps – For adjustable fins, once you get the right size, spring straps "auto adjust" for a proper fit every time and are highly unlikely to wear out.

To prepare your fins, adjust the strap on adjustable fins for a comfortable fit with your wet suit boots on. Many buckles let you put your fins on with the straps loose, then pull them snug. Full-foot fins typically require little or no preparation.

Exercise 1-10

1. Fins provide a large surface area so my legs can push against the water effectively.
   - ☐ True
   - ☐ False

2. The two basic fin styles are _____ fins.
   - ☐ a. large blade and small blade
   - ☐ b. freshwater and marine
   - ☐ c. vented and split
   - ☐ d. adjustable and full-foot

3. My primary considerations when choosing fins are fit and
   - ☐ a. blade size.
   - ☐ b. material.
   - ☐ c. splits.
   - ☐ d. vents.

4. To prepare adjustable fins, I should adjust the straps wearing my wet suit boots.
   - ☐ True
   - ☐ False

How did you do?
1. True. 2. d 3. a. 4. True.

By the end of this section, I should be able to answer these questions:

1. What four equipment systems combine to make my scuba kit (scuba unit), and what is the purpose of each?

2. What should I consider when choosing my scuba kit?

1 **BCD (Buoyancy Control Device)** – Holds your kit together and allows you to adjust buoyancy throughout the dive.

2 **Regulator** – Delivers breathing air at the surrounding pressure when you inhale and directs exhaled air into the water.

3 **Cylinder** – Holds the high-pressure breathing air supplied by your regulator during the dive.

4 **Weight system** – Holds lead weight to counteract the positive buoyancy of your body and some of your equipment, with a mechanism for dropping some or all the weight in an emergency.

Scuba Kit

Your scuba kit (or "scuba unit") forms the core of your underwater life support and is actually *four* equipment systems integrated into a single package.

Scuba equipment
is generally interchangeable, but building your kit together helps assure that it meets your preferences.

Each of these systems is made up of individual components as well, each with a specific purpose, which we'll look at shortly.

Choose your scuba kit based on your size, preferences and the types of dive adventures that appeal to you. Because this equipment integrates, invest in the entire scuba kit as a package. Scuba equipment is generally interchangeable, but building your kit together helps assure that it best meets your preferences.

The best way to put a system together is with professional guidance at your local PADI Dive Center or Resort. Most scuba kit components require regular professional servicing and inspection; consider this when choosing your gear. Most dive operators service the models they sell.

As you'll learn later, electronic dive logs such as those found via your PADI Mobile App make it easy for you to keep a file on your dive equipment serial numbers, service dates and notes on personal configurations.

Exercise 1-11

1. Identify the four systems that make up a scuba kit.

   ☐ a. A = cylinder
      B = regulator
      C = BCD
      D = weight system

   ☐ b. A = BCD
      B = regulator
      C = cylinder
      D = weight system

   ☐ c. A = cylinder
      B = regulator
      C = weight system
      D = BCD

   ☐ d. A = regulator
      B = cylinder
      C = weight system
      D = BCD

2. There's no real benefit to choosing the components of my scuba kit as an integrated package.

   ☐ True
   ☐ False

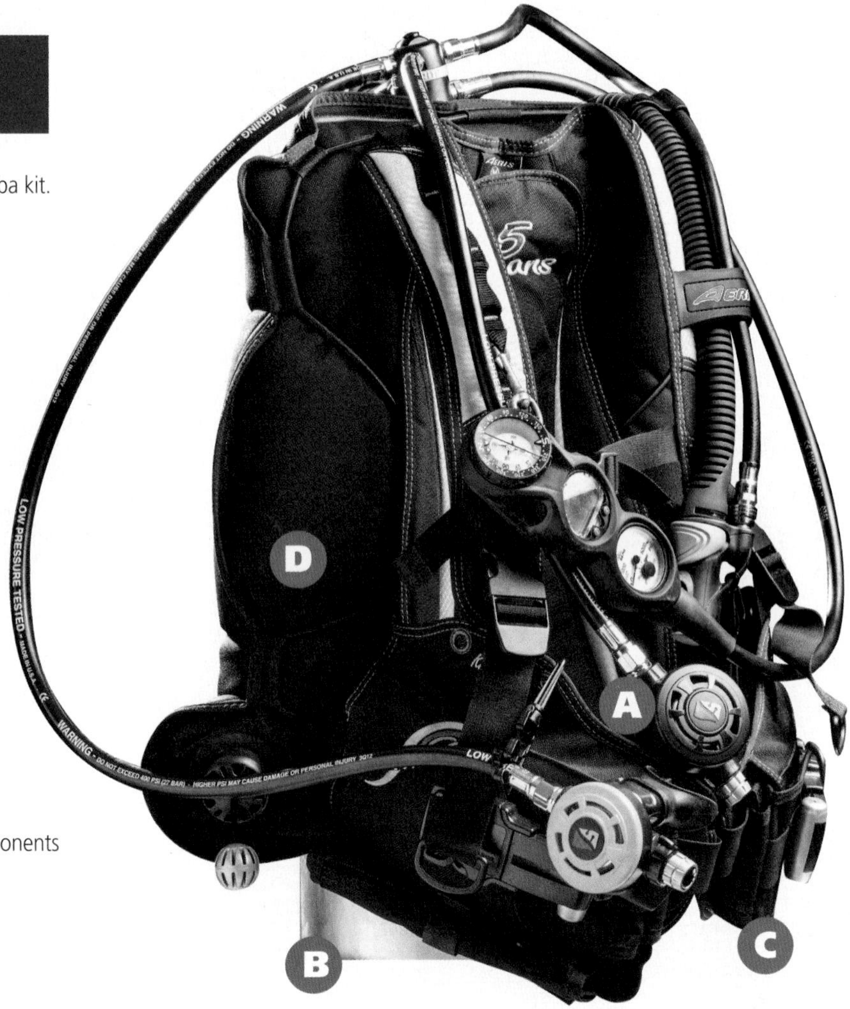

How did you do?
1. d. 2. False. Although the components are generally interchangeable, choosing your scuba kit as a package helps you best meet your preferences.

INTEGRATED SELECTION

It's a good strategy to choose integrated packages rather than individual items. Your PADI Dive Center or Resort can help you put together equipment packages, and may even have kits prepackaged as a start.

Choose equipment based on the type of dives you plan to make and how it fits in with equipment you have, or will have. You have lots of choices, and popular gear usually works well for a broad range of divers. Here are some examples of gear packages:

- Mask, fins and snorkel. You can have a lot of fun with just these. Don't forget mask defog, wet suit boots for open-heel fins, spare straps and a mesh carrying bag.
- Regulator (with alternate air source, submersible pressure gauge and dive computer), BCD, weight system, cylinder – your scuba kit. Don't forget an equipment bag, hose protectors, clips and accessories for rigging, spare o-rings, etc.
- Exposure suit, exposure suit accessories, BCD. The BCD appears here because if you're looking at cooler water diving, you may need a BCD with greater buoyancy and/or higher weight system capacity. Don't forget a mesh bag for carrying a wet exposure suit, suit repair cement, wet suit detergent, and plastic hangers.

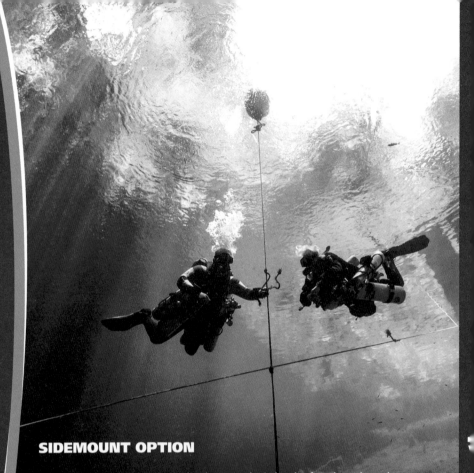

SIDEMOUNT OPTION

Divers have worn scuba cylinders on their backs for decades – but there's a "newer" option: sidemount. In sidemount, you wear at least one, but usually two, cylinders on your sides instead of your back.

It may look awkward, but a well-designed sidemount package is highly streamlined, well-balanced and comfortable. It has several benefits that some divers like:

- Out of the water, it is often easier to transport two smaller cylinders instead of one large one.
- Since you usually put the cylinders on after entering the water, sidemount is a good option for people with lower-back issues and some types of limited mobility.
- You can use two normal sized cylinders for long dives in warm, shallow water.
- Two cylinders and regulators are ideal for air supply emergencies.

To learn more, ask your instructor about the PADI Sidemount Diver course, or visit padi.com and check out the PADI Sidemount Diver

LEARNING OBJECTIVES

By the end of this section, I should be able to answer these questions:

1. What five components make up a BCD, and what does each do?

2. What considerations and options do I have when choosing a BCD?

3. How do I prepare my BCD for use?

4. What two special maintenance considerations do BCDs have?

BCD components. BCD options include:
1 bladder capacity
2 pockets
3 D-rings for accessories
4 shoulder quick releases, as well as color and style choices

BCD – Buoyancy Control Device

The modern BCD has evolved from separate components that function best as a single unit. Its components include:

Inflatable bladder – This is a very durable bag that you inflate or deflate to change your buoyancy.

Cylinder band and harness/jacket – The bladder integrates with an adjustable harness that holds the cylinder on your back. The bladder may be entirely behind you, or wrap partially around your waist and/or over your shoulders. With some systems, you can interchange harnesses and bladders to accommodate sizing and preferences.

LPI (low-pressure inflator) mechanism – Usually at the end of a large-diameter hose, the LPI inflates the bladder with air from your cylinder, via the regulator, when you press a button. Another button allows you to deflate the bladder, or inflate it orally.

Overpressure/quick exhaust valves – To prevent rupturing the bladder due to overfilling, BCDs have one or more overpressure valves that automatically vent if the BCD is too full. Some may have "quick dump" valves that let you manually release air, which is sometimes easier (due to your position in the water) than using the LPI exhaust.

Weight system – Many BCDs have special weight pockets that you can release and drop in an emergency. The more weight you need (like when wearing a buoyant dry suit), the more useful these are. (More about weight systems shortly.)

BCD inflator, deflator and weight systems vary. Your instructor will show you the specifics for the BCD you use.

BCD Options

Among BCDs that fit and are comfortable, choose from the following options:

Buoyancy capacity – Most BCDs cover a wide range of diving circumstances. Your BCD should have ample buoyancy to easily float you and all your equipment at the surface. You sometimes hear the amount of buoyancy called "lift" capacity.

Pockets and D-rings – Many BCDs have pockets for storing and D-rings for attaching accessories.

Shoulder quick release – A quick-release buckle on one or both shoulders makes it easier to get out of your kit.

Colors and style – Choose a look that matches the rest of your gear.

BCD Setup and Care

Prepare your BCD by adjusting it to fit snugly, but not too tightly, ideally while wearing your exposure suit – your instructor will help you with this. After adjusting the BCD, fully inflate it to be sure it doesn't restrict breathing; if it does, it's too tight. Attach a whistle near the low pressure inflator where you can get to it easily, and as necessary, attach hose retainers for regulator components.

Besides general maintenance, BCDs have two additional steps. The first is to rinse the *inside* of the bladder with fresh water as well as the outside. Fill it about 1/3rd with water, then the rest of the way with air. Slosh the water around, then drain it through the LPI exhaust and through each quick dump (if you can manually activate them). You may need to reinflate it a couple times to get out all the water.

The second consideration is that you store most BCDs partially inflated. This helps keep the bladder from sticking together inside.

Prepare your BCD
by adjusting it to fit snugly, but not too tightly. After adjusting it, fully inflate the bladder to be sure it doesn't restrict breathing.; if it does, it's too tight.

Exercise 1-12

1. The LPI mechanism inflates the BCD with air from my scuba cylinder.
   - ☐ True
   - ☐ False

2. My BCD should have adequate capacity to easily float my equipment and me at the surface.
   - ☐ True
   - ☐ False

3. My BCD should fit
   - ☐ a. very tightly and restrict breathing when fully inflated.
   - ☐ b. fit snugly but not restrict breathing when fully inflated.

4. My buddy is rinsing a BCD and partially fills the bladder with water. Is this consistent with recommended BCD care?
   - ☐ Yes
   - ☐ No

How did you do?
1. True. 2. True. 3. b. 4. Yes

By the end of this section, I should be able to answer these questions:

1. What five components make up a regulator, and what does each do?

2. What is the most important consideration in choosing a regulator? What considerations and options do I have when choosing a regulator?

3. What are my considerations and options when choosing an alternate air source?

4. What are my considerations and options when choosing an SPG?

5. How do I prepare my regulator for use?

6. Where do I place or secure each regulator component when diving? Why is this important?

7. What three special maintenance considerations do regulators have?

Your regulator consists of five components: ❶ The first stage is the "hub" of your regulator and supplies air to the components. ❷ Second stage, ❸ alternate air source, ❹ low-pressure inflator hose and ❺ the SPG/computer.

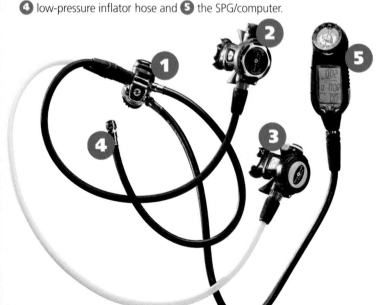

Regulators

Your scuba regulator regulates the air flow from your cylinder (hence the name). When you select "a regulator" at your PADI Dive Center, you start by choosing the first and second stage together, then select the other components for a total of five.

The **first stage** is the "hub" of your regulator. It is a simple and reliable device that supplies air to all the other components. It connects to the cylinder valve either by screwing into it, or with a yoke (clamp system). Either way, an o-ring forms the air-tight seal between the first stage and the cylinder valve. The first stage reduces cylinder pressure to an intermediate pressure, which is 7-10 bar/100-150 psi above the surrounding pressure.

You breathe from the **second stage**. It reduces the first stage intermediate pressure to the pressure around you and delivers air only when you inhale – on demand. It has one-way valves that vent your exhalation. The purge button lets you manually release air from your cylinder.

The **alternate air source** (or "octopus") is an extra second stage you use for sharing air with a buddy should the need arise. The most popular alternate air source is a standard second stage on a longer hose. If needed, you pass it to your buddy to share air. Many are brightly colored so a buddy can locate them easily.

Some divers prefer an **alternate inflator regulator**, which combines a second stage with your BCD low-pressure inflator. If needed, you switch to it and pass your buddy the primary second stage from your mouth. This is usually a part of your BCD when your kit is disassembled.

Pony bottles and **self-contained ascent bottles** are small cylinders with their own regulators, so they're completely separate from your main scuba kit. You can use them yourself or share them with another diver. A self-contained ascent bottle has just enough air to reach the surface and usually attaches to your BCD harness. Pony bottles hold more air, but they're bigger. You typically strap them to your main cylinder or clip them to BCD D-rings.

The **low-pressure inflator (LPI)** *hose* is the hose that supplies air to your BCD inflator. When diving with a dry suit, you have two. You use the second to add air to the suit as you descend (more about this later).

The **Submersible Pressure Gauge (SPG)** tells you the air pressure remaining in your cylinder so you can manage your air supply. The simplest SPG is a hose with a mechanical gauge that reads the pressure in bar (metric) or psi (imperial, pounds per square inch). It may have other instruments attached in a console. Your SPG may also be built into your dive computer (called an *air-integrated* computer) rather than be a separate instrument. Some air-integrated computers are hoseless and use a transmitter to send air supply information from the first stage to your dive computer.

Regulator Options

The most important consideration in choosing a regulator is *ease of breathing.* All modern regulators from reputable manufacturers meet the breathing requirements for diving within normal recreational limits. Higher-end models usually have the highest performance and breathe the easiest. Other considerations and options include:

Yoke or DIN – The yoke system holds the first stage to the cylinder with a clamp system. With the DIN system, the regulator threads into the valve. The yoke system is older and more widely established, while the DIN system – which is growing in popularity – is widely used in Europe and Asia, and has a higher pressure rating. Your instructor or

dive shop can advise you which system is the most popular where you are, but you can be ready for both systems. To do this, a common option is to choose a DIN regulator with a yoke adapter, useable on either type valve.

Adjustable second stage – A knob allows small air flow adjustments; this option lets you keep the regulator breathing its best over the course of its maintenance cycle.

Dive/Predive switch – This switch reduces freeflow (air released without control) when the second stage isn't in your mouth.

Cold-water first stage – In cooler climates, the first stage can freeze, resulting in a freeflow. Special cold-water regulators reduce the likelihood of this by surrounding the first stage with a special liquid.

The second stage delivers air only when you inhale – on demand – or when you press the purge button **1** to manually release air.

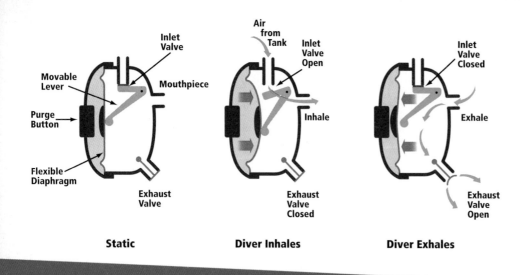

Inlet Valve

Movable Lever

Mouthpiece

Purge Button

Flexible Diaphragm

Exhaust Valve

Static

Air from Tank

Inlet Valve Open

Inhale

Exhaust Valve Closed

Diver Inhales

Inlet Valve Closed

Exhale

Exhaust Valve Open

Diver Exhales

How It Works. The second stage is basically a cup with a flexible diaphragm. When you inhale, you pull the diaphragm inward, which depresses a valve lever. This releases air flow from the first stage. When you exhale, the diaphragm relaxes and the lever lifts, allowing the valve to close. Your exhaled breath flows into the water through one-way exhaust valves.

An alternate inflator regulator combines a second stage with your BCD low-pressure inflator.

Alternate Air Source Options

Your primary consideration when choosing an alternate air source is deciding between simplicity and independence. The extra second stage and the alternate inflator regulator are the simplest alternate air sources regarding setup and care because they're part of your regulator and/or BCD. They add the least bulk to your kit and you typically select these with your regulator. Your PADI Professional can confirm compatibility.

Some divers choose a self-contained ascent bottle or a pony bottle to handle an air supply problem independently. This allows them to manage an air supply problem without buddy assistance (but doesn't replace diving with a buddy, of course).

The alternate air source is an extra second stage you use for sharing air with a buddy should the need arise. The most popular alternate air source is a standard second stage on a longer hose.

Most recreational divers find the alternate second stage or alternate inflator regulator more than adequate, making them the most popular. Divers who choose self-contained ascent bottles or pony bottles usually have one of these as well.

SPG Options

Considerations and options for choosing your SPG are usually driven at least partly by your choice of dive computer. If you choose a computer that isn't air-integrated, you will probably choose a standard mechanical SPG. As mentioned earlier, it may be independent or combine with other instruments in a console. It typically secures to the left side of your BCD in the hip or torso area.

If your SPG is part of an air-integrated computer on a hose, it secures similarly and may also have other instruments in the console. If it is a hoseless computer, it will be on your wrist and receive your air supply information wirelessly from a transmitter mounted on the first stage (more about computers in Section Two). Note that some manufacturers recommend

Pony bottles and self-contained ascent bottles are small cylinders with their own regulators, so they're completely separate from your main scuba kit.

The low-pressure inflator (LPI) hose supplies air to your BCD inflator.

The SPG shows your remaining air pressure in bar (metric) or psi (imperial, pounds per square inch).

having a separate conventional SPG even when using their air-integrated computers.

Regulator Setup and Care

To prepare a new regulator, have a scuba professional attach all the components to the appropriate ports (hose connections). This is normally handled by the dive operator when you get your regulator.

Setting up your scuba kit will be one of the first things you learn and practice during Confined Water Dive One. With respect to your regulator, pay attention to these points in particular:

- Your primary second stage – the one you breathe from – comes over your right shoulder (under with a few models) and is not secured, because it is normally in your mouth.

- Regardless of type, your alternate air source second stage attaches with a quick release in the triangle as shown on the next page. Placement, marking and securing it with a quick release are important so your buddy can locate it quickly if needed. It's also why many divers choose brightly colored models.

- Do not let your alternate air source dangle because doing so may allow it to fill with mud or sand, damage it, or damage fragile aquatic organisms.

- An SPG with a hose normally routes under your left arm and secures with a clip or hose retainer as shown on the next page. You should be able to read it easily. Don't let it dangle. Doing so may damage it and/or the environment. It also creates drag that wastes energy. Some divers simply route it through the BCD jacket sleeve to secure it.

SPG ACCURACY

Submersible pressure gauges usually give years of reliable service when you take care of them according to manufacturer recommendations. Have your SPG's accuracy checked if it does not read zero (0) while unpressurized, or if you have any other reason to question its accuracy.

57

The yoke system (right) holds the first stage to the cylinder with a clamp system. With the DIN system (left), the regulator threads into the valve.

Dive/Predive Switch

Flow Adjustment

Adjustable second stages allow you to make minor flow adjustments so your regulator keeps breathing its best over the course of its maintenance cycle. Dive/predive switches reduce freeflow when the second stage isn't in your mouth.

The extra second stage and the alternate inflator regulator are the simplest alternate air sources regarding setup and care because they're part of your regulator and/or BCD.

There are three special considerations when taking care of your regulator and its components. First, when rinsing it, use a gentle fresh water flow with the first stage dust cap tightly in place, or with the first stage still attached to a cylinder. Don't allow water to enter the air inlet where it meets the cylinder valve. Second, run water through the second stages while rinsing, but do not press the purge button. This could allow water to flow up the hose to the first stage. Third, regulators require periodic overhauls by a professional every year to two years. Have this done as required, even if it seems to be working fine.

A final point: Do not use a regulator if it has high breathing resistance, leaks water, appears damaged or seems not to function properly in any way. Have a professional inspect and service it.

Your alternate air source second stage ➊ attaches with a quick release in this triangle area, and a hose-mounted SPG ➋ typically secures on your lower to mid left torso, as shown. Avoid letting your alternate air source, SPG – or anything else – dangle unsecured from your kit.

Your standard mechanical SPG may be independent or combine with other instruments in a console. It typically secures to the left side of your BCD in the hip or torso area.

Exercise 1-13

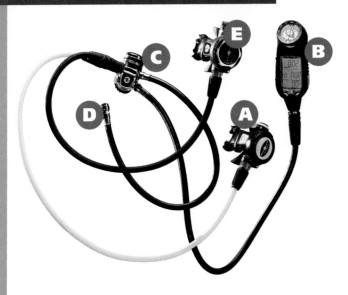

1. Identify the following components:
   - ☐ a. A = SPG/computer
     B = low-pressure inflator hose
     C = first stage
     D = primary second stage
     E = alternate air source
   - ☐ b. A = low pressure inflator hose
     B = SPG/computer
     C = primary second stage
     D = first stage
     E = alternate air source
   - ☐ c. A = alternate air source
     B = SPG/computer
     · C = first stage
     D = low pressure inflator hose
     E = primary second stage
   - ☐ d. A = SPG/computer
     B = primary second stage
     C = first stage
     D = low pressure inflator hose
     E = alternate air source

2. The *most* important consideration when choosing a regulator is
   - ☐ a. ease of breathing.
   - ☐ b. color.
   - ☐ c. dive/predive switch.
   - ☐ d. adjustable second stage.

3. When choosing an alternate air source, a primary consideration involves deciding
   - ☐ a. whether to let it dangle.
   - ☐ b. where to secure it.
   - ☐ c. between independence and simplicity.
   - ☐ d. whether you really need one.

4. My SPG is always part of my dive computer.
   - ☐ True
   - ☐ False

5. My local dive pro will usually set up my regulator components.
   - ☐ True
   - ☐ False

6. When setting up and wearing my kit, the alternate air source
   - ☐ a. dangles on either side.
   - ☐ b. secures in the triangle formed by my hips and chin.
   - ☐ c. goes in a pocket on my left.
   - ☐ d. goes in a pocket on my right.

7. Regulators need periodic overhauls, typically every year to two years.
   - ☐ True
   - ☐ False

How did you do?
1. c. 2. a. 3. c. 4. False. Your SPG may be an independent instrument or it may be integrated into your dive computer. 5. True.
6. b. 7. True.

section one

By the end of this section, I should be able to answer these questions:

1. What two components make up a scuba cylinder? What does the burst disk do?

2. What considerations and options do I have when choosing cylinders and valves?

3. What do the markings on a cylinder tell me?

4. What three safety precautions for handling scuba cylinders should I follow?

5. What six special maintenance considerations do cylinders have?

6. Where do I get scuba cylinders filled? Why?

Cylinders

Your scuba cylinder (tank) is an aluminum or steel alloy container made specifically for storing high pressure air. It consists of two components – the cylinder itself, and the valve.

The valve, made of chrome-plated brass, controls air flow to and from the cylinder. In many countries, the valve also has a *burst disk*. The burst disk is a safety device that relieves accidental overpressure by rupturing and releasing the air well before the cylinder would fail.

Cylinder and Valve Options

You have several options in choosing cylinders and valves, though in most areas one or two types tend to be most popular. When traveling by air, you take most of your kit with you, but rent a cylinder at your destination. So, you may find yourself diving with different cylinder types depending upon where you are.

Material – Both steel and aluminum make excellent scuba cylinders. Aluminum resists corrosion in wet climates, making it very common in tropical locations. Steel cylinders usually hold the same amount of air with a smaller size and/or lower pressure.

Size and capacity – You have size and capacity choices. In the metric system, you refer to cylinders by their internal (liquid) capacity. Common sizes are 8, 10, 12 and 15 litres. In the imperial system, you refer to cylinders by the amount of air held when full, if you released the air at the surface. Common sizes are 50, 63, 71.2 (commonly known as 72) and 80 cubic feet.

How much your cylinder holds depends on its internal capacity and its rated working (maximum) pressure. One cylinder can have a higher working pressure than another, but hold less air because the internal capacity is lower.

Yoke or DIN – You learned about yoke/DIN in the regulator discussion. Choose your cylinder valve and regulator first stage. If in doubt about what type regulator you may need – a common situation for dive resorts that hire out cylinders to traveling divers – a good option is a DIN valve that accepts a yoke insert, which takes either type of regulator.

Your scuba cylinder (tank) is an aluminum or steel alloy container made specifically for storing high pressure air. It consists of two components – the cylinder itself, and the valve. In many countries, the valve also has a burst disk, which relieves accidental overpressure by rupturing and releasing the air well before the cylinder would fail.

Reserve or nonreserve valve – Before the invention of the SPG, valves with reserve mechanisms were standard. Today, they're the exception and you don't see them much, but a few regions still use them. A reserve valve (often called a "J" valve) is a *warning* device; it does *not* give you any more air than a nonreserve valve. To alert a diver of low air, these valves have a spring mechanism that restricts the air when about 20-40 bar/300-500 psi remains. You release the remaining air by pulling down a lever. Even in regions that use reserve valves, you manage your air supply with your SPG.

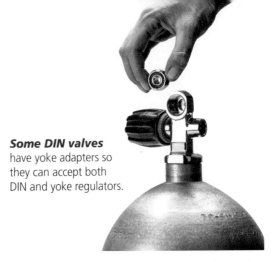

Some DIN valves have yoke adapters so they can accept both DIN and yoke regulators.

Cylinder Markings

All scuba cylinders have several markings. Some of these are stamped into the metal; others are labels stuck on the side.

The following are typically stamped into the metal (varies internationally):

- Cylinder alloy – typically a code number

- Serial number – record in case your cylinder is lost or stolen

- Working pressure – the maximum allowed fill pressure

- Manufacturer's identification

- Manufacture date

- Test pressure – the pressure used for periodic hydrostatic tests (more about hydrostatic tests shortly)

- Hydrostatic test date – there will be at least one, with additional dates for each test over time

1. Government Specification
2. Serial Number
3. Water Capacity
4. Hydrostatic Test Date
5. Tare Weight
6. Working Pressure
7. Test Pressure

Australian Cylinder Neck Markings

You are primarily interested in the serial number, working pressure and the hydrostatic test date. Local laws or regulations may require other markings.

Scuba cylinders that are in service have at least one label. All have a visual inspection decal, which shows the date of their last annual visual inspection. Your dive operator will not fill a cylinder that lacks a current inspection.

You may also see cylinders with an Enriched Air Nitrox (EANx) or Nitrox band just below the cylinder shoulder, which indicates the cylinder is filled with enriched air nitrox. This is air with additional oxygen added to it.

1. Government Agency
2. Metal Type
3. Working Pressure
4. Serial Number
5. Manufacturer
6. Tester's Mark and Hydrostatic Test Date
7. 10% Overfill Allowed

American Cylinder Neck Markings

You typically find these markings stamped into the crown near the valve of scuba cylinders (varies based on local regulations).

These cylinders also have Oxygen Clean/Not Oxygen Clean decals, which tell PADI dive operators information about filling the cylinder with EANx.

You need certification as a PADI Enriched Air Diver to use enriched air. Don't use a cylinder marked this way until certified to do so, or under the supervision of a PADI Enriched Air Instructor.

You'll learn more about EANx a bit later.

Handling Scuba Cylinders

Cylinders are heavy, so there are three main handling precautions to follow.

1. Don't leave a cylinder standing unattended, particularly once you assemble your scuba kit. A falling cylinder can damage equipment and injure people. Lay it down with the BCD up.

2. Secure cylinders for transportation. Block or otherwise restrain them securely so they can't roll or slide.

3. Keep cylinders secured on boats. Cylinders can tumble from their racks when the boat rocks, posing an injury risk as well as possibly damaging gear and the boat. Have a restraining cord in place (if the cylinder rack has one), even if you step away only momentarily.

Depending upon your physical characteristics, be cautious when lifting or moving heavy cylinders, and get help if you need it.

Cylinder Care

Cylinders are highly reliable and typically last decades if properly cared for, but all types have six special maintenance requirements.

1. Have your cylinder pressure tested at required intervals. Laws and regulations require that scuba cylinders receive periodic pressure tests called *hydrostatic* tests every two to five years (varies regionally). This is the date that's stamped into the cylinder metal. Have your cylinder tested as required; never have a cylinder filled that has not been tested within the required interval. Your PADI dive operation can arrange for hydrostatic tests.

2. Have it visually inspected annually. Scuba cylinders are drained, opened and inspected internally for corrosion or other contamination/damage.

Keep cylinders secured on boats. Cylinders can tumble from their racks when the boat rocks, posing an injury risk, as well as damage gear and the boat. If the rack uses restraining cords, put the cord on your cylinder even if you only need to step away momentarily.

An Enriched Air Nitrox (EANx) or Nitrox band indicates the cylinder is filled with enriched air nitrox. Don't use a cylinder marked this way until certified to do so, or under the supervision of a PADI Enriched Air Instructor.

All scuba cylinders have a visual inspection decal, which shows the date of their last annual visual inspection.

Have your cylinder hydrostatically tested and visually inspected at required intervals. Your dive center will not fill a cylinder without a current hydrostatic test date and visual inspection sticker.

Only have your cylinder filled with air from a reputable scuba air station like a professional dive center or resort.

Never have a cylinder filled that doesn't have a current visual inspection sticker. Your PADI Dive Center can conduct the inspection for you.

3. Close and open the valve gently. You don't need to use excessive force when opening and closing the valve. Doing so may damage it.

4. To prevent moisture from entering a cylinder, never completely empty it. Keep 20 bar/300 psi or so in it. (If you accidentally drain it completely, have your PADI Dive Center or Resort visually inspect it). Note that draining air quickly can cause condensation even if you don't drain it completely.

5. Store the cylinder in a standing position in a safe place where it won't get knocked over. This is so if moisture does get in, it will accumulate on the bottom, which is the thickest part.

6. Keep your cylinder out of high heat. Increased temperature raises the air pressure and could blow the burst disk. *Very* high heat (like being in a fire) can damage the metal alloy itself, reducing its strength. If a cylinder has been in a fire, it needs professional testing before reuse (aluminum cylinders are usually condemned). Note that if you want to paint your cylinder, you should see your PADI Professional for guidance. Some metal painting processes use heat (like automotive painting) and will damage the alloy, making the cylinder unsafe even though it looks unaffected.

Filling Cylinders

Get your cylinder filled only at a reputable scuba air station, such as a PADI Dive Center or Resort. Scuba air must be specially filtered, and filled by compressors designed specifically for breathing air. This is important, because contaminants in air that may be harmless at the surface can be toxic at depth due to the pressure. Reputable scuba air stations meet standards for air purity.

Also, have your cylinder filled only with *air*. Under pressure, oxygen can become toxic. This is why you need special training to use enriched air nitrox, which has more oxygen than air. Some forms of diving use pure oxygen, which can be toxic as shallow as 6 metres/20 feet. These require additional training and certification. Unless specifically trained and certified to do so, diving with anything other than air from a reputable scuba air source can be hazardous, with risks including death or permanent injury. As a PADI Open Water Diver, you can become a PADI Enriched Air Diver and use enriched air nitrox, which lets you stay underwater longer in many circumstances. This training teaches you how to manage the problems related to its higher oxygen content.

Exercise 1-14

1. The _____ is a safety device that relieves accidental overpressure by releasing air before reaching the pressure at which the cylinder would fail.
   - ☐ a. DIN valve
   - ☐ b. burst disk
   - ☐ c. cylinder alloy

2. A cylinder with a higher working pressure always holds more air than a cylinder with a lower working pressure.
   - ☐ True
   - ☐ False

3. I'm renting a scuba cylinder at a dive resort. Among the cylinders for hire, some have green and yellow bands that read "Nitrox." As a PADI Open Water Diver with no other training or instructor supervision, am I qualified to use one of these cylinders?
   - ☐ a. Yes.
   - ☐ b. No.

4. I bring a cylinder aboard a dive boat in preparation for a trip out to a nearby reef. The normal procedure would be to
   - ☐ a. stand the cylinder on the deck.
   - ☐ b. lay the cylinder on the deck.
   - ☐ c. secure the cylinder in a rack.

5. Scuba cylinders require pressure testing _____ and visual inspection _____.
   - ☐ a. annually, annually
   - ☐ b. annually, every 2-5 years
   - ☐ c. every 2-5 years, annually
   - ☐ d. every 2-5 years, every 2-5 years

6. I should have my scuba cylinder filled
   - ☐ a. from any compressed air source.
   - ☐ b. with pure oxygen.
   - ☐ c. with pure nitrogen.
   - ☐ d. only by reputable scuba air stations.

How did you do?
1. b. 2. False. A cylinder's capacity depends upon both its working pressure and its internal capacity. 3. b (until you are a PADI Open Water Diver and a PADI Enriched Air Diver).
4. c. 5. c. 6. d.

THE PADI ENRICHED AIR DIVER COURSE

The Enriched Air Diver course is PADI's most popular specialty diver course. Why? Because in many circumstances, it lets you dive longer – especially when making two or more dives in a day.

Enriched air (also called "nitrox," "enriched air nitrox" and "EANx") is air with oxygen added to it. The purpose isn't to have more oxygen, but to have less nitrogen (air is made mainly of oxygen and nitrogen). As you'll learn in Sections Four and Five, nitrogen can limit your allowable dive time. Adding oxygen and reducing nitrogen can therefore provide longer dives.

But high amounts of oxygen can be toxic while diving, and have special equipment requirements. The PADI Enriched Air Diver course teaches you how to benefit from the extended dive times while avoiding problems associated with increased oxygen. Ask your instructor for more information about the PADI Enriched Air Diver course, or visit padi.com.

TECHNICAL DIVING

In many areas, it's likely you'll see divers kitted up in equipment that differs significantly and is far more complicated than what you learn to use as a recreational diver. These divers may go well beyond the limits you learn as well.

These are technical divers, or "tec" divers for short. Tec divers are sport divers who use extensive technology, and have substantial additional training and experience, to exceed the accepted limits of recreational diving. The hardware and training help them manage the complexity and added risk their diving involves.

If tec diving interests you, talk to your instructor about PADI's tec diver courses, the PADI TecRec program, and how you can qualify for them. In the meantime, stay within the limits and use the kit you learn with in this course.

Tec divers go outside the limits you have as a PADI Open Water Diver, but they are not breaking the rules. They are diving by a *different set* of rules, which imposes different limits and equipment requirements.

Visit the TecRec program pages of padi. com to learn more about tec diving.

LEARNING OBJECTIVES

By the end of this section, I should be able to answer these questions:

1. What is the most important feature in my weight system?

2. In an emergency, is it necessary to drop all my weight?

3. What is trim? Why is it important?

4. Why might I use more than one weight system?

5. What are my considerations and options when choosing one or more weight systems?

Weight Systems

There are several types of weight systems. Regardless of type, the most important feature is a quick release that enables you, in an emergency, to drop enough weight to float even with an uninflated BCD. This is an important safety consideration so that if you have a BCD problem, you could still make yourself float quickly.

When wearing a full wet suit or dry suit, dropping only part of your weights will accomplish this. Wearing no exposure suit or a partial wet suit, you don't need much weight, so you should be able to drop all, or nearly all your weight. Most BCD weight systems have two quick releases so you can drop your weight in two amounts. Some BCDs have *non*releasable weight pockets. You use these for trim, but you should have enough releasable weight to assure positive buoyancy. (More about trim shortly.)

You'll practice proper weighting during your training dives. Proper weighting has two aspects. The first is the right *amount* of weight – you want to wear just enough to offset your positive buoyancy, but not more. The second is the right *distribution* of weight. This is called *trim*. Trim is your orientation and balance in the water – generally, the desired trim is a natural horizontal swimming position with your feet parallel to the bottom or slightly elevated.

Your weight system's most important feature is a quick release that enables you, in an emergency, to drop enough weight to float.

Most BCD weight systems have two quick releases so you can drop your weight in two amounts.

Some BCDs have nonreleasable weight pockets. You use these for trim, but you should have enough releasable weight to assure positive buoyancy.

Some divers use more than one weight system. This helps distribute weight for the best trim, and it's often easier than wearing one heavier system when wearing a buoyant exposure suit.

The weight belt is the oldest weight system. Many divers still prefer it, and it's a good option when you don't need much weight. Some divers wear it in addition to integrated weights when they need a lot of weight.

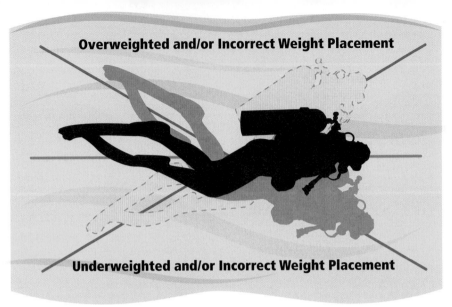

Overweighted and/or Incorrect Weight Placement

Underweighted and/or Incorrect Weight Placement

Trim is your orientation and balance in the water. Generally, you want trim that balances you for a natural swimming position.

Your BCD and weight placement determine trim. Trim is important because it helps you maintain the optimum body position in the water, save energy, reduce accidental damage to fragile organisms and enjoy diving more.

To help with their trim, some divers use more than one weight system to help distribute weight. When wearing a buoyant exposure suit (like a dry suit), it's often easier to handle two or three weight systems rather than one relatively heavy one. This doesn't compromise emergency weight ditching, provided that with at least one system you can quickly release enough weight to be sure you'll float.

Weight System Options

Choose weight systems depending upon your preferences, weight required and trim requirements; your instructor or dive center can help you. Because weight-integrated BCDs have become the most common system, selecting your weight system is usually part of selecting your BCD. BCD weight systems are popular because they:

- Simplify kitting up.

- Eliminate a separate piece of equipment.

- Provide more comfort.

- Commonly include trim pockets.

The weight belt is the oldest weight system, and many divers still prefer it. Weight belts include weights that thread onto a nylon belt and belts that include zippered pockets that hold the weights. It's a good option when you don't need much weight, or (ironically) when you need a lot of weight. In this case, some divers wear it in addition to a BCD integrated-weight system.

HOW TO SET UP A WEIGHT BELT

If you use a weight belt that requires you to thread weights onto it, set it up so that it's comfortable and the weights stay where you put them. Start by determining how long you need the belt to be. You may need to trim yours, but don't do it until you've figured out how much weight you need. This is important, because each weight takes up some of the slack. Rather than cutting your belt, many weight belt buckles let you run any slack back under the belt so you don't have to buy a new belt if you need more weight (and therefore length) later.

Put the weights you need on it, then buckle the belt around you while wearing the exposure suit you'll use. Adjust the length so the free end protrudes about 15 to 20 cm/6 to 8 inches from the buckle when it's snug, but not too tight. Leave room to tighten or loosen it a bit. If you do need to cut the belt because it is much longer than necessary, round the cut edge then melt it with a lighter to keep it from unraveling.

Distribute weights on the belt as evenly as possible, leaving a space in the center of your back where the cylinder goes. Leave about 10 cm/4 inches next to the buckle so you can work it easily. Finally, after you're happy with the weight distribution, use retaining clips as shown in the illustration to keep the weights in place.

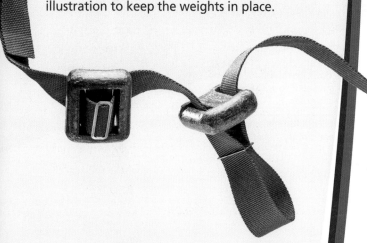

Accessory weights are used to adjust your trim. These are small, specialized weights with clips or devices for attaching around ankles or cylinder valves for better distribution. They don't usually quick release, but should make up only a small portion of your weight so this isn't an issue.

Once you have properly adjusted your weight and trim, log the amount and placement for the equipment and exposure suit you are wearing. This will save you equipment set up time in the future. Access your PADI eLog with the PADI Mobile App or online at padi.com.

Exercise 1-15

1. The most important feature in my weight system is its
   - ☐ a. comfort.
   - ☐ b. quick release.
   - ☐ c. size.
   - ☐ d. trim.

2. I must be able to quickly release enough weight to float reliably in an emergency, but not necessarily all my weight.
   - ☐ True
   - ☐ False

3. Trim means having the right _____ of weight.
   - ☐ a. distribution
   - ☐ b. amount
   - ☐ c. shape

4. One reason for wearing more than one weight system is that it is sometimes easier than handling a single, heavier one.
   - ☐ True
   - ☐ False

5. Accessory weights
   - ☐ a. must have quick releases.
   - ☐ b. can help you adjust your trim.
   - ☐ c. require special training.

How did you do?
1. b. 2. True. 3. a. 4. True. 5. b.

HOW TO DEFOG YOUR MASK

If you don't defog your mask, it will usually fog up during the dive. Most divers have their own "recipes," though your best bet is to follow the directions on the defog product you purchased from the dive center. If there are none, this works for most types:

- Rinse the mask.
- Apply two drops of defog (or one on each side of a split pane mask).
- Spread the defog around with your fingers until it coats the inner surface.
- Dip the mask *once,* briefly, and then pour away any excess water.

This should keep your mask from misting up *unless* the defog compound gets washed out. This may happen if you flood your mask or take it off while still in the water.

❶ *Setting up your gear* is foundational to having fun and diving safely, because doing so correctly is necessary for your gear to fit comfortably and work properly.

❷ *If your physical characteristics* make lifting, standing and/or walking in scuba equipment unreasonable and/or unsafe, don't do it! Ask for help as necessary; there are plenty of other methods for getting into your kit.

❸ *Use proper lifting techniques* whenever you move scuba gear. Bend at the knees and lift by standing with your back straight with its normal curve as shown, upper chest raised and buttocks out slightly. Never bend your back to lift scuba gear, or anything else that's heavy.

❹ *Your first breaths* underwater are exhilarating and exciting. You will never forget them.

Your Skills as a Diver I

Let's look at some of the skills you'll learn. This subsection covers *why* each skill is important and reviews some important points. You'll learn *how* to perform them by watching the demonstration in the PADI *Open Water Diver Video,* followed by your instructor's demonstration, and then by practicing each skill until you can perform it competently and reliably. Important: There are several correct ways to accomplish most dive skills. The methods you see in the video are some of the most popular ways to perform the skills you're learning, but your instructor may show you different or additional ways of doing the same skills.

Setting Up Your Scuba Kit

Setting up your gear involves more than connecting everything together. It's foundational to having fun and diving safely because correct setup is necessary for your gear to fit comfortably and work properly. After you've done it a few times, you'll be able to set up your kit correctly, without rushing, in surprisingly little time.

Gearing Up With Your Buddy(ies)

There are lots of ways to get into your gear, depending upon where you're diving, your physical characteristics and the circumstances. Sometimes you put it on while seated, sometimes buddies help each other while standing, and then you often walk to the water in your gear . . . **but only if you're able.**

⚠ **If your physical characteristics make lifting, standing and/or walking in scuba equipment unreasonable and/or unsafe, don't do it!** Ask for help as necessary; there are plenty of other methods for getting into your kit.

⚠ Dive gear is moderately heavy, so **use proper lifting techniques whenever you move it**. This means bend at the knees and lift by standing. Keep your back straight with its normal curve. Raise your upper chest and stick out your buttocks slightly to keep your back in the right position. Exhale as you lift. Never bend your back to lift scuba gear, or anything else that's heavy.

Besides preventing strains or injury, gearing up in the proper order helps you and your buddies get ready at about the same time. It also helps avoid overheating in hot climates and having to take stuff off because you forgot something.

Inflating and Deflating Your BCD

You use your BCD constantly, so this is an important skill to master. Start developing these habits now:

- Generally, inflate your BCD before entering the water.
- Inflate your BCD when you return to the surface.
- Inflate your BCD if you have a problem at the surface.
- Add or vent air from your BCD in small amounts while underwater.

In Confined Water Dive Two, you will also practice using breathing to fine-tune your buoyancy.

Breathing Underwater

When you're ready, your instructor will also have you go underwater using scuba in shallow water.

- Relax and enjoy the experience – it is unique.
- Breathe slowly and deeply.
- Don't hold your breath!

Hand Signals

Underwater communication is important. Hand signals are the primary way you communicate with other divers. Begin by getting your buddy's(ies') attention. You can rap on your cylinder with a clip, slate edge, finger ring or other hard object. You can also get simple "cylinder clangers" made especially for making attention-getting sound.

Among others, you'll learn these signals:

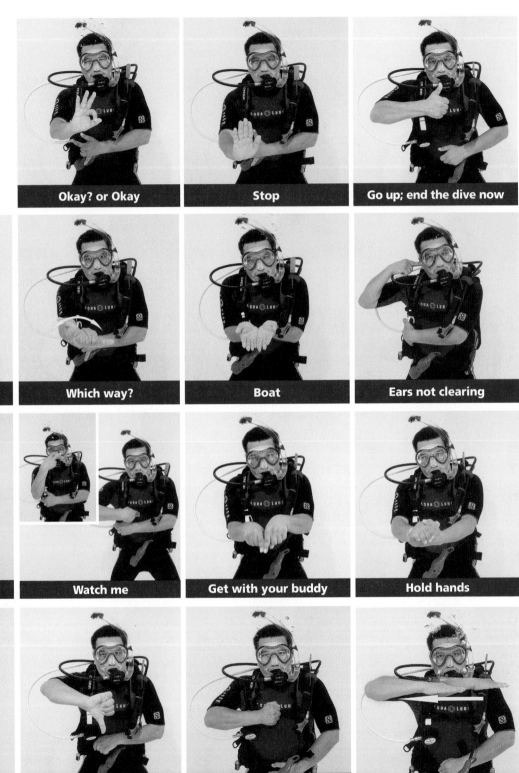

Okay? or Okay

Stop

Go up; end the dive now

Something's wrong

Which way?

Boat

Ears not clearing

Come here

Watch me

Get with your buddy

Hold hands

You lead, I'll follow

Down; descend

Low on air

Out of air

Share air

Slow down, calm down

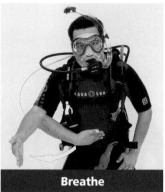
Breathe

How much air do you have?

Danger; hazard

Turn the dive; go back

I'm cold

Use these signals at the surface to communicate with people on the boat or shore:

Okay? or Okay

Okay? Okay, one hand occupied

Distress – help me

71

When learning to recover your regulator, remember to blow a slow, steady bubble stream when it's not in your mouth.

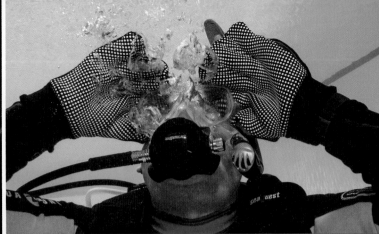

It's easy to clear water out of your mask. Your instructor will show you how to hold the top, blow through your nose and tilt your face upward so your breath pushes the water out the bottom.

Regulator Clearing

When your regulator leaves your mouth for some reason, it fills with water. You need to clear the water so you can resume breathing. This is easy, and your instructor will guide you through the *exhalation* method and the *purge* method. You'll use these skills frequently.

- Blow a small, continuous stream of bubbles when the regulator is out of your mouth.

- After clearing, take your first breath gently and cautiously in case there's a little bit of water left in your regulator.

Regulator Recovery

If you let go of your second stage while it's not in your mouth, depending upon your position it often swings away, out of sight. Your instructor will teach you the *arm-sweep* and the *reach* methods of recovering it.

- With the arm-sweep method, you need to be relatively upright and lower your right shoulder.

- With the reach method, it helps to lift the cylinder with your left hand.

- Blow a slow, steady stream of bubbles when the regulator isn't in your mouth.

- If you have difficulty, don't waste time. Locate your alternate air source and breathe from it, then locate your primary second stage.

Clearing Water Out of Your Mask

It is normal for water to trickle into your mask, and sometimes it can fill entirely by accident. It's easy to clear the water out. Your instructor will show you how to hold the top, blow through your nose and tilt your face upward so your breath pushes the water out the bottom.

- Blow through your nose, not your mouth.

- Start blowing before you look upward.

- Close your eyes if you wear contacts.

- Look downward if your mask has a purge valve.

Managing Your Air Supply

You use your SPG to manage your air supply at all times while diving. With good air monitoring and management habits, you avoid running out of air.

- The caution zone – 50 bar/500 psi remaining – indicates that you should reserve at least this much of your air supply.

Check your air frequently – you should know your remaining pressure within 20 bar/300 psi at all times.

Equalize gently and often – every metre/few feet. If you have difficulty equalizing, stop your descent and signal your buddy and instructor.

- Alert your instructor if you near the caution zone. Your instructor may ask you to indicate when you reach a different, higher pressure.

- Check your air frequently – you should know your remaining pressure within 20 bar/300 psi at all times.

- You will learn to *turn the dive* – that is, head back to the boat or shore – based on how much air you have.

Descending and Equalizing

After using scuba in water shallow enough in which to stand, your instructor will have you practice descending deeper, equalizing as you do so. When you can do this effectively in confined water, you'll be ready to do so during your open water dives.

- Equalize gently and often – every metre/few feet.

- Blow into your mask to equalize it.

- Descend slowly.

- If you can't equalize, stop your descent and signal your buddy and instructor.

- Never continue descending if you can't equalize.

Swimming Underwater

You can use different kicks while diving, but the *flutter kick* is the most common.

- Kick from the hip with very little bend to the knee, and avoid other body movements.

- Use long, slow deep kicks.

- Keep your arms at your sides.

- Your instructor may teach you other kicks.

Alternate Air Source (AAS) Use

With proper air management, running out of air is very unlikely, but you should know how to handle the situation. If possible, you want to respond to an air supply problem by using an alternate air source. The most common type is a second stage supplied by a buddy, which is what you will practice.

- Signal "out of air" and "share air."

- If your buddy doesn't give you the alternate air source, secure it yourself.

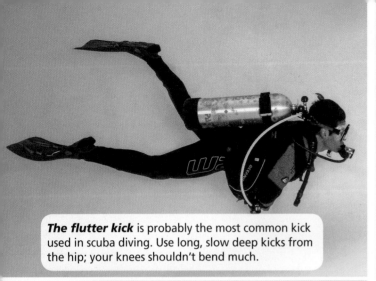

The flutter kick is probably the most common kick used in scuba diving. Use long, slow deep kicks from the hip; your knees shouldn't bend much.

After securing the alternate air source, you and your buddy maintain contact and ascend together at a normal, safe rate.

- With alternate inflator regulators, your buddy switches to the alternate and passes the primary.
- You and your buddy maintain contact.
- Take a moment to get settled, then signal "up" and ascend at a normal, safe rate.

Ascents and Returning to the Surface

Your instructor will teach you the steps to ascend at a safe rate, stay with your buddy and change smoothly to being on the surface.

- Signal "up" to your buddy.
- Swim up – you should not need to inflate your BCD.
- Look up and breathe normally as you swim up.
- Ascend slowly.
- Vent expanding air from your BCD in small amounts frequently (your instructor may do this for you during the first confined water dive).
- Reach up as you break through the surface, and continue to breathe from your regulator while inflating your BCD.
- Have either your snorkel or regulator in your mouth while at the surface.
- Keep your mask on.

Emergency Weight Drop

To be sure you can float in an emergency at the surface, one option is to drop your weights. This is an important option if you have no air in your cylinder, or if there is some problem with your BCD.

- It is never wrong to drop your weights at the surface. **If in doubt, don't hesitate: drop your weights.**
- Quick-release the weights and pull them clear of your body before dropping them.
- Dropping weights underwater risks an uncontrolled rapid ascent, so only do so if you're unsure you could reach the surface any other way.

- When practicing, make sure the area below is clear.

- If you have difficulty when practicing, inflate your BCD so you float and sort out the difficulty.

- For practicing, your instructor may have you use soft weights, attach a capture line or use another method that keeps your weights from dropping to the bottom.

BCD Oral Inflation at the Surface

You need to know how to inflate your BCD orally rather than with the low-pressure inflator, because if your low-pressure inflator had a problem you would disconnect it. You also would not be able to use the low-pressure inflator after surfacing in an out-of-air emergency.

- As you blow into the BCD, press the button you normally use for deflation.

- Release the button between breaths, or else the air will flow back out.

- Kick upward as you take a breath to get well above the surface. This helps you get a good breath in rough conditions.

- Two or three breaths usually floats you adequately (unless you're overweighted).

- Don't dive with a malfunctioning low-pressure inflator. Only use oral inflation to abort the dive.

Exiting the Water

There are different methods for exiting the water, depending upon the situation and your personal needs. You'll probably learn and practice several techniques during the course.

- Inflate your BCD before switching from regulator to snorkel.

- Remove your fins before exiting (if appropriate).

- Keep your mask on.

- Breathe from your snorkel or regulator until out of the water, or in calm water shallow enough in which to stand.

Never hesitate to drop your weights at the surface in an emergency. Quick-release the weights and pull them clear of your body before dropping them.

As you ascend slowly, breathe normally and vent expanding air from your BCD in small amounts. Look up and reach up to avoid overhead obstructions.

You need to know how to inflate your BCD orally in case you have to disconnect the low-pressure inflator, or so you can inflate it with no air in your cylinder.

Remove your fins before exiting if appropriate for your exit technique. This helps avoid walking with fins on.

After the Dive

Once you're out of the water, sit or have a buddy help you remove your fins if you didn't before exiting. If you must walk with them on, walk backward carefully and remove them as soon as you can. Your instructor will demonstrate how to get out of your kit and take it apart.

- It's easiest to get out of your gear while seated.

- On boats, remember to secure your gear so it can't fall or roll.

- Use proper lifting techniques with heavy gear.

- When taking your gear apart, re-secure your cylinder (on a boat) or lay it down (ashore) after removing your BCD.

Confined Water Dive One

- ☐ Briefing – signals introduction/review
- ☐ Assemble, put on and adjust equipment, predive check (instructor)
- ☐ Inflate/deflate BCD at surface, low-pressure inflator
- ☐ Breathing underwater
- ☐ Regulator clearing (two methods)
- ☐ Regulator recovery
- ☐ Clearing a partially flooded mask
- ☐ SPG use
- ☐ Swimming on the surface
- ☐ Descending and equalizing
- ☐ Hand signals underwater
- ☐ Underwater swimming
- ☐ Alternate air source stationary
- ☐ Free time for skill practice and fun
- ☐ Ascents and returning to the surface
- ☐ Emergency weight drop (dive flexible)
- ☐ BCD oral inflation at the surface
- ☐ Exit

Note: Your instructor may modify this to some extent to meet class and logistical requirements.

Knowledge Review One

Some questions may have more than one correct answer. Choose all that apply:

1. Complete the following depth-pressure-air volume-air density table :

Depth	Pressure	Volume	Density
0m/0ft	1 bar/ata	1	x 1
10m/33ft	2 bar/ata	½	x 2
30m/99ft	4 bar/ata	¼	x 4
40m/132ft	5 bar/ata	⅕	x 5

2. As I descend, I need to equalize air spaces. Which of the following are accepted ways of equalizing my ears?
   - ☒ a. Block my nose and attempt to gently blow through it.
   - ☒ b. Swallow and wiggle the jaw from side to side.
   - ☐ c. Block my nose and blow forcefully for an extended period.

3. During a descent, I try to equalize but discover I'm having trouble doing so. Which of the following is correct?
   - ☐ a. Slow my descent, signal my buddy to slow down, and equalize more forcefully.
   - ☒ b. Stop my descent, signal my buddy, ascend slightly and try again.
   - ☐ c. Continue my descent while equalizing repeatedly.
   - ☐ d. Signal my buddy, ascend to the surface and start my descent over.

4. I should equalize
   - ☒ a. early and often, before I feel discomfort.
   - ☒ b. when I begin to feel discomfort.
   - ☐ c. only if I experience pain.

5. I should not dive with a cold, nor use medications to dive with a cold.
   - ☒ True   ☐ False

6. The most important rule in scuba diving is:
   - ☒ a. Breathe continuously and never hold my breath.
   - ☐ b. Always dive with a buddy.
   - ☐ c. Keep my mask on while in the water, even at the surface.
   - ☐ d. Check my SPG at least every couple of minutes.

7. Failure to follow the most important rule in scuba diving can cause serious lung overexpansion (lung rupture) injuries, which in turn can cause paralysis and death.
   - ☒ True   ☐ False

8. If I feel discomfort in a body air space while ascending, the correct action is to:
   - ☐ a. Continue my ascent while blowing against blocked nostrils.
   - ☒ b. Stop, descend slightly and give trapped air time to work its way out.
   - ☐ c. Descend at least 10 metres/33 feet, then resume my ascent.

9. My buddy and I are planning a dive to 18 metres/60 feet. We would expect our air supply to last shorter at 10 metres/33 feet, all else being the same.
   than
   - ☒ a. longer than
   - ☒ b. shorter than
   - ☐ c. the same as

10. During a dive, I swim hard to keep up with a fish that interests me, but shortly begin to feel like I can't get enough air. The correct action would be to:
    - ☐ a. Signal my buddy and head up to the surface.
    - ☐ b. Use the regulator purge button to boost air flow.
    - ☒ c. Stop all activity and rest to restore proper deep, slow breathing.

11. An object that is neutrally buoyant in fresh water will _____ in salt water.
    - ☐ a. sink
    - ☒ b. float
    - ☐ c. be neutrally buoyant

12. The three overall benefits of the buddy system are practicality, safety and fun.
    - ☒ True   ☐ False

13. The primary considerations when choosing any piece of scuba gear are:
    - ☒ a. suitability
    - ☐ b. brand
    - ☒ c. fit
    - ☒ d. comfort

14. I'm planning to dive the following week and am checking my gear. I put my kit together and notice that my regulator seems to breathe harder than I remember. The appropriate action would be to:
    - ☒ a. Have it inspected and serviced as needed by a professional before using it.
    - ☐ b. Go ahead and use it, but limit my dive depth to 10 metres/30 feet.
    - ☐ c. Wash it in fresh water and see if the problem persists.

15. There is no way to use a DIN regulator on a yoke cylinder valve.
    - ☐ True   ☒ False

16. It is important to master buoyancy control because it allows me to control whether I descend, float or am neutrally buoyant. I adjust my buoyancy frequently while diving.
    - ☒ True   ☐ False

Student Diver Statement: I've completed this Knowledge Review to the best of my ability and any questions I answered incorrectly or incompletely, I have had explained to me and I understand what I missed.

Name _____

Date _____

section

two

LEARNING OBJECTIVES

By the end of this section, I should be able to answer these questions:

1. How does being underwater affect the apparent size or distance of things?

2. How does water affect light intensity and color?

3. How does hearing differ underwater?

Being a Diver II

Seeing and Hearing as a Diver

Section One discussed some of the differences between being on land and being underwater that are part of what make diving unique. Let's look at how being underwater affects how you see and hear.

Apparent Size and Distance

Water is about 800 times denser than air, which causes many of the differences between the terrestrial and aquatic worlds. One effect of this is that it causes light to change direction slightly (refract) when it transfers from water into the air in your mask.

This direction change magnifies objects by about a third. Depending upon your perspective objects look larger, closer, or both, than they really are. You may reach for something and miss because it's farther away than it appears. With experience, you learn to compensate unconsciously.

Underwater, what you see is magnified about a third. This makes objects look larger or closer, or both, depending upon your perspective.

Apparent Position
Actual Position

Color Loss and Scattering

Water also affects light by reflecting, scattering and absorbing it. This means that as you go deeper, it gets darker. During the day, at most popular dive sites you usually have adequate light. On most dives, it doesn't seem dark at all, though on others, like night dives or when the visibility is poor, it obviously does. In these conditions, you can use a dive light – you'll get to do this during the Night Adventure Dive in the PADI Advanced Open Water Diver course.

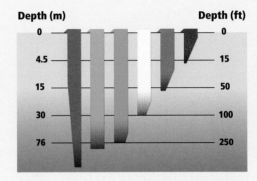

Depth (m)		Depth (ft)
0		0
4.5		15
15		50
30		100
76		250

As you go deeper, red is the first color absorbed, followed by orange, yellow, green and finally blue. You experience the same color loss when looking at distant objects.

Water also absorbs light directly, but not uniformly. As light travels through it, water absorbs some colors before others. The farther light travels through water, the more color it loses. As you go deeper, red is the first color absorbed, followed by orange, yellow, green and finally blue. You see the same color loss when looking at distant objects. Distant objects tend to become more colorful as you get closer.

Your eyes adjust somewhat for the color change, but shining a light at depth brings back lost color and shows the difference.

Hearing Underwater

Water affects what and how you hear underwater, because it transmits sound more efficiently than does air. You will hear many new sounds from aquatic life, boats, divers and other sources.

section two

Underwater sound travels over longer distances. For example, a boat that you can't hear at the surface may sound relatively close underwater.

Sound travels about four times faster in water than in air. This makes it difficult to determine its source – underwater, it usually seems like sound is coming from all around, or directly overhead. You may be able to tell *relative* change in distance by a sound growing louder or fainter, even though you can't tell the direction.

Exercise 2-1

1. Underwater objects appear
   - ☐ a. larger and/or closer.
   - ☐ b. smaller and/or more distant.
   - ☐ c. the same as they do in air.

2. My buddy has a bright red shoulder patch on his wet suit. If we're diving together in very clear water on a sunny day, at 12 metres/40 feet I would expect the patch to appear
   - ☐ a. a more vivid red.
   - ☐ b. less red than at the surface.
   - ☐ c. blue.

3. While my buddy and I are diving, a motorboat passes by about 300 metres/yards away. Which of the following statements is true?
   - ☐ a. It will sound farther away (quieter) than in air.
   - ☐ b. I may have difficulty determining where the boat is based on the sound.
   - ☐ c. It will sound like it is straight below me.

How did you do?
1. a. 2. b. 3. b.

LEARNING OBJECTIVES

By the end of this section, I should be able to answer these questions:

1. How does water's density affect moving in water?
2. How do I move efficiently as a diver?
3. How does streamlining benefit me as a diver?
4. Why is trim important to streamlining, moving efficiently and protecting the underwater environment?
5. What skill allows me to use water's density to make moving in water more efficient?

Swimming and Moving

Because water is so much denser than air, it takes more effort to move in it. The faster you try to swim or move, the more energy you use and the faster you tire because it takes four times as much energy to double your speed.

There's no reason to rush while diving. To move efficiently as a diver, move slowly and steadily. Avoid rapid and/or jerky moves, which waste your strength. You'll go much farther and enjoy the dive more if you relax and take your time.

Streamlining reduces drag, which in turn reduces the energy you use underwater. This makes the dive more relaxing and helps you save air. Streamlining is simply the process of wearing your gear close, with nothing dangling, and swimming relatively level in the water. Your instructor will help you during your confined and open water dives.

Trim

You learned in Section One that trim is your balance in the water – whether, when neutrally buoyant, you tend to hover feet up or down – and depends upon having both the correct amount of weight and correct weight *placement*. With ideal trim, you float with your feet and head relatively level, which is part of being streamlined.

If you have more weight than you need, you compensate by inflating your BCD. This raises your torso and lowers your feet. Too little weight tends to do the opposite. Even the correct amount of weight may be distributed too high or low on your body for proper trim.

With correct trim, buoyancy control makes water's density work *for* you to move efficiently. As you dive, stay neutrally buoyant – almost weightless – so you glide smoothly through the underwater world, and avoid accidental damage to it with fin kicks or other contact. At the surface, inflate your BCD so you float effortlessly. The ability to change your buoyancy is what makes diving a unique, fun experience.

Exercise 2-2

1. Because water is denser than air, it takes more effort to move through water.
   ☐ True   ☐ False

2. To move efficiently as a diver, I should move
   ☐ a. quickly and steadily.
   ☐ b. quickly and sporadically.
   ☐ c. slowly and steadily.
   ☐ d. slowly and sporadically.

3. Streamlining benefits me as a diver because it reduces drag, which helps me save energy.
   ☐ True   ☐ False

4. Trim is important for streamlining because
   ☐ a. poor trim raises or lowers my feet, causing drag.
   ☐ b. it means I have the correct amount of weight.

5. Water's density works best for me when I use the skill of
   ☐ a. shallow, rapid breathing.
   ☐ b. clearing water from my mask.
   ☐ c. equalizing my ears, sinuses and mask.
   ☐ d. controlling my buoyancy.

How did you do?
1. True. 2. c. 3. True. 4. a. b is incorrect because you can have poor trim with the correct amount of weight. 5. d.

When you have correct trim, buoyancy control makes water's density work for you to move efficiently. The ability to change your buoyancy is what makes diving a unique, fun experience.

By the end of this section, I should be able to answer these questions:

1. Why do I chill faster in water than in air at the same temperature?

2. What do I do to stay comfortably warm while diving?

3. What should I do if I'm not warm enough while diving?

4. What should I do if I start shivering uncontrollably?

Staying Warm

Water absorbs more heat than air of the same temperature, and absorbs it about 20 times faster. This means you can chill rapidly even in water as warm as 30°C/86°F. Without an exposure suit, you will get cold after a while, though you may stay comfortable long enough to enjoy a dive.

To stay comfortably warm while diving, you choose an appropriate exposure suit – a wet suit or dry suit – to insulate you. Generally, you *need* one when diving in water 24°C/75°F or cooler, but even in warmer water most divers still use an exposure suit.

The type of exposure protection depends upon the water temperature and how long you plan to dive (or be in the water).

- Dry suits provide the most insulation. You use these for the coolest water/longest dives.

  - Wet suits allow diving in a wide temperature range because you can choose different thicknesses, and select styles that cover more or less of your body.

    If you are not warm enough while diving, end the dive and use more exposure protection next time. It makes no sense to keep diving if you're not enjoying yourself. With the proper exposure suit, you don't have to get cold while diving – even in relatively cool water.

Hypothermia

Exposure suits work very well, but in all but the warmest water you still gradually lose heat. You may be insulated for most of the dive, but if you are in the water long enough you will eventually get cold. Normally, you'll end the dive if you start to get too cool for comfort. However, be aware that if uncontrollable shivering begins, it is a sign/symptom of *hypothermia*.

Normally, you'll end the dive if you start to get too cool for comfort. But if you begin to shiver continuously, exit the water immediately, dry off and seek warmth.

⚠️ Hypothermia is a serious condition in which your body cools so much it can no longer function properly. **If you begin to shiver continuously, exit the water immediately, dry off and seek warmth.**

Exercise 2-3

1. I chill faster in water than in air of the same temperature because water absorbs more heat than air does
   - ☐ True
   - ☐ False

2. To stay comfortably warm during a dive, I
   - ☐ a. wear an appropriate exposure suit.
   - ☐ b. never dive in water colder than 24°C/75°F.

3. After 30 minutes underwater, I start to feel a bit too cool and uncomfortable. I should
   - ☐ a. increase my activity.
   - ☐ b. keep my arms by my sides.
   - ☐ c. end the dive.

4. While diving, I start to feel cool and shortly begin to shiver uncontrollably. I should
   - ☐ a. increase my activity.
   - ☐ b. keep my arms by my sides.
   - ☐ c. end the dive immediately, dry off and seek warmth.

   How did you do?
   1. True. 2. a. 3. c. 4. c.

The type of exposure protection depends upon the water temperature and how long you plan to dive (or be in the water). Dry suits (right) provide the most insulation for the coolest water/longest dives. Wet suits cover a wide temperature range by having different thicknesses and styles.

By the end of this section, I should be able to answer these questions:

1. What is the most effective way to breathe while diving? Why is it important?

2. What is "airway control"? What are two techniques for it?

3. What are eight symptoms of overexertion while diving?

4. What causes overexertion while diving? How do I prevent it?

5. What should I do if I think I'm becoming overexerted at the surface and underwater?

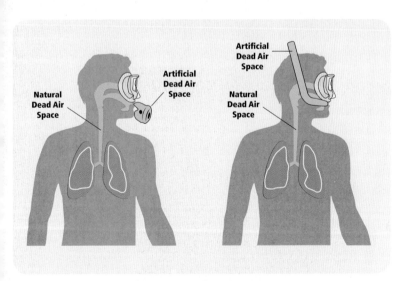

Equipment increases the amount of dead air space. Slow, deep breathing reduces the proportion of dead air in each breath.

Breathing Effectively Underwater

Air Density and Dead Air Space

You'll remember that when scuba diving, it is most effective to *breathe slowly and deeply,* because the air you breathe while underwater is denser than at the surface and requires more effort to breathe. And the denser the air and the faster you breathe, the more energy you use breathing.

Breathing slowly and deeply is also important for effective gas exchange. When you breathe, your body absorbs the oxygen it needs and releases waste carbon dioxide, but this occurs only in the lungs. Not all of the breathing passages take part in gas exchange. We call these air passages dead air space. The first air you inhale ("dead" air) with each breath is the air from your last exhalation, so it is higher in carbon dioxide.

Dive equipment adds dead air space. If you breathe shallowly and rapidly, you rebreathe a much greater proportion of dead air with each breath, and you have to use more energy to meet your body's gas exchange needs. On the other hand, breathing slowly and deeply reduces the proportion of dead air in each breath.

You breathe slowly and deeply when you're relaxed. Making a point of breathing slowly and deeply helps you stay relaxed, and it can help you calm down if you begin to feel anxious. Proper breathing also helps you stay clear-headed and make better decisions.

Airway Control

It is common to have some residual water in your regulator or snorkel, especially after clearing it. *Airway control* is the skill of breathing past this remaining water without drawing any into your throat. There are two basic techniques – after clearing your regulator or snorkel, assume it will have a little water left and use one or both.

The first technique is to inhale slowly. If you inhale slowly, water tends to stay in the mouthpiece while the air gurgles past into your mouth and lungs. It helps to look downward a bit.

The second technique is to touch your tongue to the roof of your mouth as you inhale. Your tongue will tend to block water as air flows around it. Again, looking a bit downward helps, and you can combine both methods.

Sometimes you get a few drops of water in the back of your throat, which create the urge to cough. Go ahead and cough – simply hold your regulator or snorkel in place as you do.

Overexertion

⚠️ **Overexertion while diving can be alarming, and may lead to panic and accidents.** You can avoid and/or stop overexertion by recognizing its symptoms, causes and prevention, and by knowing what to do if you experience it.

Overexertion symptoms include:

- Fatigue
- Labored breathing
- A feeling of suffocation or air starvation
- Weakness
- Anxiety
- Headache
- Muscle cramping
- A tendency to panic

Overexertion usually results from prolonged elevated effort, like fighting a current. It is caused by trying to breathe dense air rapidly, faster than equipment can deliver it.
You prevent overexertion by breathing slowly, deeply and continuously. Avoid lengthy, strenuous exertion while diving. If your breathing rate begins to rise, stop and rest before it becomes labored.

If you experience overexertion, stop *all* activity, signal your buddy and rest. Further activity makes it worse. If you're at the surface, inflate your BCD and/or drop your weights so you

The first airway control technique is to inhale slowly while looking downward a bit. Water tends to stay in the mouthpiece as the air gurgles past.

The second airway control technique is to raise your tongue to the roof of your mouth. This helps block water as air flows around it.

If you experience overexertion, stop all activity, signal your buddy and rest. If you're underwater, hold on to something or rest on insensitive bottom.

PEAK PERFORMANCE BUOYANCY

You'll quickly notice that the most skilled divers have excellent buoyancy control. They seem to descend, ascend or hover midwater just by *thinking* about it. There's more to it than that, but you're witnessing Peak Performance Buoyancy.

Although you master the fundamentals of basic buoyancy control as part of earning your PADI Open Water Diver certification, the Peak Performance Buoyancy course fast-tracks you to this skill level. You learn to apply center-of-gravity and center-of-buoyancy concepts to refining weight placement and trim, as well as breathing and streamlining techniques. Because it helps raise your skills so quickly, it's one of the first specialty diver courses new divers take after certification. See your instructor, PADI Dive Center or Resort, or visit the Peak Performance Buoyancy page at padi.com.

don't have to fight to stay there. Signal the boat to pick you up, if appropriate. If you're underwater, hold on to something or rest on the bottom where you won't damage sensitive aquatic life.

After restoring normal breathing, resume activity at a lower pace, avoiding the effort that caused the problem. Remember that your goal is to always breathe slowly, deeply and continuously.

Exercise 2-4

1. While scuba diving, I should breathe
   ☐ a. rapidly and shallowly.
   ☐ b. slowly and deeply.

2. One method of airway control is to inhale slowly. I can also _____ to help breathe past small amounts of water in my regulator.
   ☐ a. tilt my head upward
   ☐ b. press the purge button
   ☐ c. close and reopen the cylinder valve
   ☐ d. raise my tongue

3. If I'm tired, have labored breathing and feel air-starved and anxious during a dive, it is likely I am experiencing overexertion.
   ☐ True
   ☐ False

4. Overexertion results from
   ☐ a. slow, deep breathing.
   ☐ b. a prolonged increased effort.
   ☐ c. normal swimming.

5. If I think I'm overexerting while underwater, I should stop, signal my buddy and
   ☐ a. rest.
   ☐ b. ascend immediately.
   ☐ c. use purge-assisted breathing.
   ☐ d. fully inflate my BCD.

How did you do?
1. b. 2. d. 3. True. 4. b. 5. a.

LEARNING OBJECTIVES

By the end of this section, I should be able to answer these questions:

1. How do my buddy(ies) and I plan dives together? What nine points should a dive plan normally include?

2. How do my buddy(ies) and I kit up together?

3. How and when do we conduct the predive safety check?

4. What do I do if I get separated from my buddy(ies) during a dive?

5. Whose responsibility is the buddy system?

The Buddy System (continued)

You've learned that as a diver, you will plan and make dives with your buddy or buddies. Plans don't have to be complex or lengthy, but they help avoid problems and make the dive enjoyable.

Plan your dives by discussing what you want to accomplish, the best techniques, hazards to avoid and what to do if problems occur. There may be more, but dive plans usually address these nine points:

1. Agree on the best entry and exit techniques for the environment.

2. Decide what course you'll follow.

3. Agree on the maximum time and depth.

4. Review underwater signals and other communications.

5. Determine when you will turn the dive and head back based on your remaining air, time and/or other factors – whichever comes first.

6. Agree on how you'll stay together during the dive (e.g., swim side by side, one leads while the others follow, etc.).

7. Establish what you will do if you become separated.

8. Discuss emergency procedures.

9. Agree on an objective. An objective may be detailed, such as "shoot videos of butterfly fish pairs," or as simple as, "let's go for a look."

Predive Safety Check

You and your buddy(ies) gear up at the same time so you're ready to get in the water together. You may assist each other with zipping exposure suits, adjustments, holding scuba kits for each other, etc. Sometimes divers get into their kit with little assistance and at other times they benefit from some help. When everyone's ready and kitted up (except for mask, snorkel and fins in many instances), you go through the predive safety check. The check helps make sure everything's good to go, and everyone's familiar with each other's kit.

When everyone's ready, you go through the predive safety check. The check helps make sure everything's good to go, and everyone's familiar with each other's kit.

The recall phrase for the predive safety check is **Begin With Review And Friend,** but you can use any other phrase that helps you remember BWRAF.

Begin – B – BCD: Check adjustment, how to operate it, low-pressure inflator connection, and that your cylinder is firmly in the band. If appropriate for the entry technique, make sure it's partially inflated. Confirm that your visual and audible surface signaling devices, which are usually attached to your BCD or in a BCD pocket, are in place.

With – W – Weight: Check that you have the right amount of weight, that it's properly distributed for trim, and that the quick release is clear so that you can, in a single motion, release enough weight to be sure you float.

Review – R – Releases: Confirm everyone's releases are secure, and that all buddies know how to work each other's releases in case they need to do so in an emergency.

And – A – Air: Test breathe your regulator two or three breaths. Check your air pressure to be sure it shows a full cylinder. All buddies make sure they know how to find and use each other's alternate air sources so they can share air should they need to do so.

Friend – F – Final Check: Look each other over for anything that seems to be missing, out of place, not adjusted correctly, etc.

Perform the predive safety check before every dive. With practice, you'll find it takes only a few moments, yet it can prevent inconveniences, disappointments and accidents.

Avoiding and Dealing with Buddy Separation

During the dive, you and your buddy(ies) need to stay close together – ideally within a couple metres/few feet. If you find yourself farther apart than that, get back together. A good rule of thumb is to be able to reach each other in two seconds. Usually, it's easier to stay together if you discuss how to do so during dive planning.

Buddy separation occurs when buddies can't see each other, but it's also possible when they can. In very clear water, you may be able to see your buddy, but be too far away to provide assistance quickly. In lower visibility, it is easier to lose sight of each other; for example, when your buddy stops to look at something while you keep swimming. In either situation, staying close and checking each other frequently reduces accidental separation and/or being too far apart.

Although you shouldn't get separated from your buddy, you should know what to do if it happens. During dive planning, discuss what to do if you get separated – how you will reunite (meet some place, etc.).

The *general* procedure is to look for each other for no more than a minute, then if unable to relocate each other, carefully ascend and reunite on the surface. But this procedure may not be practical in some environments, so in those instances it's important to plan what you would do if buddy separation occurs.

Note that when three people dive together, if one gets separated all divers follow the procedures for reuniting. Even though two divers are still together, they must take action to rejoin the isolated buddy.

The PADI Skill Practice and Dive Planning Slate provides a handy checklist for basic dive planning steps. Use it during the course to develop your ability to plan dives, and after the course as a planning checklist.

The buddy system works well when divers plan their dives together, conduct the predive safety check together, stay together and manage their air together. **It's *your* responsibility to stay with your buddy and follow the rules, guidelines and recommendations for each other's dive safety.** No one can do it for you.

Exercise 2-5

1. My buddies and I are planning a dive. Among other things, we should address how to enter and exit the water, the maximum depth and time, when to turn the dive and what to do if we get separated.
   - ☐ True
   - ☐ False

2. As my buddy and I kit up, the normal practice is to be entirely independent. Helping each other is discouraged.
   - ☐ True
   - ☐ False

3. When I conduct a predive safety check, the "A" in the recall phrase includes
   - ☐ a. assuring that all releases are secure.
   - ☐ b. confirming adequate air pressure for the dive.
   - ☐ c. adjusting the BCD.
   - ☐ d. addressing weight system issues.

4. If my buddy and I get separated, the *general* procedure is to
   - ☐ a. return to where I last saw my buddy and wait.
   - ☐ b. search until we reunite or until I run low on air.
   - ☐ c. bang on my cylinder to get my buddy's attention with sound.
   - ☐ d. look for each other for no more than a minute, then reunite on the surface.

5. The buddy system is _____ responsibility.
   - ☐ a. my
   - ☐ b. the divemaster's
   - ☐ c. my buddy's
   - ☐ d. no one's

How did you do?
1. True. 2. False. Buddies normally help each other. How much you assist each other depends on the situation.
3. b. 4. d. 5. a.

During the dive, you and your buddy(ies) need to stay close together – ideally within a couple metres/few feet. A good rule of thumb is to be able to reach each other in two seconds.

In very clear water, you may be able to see your buddy, but be too far away to provide assistance quickly.

Note that when three people dive together, if one gets separated, all divers follow the procedures for reuniting. Even though two divers are still together, they must take action to rejoin the isolated buddy.

By the end of this section, I should be able to answer this question:

1. How do my buddy(ies) and I manage our air supply together while diving?

In reality, with appropriate conservative dive planning and habits, you will often use a bit less air than planned coming back. In many circumstances, you can adjust and delay your ascent to enjoy your "extra" air. If the unexpected causes you to reach your ascent pressure before you reach your planned ascent point, surface where you are. **Do not risk running out of air underwater.**

Managing Your Air Supply as a Buddy Team

You manage your air supply while diving, but you interact with your buddies as you do so. This is important because people use air at different rates. Someone will always use air the fastest, and someone the slowest. Throughout the dive, you and your buddy(ies) share air supply information, then turn the dive and head back based on the diver who's using it the fastest.

On many shallow dives, where air supply is the usual limiting factor (you'll learn some other factors in Section Four), you can plan your air use something like this (Note: Metric and imperial figures are not equivalent; the example uses pressures commonly used by divers in the respective systems.):

- You and your buddies are diving from a boat and have the same size cylinders. You all start the dive with 200 bar/3000 psi.

- You agree that 50 bar/500 psi is ample reserve pressure – the minimum you want to have left at the end of the dive.

- Now plan for the air you'll use during your ascent and safety stop. Based on the depth, you agree that you want to save 20 bar/300 psi for this. Put this with your reserve so you know the pressure at which you should be heading up – in this case, 70 bar/800 psi (50 bar + 20 bar = 70 bar/500 psi + 300 psi = 800 psi).

- Take this from your starting pressure, and what's left is the pressure you can use for the main part of the dive. In this case, you have 130 bar/2200 psi (200 bar – 70 bar = 130 bar/3000 psi – 800 psi = 2200 psi).

- To simplify, you agree to use half of this swimming out, then turn the dive and use the other half for the return. This means you'll turn around when one of you has used 65 bar/1100 psi. (Half of 130 bar is 65 bar; half of 2200 psi is 1100 psi.)

- Take this pressure away from your starting pressure to find the pressure at which you head back. You'll turn the dive when either you or your buddy's SPG reads 135 bar/1900 psi. (200 bar – 65 = 135 bar, or 3000 psi – 1100 psi = 1900 psi.) This is called your *turn pressure* – the SPG pressure at which you turn around.

- Note your starting air pressure, planned reserve and planned turn pressure on the PADI Skill Practice and Dive Planning Slate for reference during the dive.

Turning the dive at 135 bar/1900 psi leaves 65 bar/1100 psi for swimming back. When you get there, you should have at least 70 bar/800 psi for your ascent, safety stop and reserve. After you surface, you should have at least 50 bar/500 psi – your reserve – remaining.

In reality, with appropriate conservative dive planning and habits, you will often use a bit less air than planned coming back. In many circumstances, you can adjust and delay your ascent to enjoy your "extra" air. For example, suppose you and your buddy reach the mooring line with 100 bar/1100 psi remaining. You can explore the immediate area around the mooring until you have to head up at 70 bar/800 psi.

On the other hand, suppose something unexpectedly delays your return or causes you to use more air than normal. With conservative planning and habits, you will still likely reach your ascent area within your planned air supply. But if the unexpected causes you to reach your ascent pressure before you reach your planned ascent point, surface where you are and swim the rest of the way on the surface using your snorkel.

 Do not risk running out of air underwater.

Sometimes buddies use different sized cylinders or start with different pressures. To conservatively adjust for slight differences in cylinder sizes and starting pressures, plan your air management based on the smallest air supply.

Exercise 2-6

1. My buddy and I are planning a boat dive with the same type cylinders filled to 200 bar/3000 psi. Due to conditions, we are planning very conservatively. We agree on 60 bar/800 psi for our reserve. We agree that we also want an additional 30 bar/500 psi for our ascent and safety stop. This means we should begin our ascent when either of our SPGs reads

   ☐   a. 50 bar/800 psi.

   ☐   b. 70 bar/1000 psi.

   ☐   c. 90 bar/1300 psi.

   ☐   d. 110 bar/1700 psi.

   How did you do?   1. c.

By the end of this section, I should be able to answer these questions:

1. Why is it a good habit to keep my mask on and a snorkel or regulator in my mouth while at the surface in water too deep in which to stand?

2. What are three reasons why I may swim on the surface while scuba diving?

3. What are two methods for surface swimming while scuba diving?

4. How do I maintain the buddy system while swimming at the surface?

Swimming at the Surface

You commonly spend time at the surface with your BCD partially inflated at the start of a dive before you descend, and at the end after you ascend. You may do this waiting for your buddies to enter, or when getting out, while waiting your turn to exit. Sometimes you descend and ascend some distance from where you enter and exit the water.

It is a good habit to keep your mask on and a mouthpiece (snorkel or regulator) in place whenever you're in water too deep in which to stand. This is because under stress, you tend to do what you do by *habit*. When in difficulty, you may need to see and breathe effectively with your face in the water. If your mask is off and/or you have no mouthpiece in, you respond more slowly if you must put them back on to deal with a problem. Therefore, the habit that helps reduce and handle problems is having your mask on and a mouthpiece in your mouth, even when it might seem unnecessary. If in an emergency it is better to have your mask off and/or mouthpiece out, you can remove either or both *much* more quickly than you can put them on.

section two

Keeping your mask on and your mouthpiece in place has other benefits. It protects your vision and airway from unexpected splashes or waves. You're less likely to lose a mask that is on your face. If you need to talk, do so – then replace your mouthpiece.

If you will be at the surface for more than a few minutes, use your snorkel to conserve your air supply. At the end of a dive with your cylinder nearly empty, you need a snorkel to breathe with your face in the water or in choppy conditions.

There are three common reasons why you may swim on the surface while scuba diving.

1. *To save air when you must enter the water some distance from where you want to descend and/or ascend.* You do this so you don't waste air on the surface swimming to and from your descent/ascent point.

2. *To save air while looking for where you want to descend.* Especially in clear water, you do this so you don't waste air looking for a particular spot you want to visit on the bottom. You look for the spot from the surface on snorkel, then descend directly to it on scuba.

3. *Because you may surface away from your exit point and must swim to it on the surface.* If you're low on air, for example, you would use your snorkel to make the swim easier.

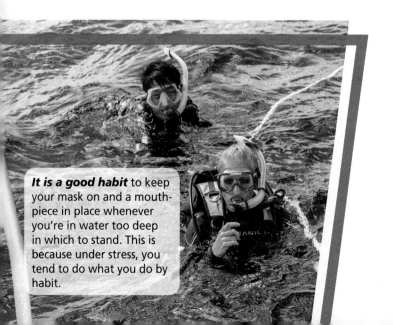

It is a good habit to keep your mask on and a mouthpiece in place whenever you're in water too deep in which to stand. This is because under stress, you tend to do what you do by habit.

Surface Swimming Methods

There are two methods you use for surface swimming. The obvious one is to swim face down breathing through your snorkel. This is good when you want to see the bottom.

For longer swims, though, you can swim on your back with your head out of the water. This can be less tiring. The only down side is it's a *little* harder to watch where you're going – but it's not that difficult. Even though your face is out of the water, breathe through your snorkel. Adjust it slightly if the tip is in the water when you're on your back.

On the surface, the buddy system still applies. Stay close enough to help each other quickly, just as you do underwater. Use the same methods for staying together at the surface that you use underwater. Generally, it works well to swim side by side.

Exercise 2-7

1. At the surface, it's a good habit to keep my mask on and my snorkel or regulator in my mouth because it helps me deal with difficulties more effectively.
    ☐ True ☐ False

2. My buddies and I plan to enter the water, but swim on the surface to a descent point about 50 metres/yards away. A primary reason we will do this is because
    ☐ a. it's easier than descending immediately.
    ☐ b. it saves our cylinder air for the dive.
    ☐ c. we enjoy the exercise.

3. For the 50 metre/yard swim, my buddies and I will swim _____ because it is less tiring.
    ☐ a. face down
    ☐ b. on our backs

4. To stay with my buddy while surface swimming, generally it works well to swim
    ☐ a. side by side.
    ☐ b. with the faster diver in front.
    ☐ c. with the slower diver in front.

    How did you do?
    1. True. 2. b. 3. b. 4. a.

By the end of this section, I should be able to answer these questions:

1. What are the five steps for a proper descent with scuba?
2. How do I descend with and without a reference?
3. When do I start equalizing when I descend? How often do I equalize?
4. What happens to my buoyancy as I descend and why?
5. How do I control my buoyancy as I descend?

Descents in Open Water

Five Point Descent

There are five steps you follow when you descend.

1. Confirm that your buddies are ready.
2. Orient yourselves to something at the surface or underwater, such as the boat or a landmark.
3. Switch from your snorkel to your regulator.
4. Check, and if necessary activate, your dive computer or timer. If in "sleep" mode, most dive computers self activate when you go underwater, but generally it's best to have them active.
5. Signal "descend" and, with your buddies, slowly deflate your BCD.

Descents With and Without a Reference

Descend slowly from the beginning. Keep your head above your feet to make equalizing easier and help you stay oriented, and stay close to your buddy.

You often have a line or slope as a descent reference. Usually, you use it as a visual reference only and control your descent rate by controlling your buoyancy. But in some circumstances, you may use the reference to help control your descent or stay in place by holding on to it. The most common example is descending in contact with a mooring line to keep a current from carrying you away from the dive boat.

Sometimes, though, you have to descend without a reference. In this circumstance, stay with your buddy and control your descent by watching the depth on your computer (or a depth gauge) while adjusting your buoyancy.

When you're ready to descend, begin by confirming that your buddies are ready, too.

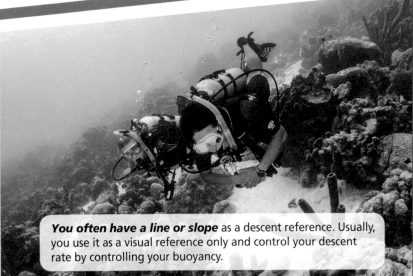

You often have a line or slope as a descent reference. Usually, you use it as a visual reference only and control your descent rate by controlling your buoyancy.

To descend without a reference, stay with your buddy and control your descent by watching the depth on your computer while adjusting your buoyancy. Begin equalizing immediately, as soon as your head submerges. Equalize frequently – every metre/few feet – before you feel discomfort. To offset the normal decrease in buoyancy as you descend, inflate your BCD in small amounts frequently. This keeps your buoyancy under control. Ideally, you arrive at the bottom neutrally buoyant.

In Section One, you learned that you equalize early and often as you descend. Begin equalizing immediately, as soon as your head goes underwater. Equalize frequently – every metre/few feet, before you feel discomfort, as you've already learned. You will equalize more on an open water dive than in confined water because you'll be going deeper.

Recall that in most circumstances, as you descend your buoyancy decreases, which makes you go down faster unless you adjust for it. This results from the pressure compressing your exposure suit (if you're wearing one), making it less buoyant. You adjust for this buoyancy loss by adding air to your BCD (or dry suit if you're wearing one).

When inflating your BCD to adjust your buoyancy as you descend, do so in small amounts, frequently. This keeps your buoyancy under control and allows you to descend slowly. This helps you equalize every metre/few feet. Ideally, you will arrive at the bottom with your buoyancy adjusted so that you're neutrally buoyant.

Exercise 2-8

1. I'm descending in open water with my buddies. After confirming they are ready, the next step is to signal "descend" and slowly deflate my BCD.
   - ☐ True
   - ☐ False

2. When descending with a reference, I would *normally*
   - ☐ a. make physical contact with it.
   - ☐ b. ignore the reference and use my dive computer.
   - ☐ c. use it as a visual reference only.

3. My buddy and I have just started our descent. I begin equalizing
   - ☐ a. immediately, as soon as my head goes underwater.
   - ☐ b. at approximately 3 metres/10 feet.
   - ☐ c. when I feel discomfort.
   - ☐ d. when I see my buddy equalize.

4. As I descend while wearing a wet suit, my buoyancy will tend to
   - ☐ a. increase.
   - ☐ b. decrease.
   - ☐ c. remain constant.

5. During my descent, to control my buoyancy I add air to my BCD
   - ☐ a. use long, infrequent bursts.
   - ☐ b. when I reach the bottom.
   - ☐ c. in small amounts, frequently.

How did you do?
1. False. You orient yourself, switch to your regulator and check your dive computer or timing device before deflating your BCD. 2. c. 3. a. 4. b. 5. c

Ascents in Open Water

Five Point Ascent

Just as there are five points when you descend, you and your buddies follow five steps when you ascend.

1. Signal "up" and confirm that your buddies are ready.

2. Check your dive computer to be sure you're within its limits. (You'll learn more about these limits later. If you're not using a computer, check the time for use with dive tables.)

3. Look up and hold up your BCD deflator hose. Do *not* add air to your BCD. If you're properly weighted and neutrally buoyant, you only need to start swimming up gently.

4. Ascend slowly – no faster than your dive computer's maximum rate. The maximum ascent rate is 18 metres/60 feet per minute, but most dive computers require a slower rate of 10 metres/30 feet per minute. Most dive computers will warn you if you ascend too fast, so use your computer to guide your speed. Release air expanding in your BCD to control your buoyancy so you don't start to rise too fast. If you're not using a computer, use your timer and depth gauge to be sure you ascend no faster than 3 metres/10 feet each 10 seconds.

5. Look up and turn as you ascend, and stay with your buddies. Watch for obstacles overhead. Reach up as you near and break through the surface.

Controlling Your Buoyancy

As you ascend, a wet suit, or the air you added to a dry suit, and your BCD will expand. Both of these changes cause your buoyancy to increase; the shallower you get, the more buoyant you become if you don't adjust for it.

To control your ascent rate, release air from your BCD (or dry suit) as you ascend. Adjust your buoyancy in small amounts, often, just as you do while descending.

You should ascend slowly and be able to pause your ascent easily. If you start to rise too fast or cannot easily pause your ascent, you're not adjusting frequently enough.

Do not add air to your BCD to start your ascent. If you're properly weighted and neutrally buoyant, you only need to start swimming up gently.

Ascents With and Without a Reference

When possible, ascend with your buddy following a reference such as a sloping bottom, mooring line or a vertical line deployed from a boat or float, much as you would use a reference when descending. A visual reference helps you control your ascent rate and maintain orientation.

Fixed references, like mooring lines, can help you slow or control your ascent rate, but this should not be necessary if you control your buoyancy properly. In some situations, however, you may ascend holding a reference line so you don't get carried away from the boat or exit point by a current.

You may also ascend in midwater without a reference. This may be intended (as will be the case for many dive sites), or may be the result of having to ascend to the surface before you planned to, away from where you'd expected to ascend. This could happen if you lose your direction, if there's an emergency or problem.

When ascending without a reference, stay with your buddy. Watch your depth and ascent rate on your dive computer, and control your buoyancy. If you're not using a dive computer, many modern depth gauges help guide your ascent rate. Otherwise, watch your depth and time. Ascend no faster than 3 metres/10 feet in 10 seconds, though slower is fine.

To control your ascent rate, release air from your BCD (or dry suit) as you ascend. Adjust your buoyancy in small amounts frequently, just as you do while descending. You should ascend slowly and be able to pause your ascent easily.

As you ascend the final distance to the surface, look up and reach up. Vent your BCD, and rotate if necessary to be sure there's nothing overhead. When you reach the surface, continue to breathe from your regulator as you inflate your BCD. Once you float comfortably, switch to your snorkel.

Sometimes you need to navigate while ascending without a reference. For example, you may run low on air before reaching your planned exit point and have to start up, but want to continue swimming in the right direction. One common technique is for one buddy to navigate while the other controls the ascent. You stay together during the ascent (holding on to each other can help). You'll learn basic navigation in Sections Four and Five.

Safety Stops

As a prudent, conservative diver, make a *safety stop* a normal part of your ascent procedure. A safety stop is simply a pause in your ascent between 6 metres/20 feet and 3 metres/10 feet (commonly 5 metres/15 feet) for three to five minutes.

A safety stop helps slow your overall ascent, then gives your body tissues extra time to release dissolved gases. Among other benefits, this helps reduce the risk of lung overexpansion injuries and decompression sickness (DCS – you will learn more about DCS in Sections Four and Five).

To make the stop, you and your buddy(ies) slow your ascent as you pass 6 metres/20 feet and fine-tune for neutral buoyancy. Pause at about 5 metres/15 feet for three minutes or longer – variations of 1 metre/3 feet above or below are not a problem. During the stop, check your computer to be sure you didn't accidentally overstay its limits.

It is easiest to make a safety stop with a reference. In many environments, you can plan the dive to follow a slope upward, so that you are still near the bottom or reef while stopped at 5 metres/15 feet. This allows you to keep exploring, watching nature, taking pictures, etc., while making the stop. But, when necessary, you can make a midwater safety stop without a reference by watching your depth gauge and hovering neutrally buoyant.

Safety stops add conservatism, but you don't make them during emergencies such as if you were assisting a diver who has an air supply problem, if you were very low on air, etc. If the maximum dive depth is very shallow – say, to 6 metres/20 feet or less – you wouldn't usually make a safety stop because you're diving in the safety stop depth range anyway.

Reaching the Surface

After completing your safety stop, signal your buddies to confirm they're also ready to ascend. If you're neutrally buoyant, you only need to swim gently upward to start ascending again.

As you ascend the final distance, look up and reach up with your BCD deflator in your left hand. You will need to vent expanding air from your BCD to control your buoyancy.

Rotate if necessary to check for obstructions overhead.

Keep your hand up as you break the surface. Continue to breathe from your regulator as you inflate your BCD. After making sure you're floating comfortably, switch to your snorkel. When diving from a boat, signal the divemaster that you're okay, and swim toward it if you didn't ascend near it (or do as the crew directs – sometimes the boat will come to you).

When possible, ascend with your buddy following a reference such as a sloping bottom, mooring line or a vertical line deployed from a boat or float, much as you would use a reference when descending.

Exercise 2-9

1. Before starting my ascent, I should check my dive computer to be sure I'm within its limits.
   - ☐ True
   - ☐ False

2. To start my ascent, I should
   - ☐ a. drop some weights.
   - ☐ b. add air to my BCD.
   - ☐ c. push off the bottom.
   - ☐ d. swim up gently.

3. When I'm ascending, I should ascend
   - ☐ a. quickly – no slower than 18 m/60 ft per minute.
   - ☐ b. slowly – at my computer's required rate.
   - ☐ c. at any speed with which I'm comfortable.

4. I'm ascending from a dive during which I'm wearing a wet suit. My buoyancy will _____ as I ascend, unless I adjust with my BCD.
   - ☐ a. increase
   - ☐ b. decrease
   - ☐ c. remain the same

5. To control my buoyancy while ascending, I should
   - ☐ a. vent my BCD in large amounts infrequently.
   - ☐ b. vent my BCD in small amounts frequently.
   - ☐ c. add air to my BCD.

6. I would never find it necessary to ascend without a reference.
   - ☐ True
   - ☐ False

7. A safety stop is a stop between _____ and _____ for three to five minutes.
   - ☐ a. 3 m/10 ft, 0 m/0 ft
   - ☐ b. 4 m/12 ft, 2 m/6 ft
   - ☐ c. 6 m/20 ft, 3 m/10 ft
   - ☐ d. 9 m/30 ft, 6 m/20 ft

8. When I reach the surface, the first thing I do is
   - ☐ a. switch to my snorkel.
   - ☐ b. signal the boat.
   - ☐ c. inflate my BCD.

How did you do?
1. True. 2. d. 3. b. 4. a. 5. b. 6. False. You may have to ascend away from a planned reference due to losing direction or to handle an emergency or problem. 7. c. 8. c.

When ascending without a reference, stay with your buddy. Watch your depth and ascent rate on your dive computer and control your buoyancy.

Make a safety stop a normal part of your ascent procedure.

You wear an exposure suit on most dives for two main reasons: warmth, and/or for protection against accidental stings, abrasions and cuts. Wet suits are the most common exposure suits. This is because they provide insulation and protection, and have the most styles and options. Multipiece suits (right) provide versatility by allowing you to wear different pieces as needed. "Shorty" wet suits (left) are popular warm water suits.

LEARNING OBJECTIVES

By the end of this section, I should be able to answer these questions:

1. What are the two reasons for wearing an exposure suit?

2. What are the three primary types of exposure suits and how do they differ? Which type requires special training?

3. Why is fit particularly important with a wet suit?

4. What exposure suit options and accessories can I choose from?

5. Why is overheating sometimes an issue with exposure suits? How do I avoid overheating?

Equipment II

Exposure Suits I

You wear an exposure suit on most dives for two main reasons: warmth, and/or protection against accidental stings, abrasions and cuts.

There are three primary exposure suit types: wet suits, dry suits and skin suits. Let's look at how they differ, and where and when you'd use each.

Wet Suits

Wet suits are the most common exposure suits. This is because they provide insulation and protection, and also come in a wide variety of styles depending upon how much insulation you need. This makes them useful in water as cold as 10°C/50°F to as warm as 30°C/86°F.

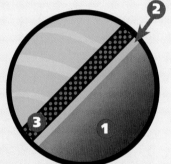

Water seeps into a wet suit around your wrists, ankles and neck and gets trapped. Your body ❶ quickly heats the trapped water ❷ and the neoprene ❸ greatly slows heat loss.

Wet suits insulate you with foam neoprene (or other insulating material), but you don't stay dry. Water seeps into the suit around your wrists, ankles and neck and gets trapped. Your body quickly heats the trapped water, and the neoprene greatly slows heat loss.

To work, though, the suit must trap the water. If your suit is too loose, water flows in and out, carrying heat with it. If it's too tight, it's uncomfortable. Have a dive professional assist you with getting a proper fit when choosing a wet suit. You get the *best* fit with a custom wet suit made specifically for you.

Dry Suits

Dry suits provide the most insulation. As their name suggests, they keep you dry. They have special watertight zippers and seals, and most types cover your entire body, except your head and hands, which you protect with a wet suit hood and gloves. Dry suits used in the coldest water (like under Polar ice) keep even your head and hands dry.

The air within the suit, as well as an undergarment and sometimes the dry suit itself (depending upon the material), provide insulation. This makes dry suits the most effective option for cooler water diving. They extend how long you remain comfortable in water cooler than about 18°C/65°F, and they're the primary option for diving in water colder than 10°C/50°F.

Dry suits provide the most insulation with a layer of air trapped by an undergarment ❶ and sometimes the suit itself ❷ slowing heat loss.

101

As mentioned earlier, a dry suit creates an air space. You must equalize this space as you descend, and vent air as you ascend to control your buoyancy. When diving in a dry suit, you use an inflator hose from your regulator to inflate it, and the suit's exhaust valve to release expanding air as you ascend.

Dry suits do not have to fit as closely as wet suits, but sizing is still important. You can choose from a variety of materials, each with different characteristics and benefits. See your PADI Professional for guidance when choosing one. It is not difficult to use a dry suit, but because you have to equalize it and control your buoyancy with it, using one does require special instruction. Ask your instructor about the PADI Dry Suit Diver course. If you'll be using a dry suit during this course, your instructor will orient you to using dry suits during your confined water dives.

Skin Suits

Skin suits – also called body suits – provide little or no insulation. You wear them in comfortably warm water to protect you from minor cuts, scrapes, stings and sunburn. Normally made of a stretchy material like Lycra®, they should fit closely to avoid drag.

In moderately warm water, you may wear a skin suit under a partial wet suit. The wet suit provides enough insulation for a comfortable dive, while the skin suit provides protection for areas not covered by the wet suit. You may also find a skin suit makes it easier to put on a wet suit, because its material easily slides against the wet suit's material.

Options and Accessories

Exposure suits have options and accessories depending upon the suit and where you use it. Your local PADI dive shop can help you sort through these based on your preferences and needs, but here are a few considerations:

Wet suits have the most styles and options. Multipiece suits give you layered insulation and versatility by letting you wear different pieces, or all of them, depending upon the temperature. "Shorty" wet suits cover your upper body and have short pant legs and sleeves. These are popular warm water suits.

Wet suits come in different thicknesses. Choose a thicker wet suit (5 or 7 mm neoprene) for more insulation. Thinner material (3 mm) is well suited to warmer water, and is less buoyant. In most styles and thicknesses, you can choose from a wide color variety, and options such as pockets, zipper location, knee pads, etc.

Dry suit options consist primarily of your choices of materials and undergarments. The dry suit materials you choose from offer advantages in terms of weight, durability and comfort.

You choose different undergarments depending upon the water temperature. You can use the same dry suit in a variety of temperatures, but with different undergarments. With most dry suits you wear a wet suit hood and gloves, but dry hoods and dry gloves are options for the coldest water.

❶ ***You wear gloves*** for warmth and protection from cuts and stings, etc. In water colder than about 18ºC/65ºF, your fingers quickly become numb and lose dexterity without insulation.

❷ ***The dry suit*** materials you choose from offer advantages in terms of weight, durability and comfort. You choose different undergarments depending upon the water temperature. You can use the same dry suit in a variety of temperatures, but with different undergarments.

Hoods are important in water cooler than about 21°C/70°F for comfort, and because you lose a significant amount of heat through your head if it's not insulated. This is true whether you're diving in a wet suit or a dry suit, and for longer dives many divers wear a hood at warmer temperatures. A professional at your PADI dive shop can show you appropriate hoods.

▶ When selecting a hood, or adjusting a dry suit neck seal, make sure it fits snugly, but not too tightly. If it's too tight, it can restrict blood flow through your neck. This can cause light-headedness and, if you keep the hood or dry suit on, fainting and unconsciousness. Your PADI dive shop can help you choose the right size. ◀

You wear gloves for warmth and for protection from cuts and stings, etc. In water colder than about 18°C/65°F, your fingers quickly become numb and lose dexterity without insulation. As the water gets colder, the choices, in order of increasing insulation, are: wet suit gloves, wet suit mitts (three finger) and dry gloves (on dry suits).

In warmer water, light "reef" gloves provide protection without sacrificing much dexterity. Some areas don't allow divers to wear gloves while diving tropical reefs to discourage touching fragile coral.

You wear wet suit boots to protect and insulate your feet. You normally wear wet suit boots with open-heel fins, regardless of the temperature. They provide foot protection from the fins and when walking to and from the water. Fin socks are soft material you can wear under wet suit boots or with full-foot fins for further comfort. Dry suits usually have integrated boots.

Although most BCDs have pockets, many divers like pockets on their wet or dry suits. The most popular location is on the thigh, with zippered or Velcro™-type closures so nothing falls out. Your PADI Dive Center or Resort can usually have pockets put on a wet or dry suit you already have.

Avoiding Overheating

Wet and dry suits are *very* effective insulators, so overheating can be an issue on a warm day especially before the dive. Your body can't cool itself as effectively when you're wearing an exposure suit, so be careful to avoid overheating.

- Set up the rest of your kit before putting on your exposure suit. Put your suit on at the last possible moment.

- Once in the suit, limit activity and stay out of the sun as much as you can.

- If you're wearing a hood, pull it back until just before you put on your mask and enter the water. This helps you eliminate excess heat through your head.

- Leave the suit unzipped as long as possible.

If you start to overheat before or after a dive, take the time you need to cool off. Get in the water, have someone spray you with a hose (common on boats), or stop and take the suit partially or entirely off to avoid overheating problems.

EXPOSURE PROTECTION AND PROTECTING THE ENVIRONMENT

Because exposure suits reduce the risk of minor scrapes and stings, sometimes divers pay less attention to contact with coral, sponges and other fragile aquatic life. Unfortunately, while the diver may be protected, contact can injure or kill these organisms.

While you wouldn't intentionally kick, kneel on or bump into fragile creatures, exposure protection can make you less aware when you do it accidentally. In some environments, breaking a 25 cm/10 in piece of coral destroys a decade of growth. (CONTINUED)

(CONTINUED FROM PREVIOUS) The following techniques help reduce incidental damage.

- Swim next to the reef rather than over it, to reduce fin damage. When you must swim over it, stay far enough above it to avoid fin contact.
- Stay neutrally buoyant with proper weighting and trim. Control your movements, and don't swim with your feet low and your torso high – this makes it much easier to do damage with your fins and legs.
- Turn sideways when you look under a ledge. Your cylinder adds height to your profile; doing this reduces the likelihood of damage through cylinder contact.
- Keep all your gauges and hoses well secured and streamlined so they don't drag.
- Remember that your exposure suit reduces but does not eliminate the possibility of aquatic life scrapes, stings or punctures. Sea urchin spines, for example, can penetrate many exposure suits. Avoiding contact with the reef and its inhabitants is the best way to reduce this risk.

In general, avoid touching living organisms underwater. Doing so almost never benefits an organism, and seldom adds to the dive.

For more about environmentally responsible diving, visit projectaware.org and download 10 Tips for Divers to Protect the Ocean Planet.

PROJECT AWARE®

LEARNING OBJECTIVES

By the end of this section, I should be able to answer these questions:

1. Why do I have a cutting tool when diving (except where prohibited by law)?
2. What are the four basic types of cutting tools?
3. Where do I wear at least one cutting tool?

Exercise 2-10

1. I wear an exposure suit while diving for _____ and _____.
   - ☐ a. streamlining, protection
   - ☐ b. streamlining, warmth
   - ☐ c. protection, warmth

2. Which type of exposure suit requires a snug fit, without which water would carry away heat or it would be uncomfortable?
   - ☐ a. wet suit
   - ☐ b. dry suit
   - ☐ c. skin suit

3. Which type of exposure suit requires special training?
   - ☐ a. wet suit
   - ☐ b. dry suit
   - ☐ c. skin suit

4. A hood is important when diving in water cooler than approximately 21°C/70°F.
   - ☐ True
   - ☐ False

5. It's a hot, sunny day but my buddy and I are diving in water that is 21°C/70°F. I'm diving in a dry suit and my buddy is diving in a full wet suit. Both of us will wear hoods. In this situation _____ is likely an issue we need to avoid before the dive.
   - ☐ a. improper weighting
   - ☐ b. hypothermia
   - ☐ c. hand protection
   - ☐ d. overheating

How did you do?
1. c. 2. a. 3. b. 4. True. 5. d.

Cutting Tools

You have a cutting tool when diving for *safety* and *convenience*. You can use it, when appropriate, to cut line, saw, pry or pound. (Don't use your cutting tool to harm aquatic life, deface a shipwreck etc., of course.)

Cutting tools' safety role is to help you handle severe entanglement should it become necessary. It's more likely you'll use your cutting tool for convenience, such as to remove a bit of fishing line that's polluting a dive site.

Contrary to cinema and television fiction, they are not weapons for protection against aquatic animals.

There are four basic cutting tool types, each with options. Some areas regulate the types and sizes of cutting tools, so some variations may not be available or legal in specific locations.

Dive knife – This is a stainless steel or titanium knife, usually with a sharp cutting edge and a serrated (sawing) edge. They range in size from very compact to large. Larger knives are the most likely cutting tools to have legal restrictions.

Dive tool – This is generally a dive knife with the sharp tip replaced with a prying tool. Other than that, dive tools have the same general options as dive knives. Local authorities may or may not classify them as knives.

Shears – Dive shears are especially suited to cutting fishing line and net. They are popular with divers likely to encounter monofilament line and net, particularly on wrecks. These are not usually restricted legally.

Z-knives – Z-knives are hooks with a blade specifically for cutting fishing line or net. They let you cut quickly, and their shape reduces the risk of accidentally cutting yourself or your equipment. Because they're not useful for heavy rope or other purposes, you generally carry a z-knife in addition to a dive knife or tool.

Dive knives

Dive tool
Note the prying tip.

Dive shears

Z-knife

Mounting Cutting Tools

Cutting tools have sheathes you can mount many places based on your preferences, such as on your BCD hose, on a waist strap, strapped inside your leg, attached to the back of a console or on your wrist. Many divers like to have two – a dive tool and a z-knife. Wear your tool where you can reach it with either hand so it is accessible with either arm entangled.

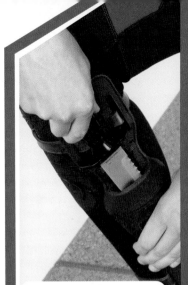

Cutting tools have sheathes you can mount many places based on your preferences, such as on your BCD hose, on a waist strap, strapped inside a leg, attached to the back of a console or on your wrist.

Exercise 2-11

1. The primary reason I carry a cutting tool is to defend myself against sharks and other aquatic animals.
   ☐ True
   ☐ False

2. Which cutting tool is a bladed hook for cutting fishing line or net?
   ☐ a. dive knife
   ☐ b. dive tool
   ☐ c. dive shears
   ☐ d. z-knife

3. I should wear at least my cutting tool
   ☐ a. on my wrist.
   ☐ b. under my BCD hose.
   ☐ c. where either hand can reach it.
   ☐ d. on my body's lower half.

How did you do?
1. False. You carry a cutting tool for safety and convenience.
2. d. 3. c.

LEARNING OBJECTIVES

By the end of this section, I should be able to answer these questions:
1. Why do I need a dive gear bag?
2. How do I choose a gear bag?

Dive Gear Bags

You need a dive gear bag to carry and protect all your equipment, except weight, cylinders and dry suits. Although many gear bags look similar to other types of luggage available, they're specifically designed for dive gear. Salt water won't ruin their zippers, nor will their material rot. Gear bags are designed to survive the stresses of transporting dive equipment. Diving quickly destroys most luggage bags not intended for this use.

You have many options in choosing a gear bag with respect to straps, configuration, pockets and wheels available at your PADI dive shop. Choose your gear bag based on your preferences, but also based on size. Select a bag *slightly larger* than you need for all the gear you have, because you tend to add gear as you gain dive experience, and this gives you room to grow.

Gear bags are specifically designed for dive gear. Salt water won't ruin their zippers, nor will their material rot. Gear bags are designed to survive the stresses of transporting dive equipment.

Exercise 2-12

1. I need a dive gear bag to carry my equipment in a bag specifically designed to survive the stresses of diving.
   - ☐ True
   - ☐ False

2. When choosing a gear bag, I should choose one _____ for the gear I have.
   - ☐ a. slightly larger than what I need
   - ☐ b. just large enough

   How did you do?
   1. True. 2. a.

LEARNING OBJECTIVES

By the end of this section, I should be able to answer these questions:
1. What are the three primary instruments I use while diving, and what do I use each one for?
2. What three optional instruments may I choose to use while diving?
3. How do I care for dive instruments?

Dive Instruments

You've already learned a bit about some dive instruments, but let's look at them more closely. There are three primary instruments you use on virtually all dives.

SPG (submersible pressure gauge) – As you've learned, this instrument tells you how much air remains in your cylinder. It may be a separate gauge or integrated into your dive computer.

Dive computer – Besides tracking your time underwater, how deep you are and other information, this instrument guides you in keeping dissolved nitrogen in your body within accepted limits. It does this by applying depth and time information to a decompression model, constantly showing how much time you have left (more about computers in Sections Four and Five).

Compass – Your compass provides a navigational reference to help you follow a course and find your way back to your exit. Compasses designed for diving are pressure resistant and have clear markings. Your compass, SPG and dive computer may be combined into a single, multifunction instrument.

Some dive computers are designed to be worn as watches. They're fully functional dive computers (many also function as your SPG).

Besides your primary instruments, there are some optional ones you may want, or need in some circumstances.

Depth gauge and dive watch – Before dive computers, these were mandatory for use with dive tables like the Recreational Dive Planner (RDP) to track dissolved nitrogen in your body and plan your dive time limits. If you use the RDP Table or eRDPML and don't have a dive computer (more about why you might do this in Section Four), you will *need* these. Although not commonly used today, there are single instruments that combine your depth gauge and timer.

Dive watches – Dive watches are popular as lifestyle accessories that identify you as a diver. Many divers wear them all the time.

Thermometer – Thermometers help you determine how much exposure protection you need. They show the water temperature, which helps you determine how much exposure protection you want on later dives. Although available as separate instruments, they are commonly part of SPGs, depth gauges and dive computers.

Care

Dive instruments have some maintenance and care considerations other than rinsing in fresh water after use. Although tough, they are instruments. Protect them from impact, and like most electronics they don't do well if exposed to direct sunlight or high heat for long periods. Keep them in the shade, and face them away from the sun or cover them when you can't.

Change the batteries in electronic instruments (primarily dive computers) as directed by the manufacturer. The requirements for this vary, so see the manufacturer literature for the details on your computer, as well as for any additional care requirements.

*If you use the RDP Table or eRDPML and don't use a dive computer, you will need a depth gauge and watch. **Dive watches** are popular as lifestyle accessories that identify you as a diver.*

Exercise 2-13

1. Of the following instruments, which three are primary instruments that I would normally have while diving?
   - ☐ a. dive watch, compass, dive computer
   - ☐ b. dive computer, depth gauge, dive watch
   - ☐ c. thermometer, compass, SPG
   - ☐ d. SPG, dive computer, compass

2. If I am using dive tables instead of a dive computer, I will need a dive timer and depth gauge.
   - ☐ True
   - ☐ False

3. It's a sunny day and I'm on a dive boat with no shade. It would be a good idea to cover my gear, including instruments, with a towel.
   - ☐ True
   - ☐ False

   How did you do?
   1. d. 2. True. 3. True.

Thermometers help you determine how much exposure protection you need. They're commonly part of SPGs, depth gauges and dive computers.

Your primary instruments are your SPG, dive computer and compass. They may be separate, or combined into a single multifunction instrument.

Remember to breathe from your regulator and hold it, and your mask, as you enter.

Your Skills as a Diver II

Let's look at some more skills you'll learn. Again, there's more than one way to execute most dive skills, and your instructor may show you a method that differs from what you learn here.

Deep Water Entry – Giant Stride

You will learn several entries into water too deep in which to stand. One may be the giant stride, which is a common entry from charter dive boats, docks and other relatively stable platforms up to a couple metres/several feet above the water.

- Enter the water fully equipped with a partially inflated BCD.

- Remember to breathe from your regulator and hold it, and your mask, as you enter. Hold them until you're stable on the surface.

- Look straight ahead and *step* in – don't jump.

- Signal that you're "okay" and clear the entry area.

- Switch to your snorkel.

Weight Check and Proper Weighting

As discussed, correct trim is important for streamlining, moving efficiently and preserving the underwater environment. Part of having good buoyancy and trim is having the right amount of weight.

- Check your weight in the water with your buddy, and make any adjustments one at a time so you can help each other.

- Check with all your equipment in place and breathe from your regulator.

- You should float at eye level with an empty BCD and holding a normal breath. When you exhale, you should slowly sink.

- After adjusting so you float at eye level, add two kilograms/five pounds if you checked with a full cylinder. This is because the air in it has weight, so you will become lighter as you use up your air. Two kilograms/five pounds adjusts for the air in a typical cylinder.

Dealing with a Loose Cylinder Band

Sometimes the band holding a diver's cylinder in the BCD comes loose. When you know how to deal with it, it is little more than an annoyance.

When you're properly weighted, you should float at eye level with a deflated BCD and holding a normal breath.

- If it comes loose while exiting, it is often simplest to ease back into the water, slip out of the kit and then lift or carry it out of the water by the cylinder valve.

- If it comes loose before the dive, help the diver remove the scuba kit for retightening.

- If it comes loose during a dive, it is not usually an emergency, because the cylinder tends to stay with the diver. Signal the affected diver so you can tighten it, or signal your buddy if it is your cylinder band that's loose.

Snorkel Clearing

Clearing your snorkel is a routine surface skill you use often during a dive, because when the snorkel is out of your mouth, it fills with water.

- Blow the water out forcefully, like using a pea-shooter. This is called the blast method of snorkel clearing.

- Take your first breath cautiously, and use airway control to breathe past any remaining water. If necessary, blast clear again to blow out the residual water.

- Practice with your face submerged, which is how you would do it if you were keeping your eyes on something underwater, or in choppy conditions when, for practical purposes, your face is always in the water.

Snorkel/Regulator Exchange

You switch from your snorkel to your regulator, and from your regulator to your snorkel, on almost every dive.

- Clear your snorkel or regulator.

- Practice the exchange with your face submerged because it may be choppy or you may want to keep an eye on something below. This teaches you to switch without choking on any water.

- During practice, take several breaths from the snorkel or regulator before exchanging again.

Neutral Buoyancy

You will begin developing neutral buoyancy by using the fin pivot or a similar technique. This teaches you basic neutral buoyancy adjustment and how your breathing affects buoyancy.

- When neutrally buoyant, you should pivot upward when you inhale and downward when you exhale.

- Be patient. Add or release air from your BCD in small amounts when adjusting for neutral buoyancy.

- Once you can reach neutral buoyancy, start thinking in terms of neutral buoyancy as your normal state and how

If a cylinder band becomes loose during a dive, it is not usually an emergency because the cylinder tends to stay with the diver.

To clear your snorkel, blow the water out forcefully, like using a pea-shooter. This is called the blast method of snorkel clearing.

you primarily function in the water. This speeds up how fast your buoyancy skills become second nature.

- Your instructor may have you use variations of the fin pivot, or a different technique entirely.

Mask Removal and Replacement, and No-Mask Breathing

It doesn't happen often, but your mask can flood completely, or come off entirely. You'll learn how to clear out the water, then to remove it, put it back on and clear it.

- Clear a fully flooded mask just as you do a partially flooded one; you just exhale a little longer.

- After removing your mask, keep your eyes open if you're not wearing contact lenses. Everything will be blurry, but you will be able to see well enough to swim and signal your buddy.

- Block your nose if it makes you more comfortable at first, but practice until you don't need to.

- You'll practice breathing without a mask for a minute or more (which is about how long it would take to reach the surface if you lost your mask and couldn't find it) then replace and clear it.

Disconnecting Your Low-Pressure Inflator

An unlikely but possible malfunction is for your BCD (or dry suit) inflator to stick. Your response is to disconnect the hose supplying air to it and vent the excess air as necessary.

- To disconnect the low-pressure hose with your regulator pressurized, push the hose toward the connection while retracting the release.

- If you can't disconnect quickly, get in a vertical position and hold open the exhaust valve while continuing to disconnect the inflator hose.

- For colder water diving, you can get low-pressure hoses with oversized release fittings to make this easier while wearing gloves.

- Be sure to reconnect the hose after finishing the exercise.

Air (Gas) Depletion Exercise

This exercise lets you experience what it feels like to run out of air, which is part of learning to respond appropriately.

- Watch your SPG as your instructor closes your cylinder valve.

You switch from your snorkel to your regulator, and from your regulator to your snorkel, on almost every dive.

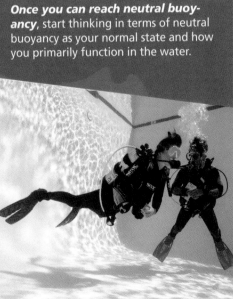

Once you can reach neutral buoyancy, start thinking in terms of neutral buoyancy as your normal state and how you primarily function in the water.

You'll practice breathing without a mask for a minute or more, which is about how long it would take to reach the surface if you lost your mask and couldn't find it.

- Breathing becomes difficult as the pressure goes down.
- Signal "out of air" when you can't get a breath.
- Your instructor reopens the valve. You'll see the SPG reading return to the previous pressure. Resume breathing.

Air Awareness and Managing Your Air Supply

Besides knowing how to read your SPG and plan your air use, develop the habit of knowing approximately how much air you have at all times.

- Your instructor will periodically ask for your SPG pressure.
- If you're monitoring your supply regularly, you should be able to answer within 20 bar/300 psi *without rechecking.*
- Your instructor will confirm that your response is within 20 bar/300 psi.
- You must demonstrate to your instructor that you are continually aware of your remaining cylinder pressure.

Deep Water Exit – Ladder Exit

Your instructor may have you practice exiting the water by climbing a ladder. This is a technique commonly used when diving from dive boats.

- Stay out from under divers ahead of you in case they were to fall back in, or have a cylinder slip loose.

❶ If you can't disconnect a stuck inflator quickly, get in a vertical position and hold open the exhaust valve while continuing to disconnect the inflator hose.

❷ The air depletion exercise lets you experience what it feels like to run out of air, so you can respond appropriately.

❸ Your instructor will periodically ask for your SPG pressure. If you're monitoring your supply regularly, you should be able to answer within 20 bar/300 psi without rechecking.

- If there's a current, you usually have a line to hold while waiting to exit.

- Keep all your gear in place and enough air in your BCD to float comfortably. Breathe from your snorkel while waiting to exit (your regulator is fine if you have a lot of air left).

- Hand up accessories before exiting.

- Hand up your fins, or put them on your wrist.

- Switch back to your regulator before exiting.

- Breathe from your regulator and keep your mask on until you're all the way aboard.

- Depending upon the ladder, the conditions and your physical characteristics, you may hand up your weights, or your entire scuba kit, before climbing the ladder.

- Some divers cannot use a ladder at all due to physical characteristics and use a different exit technique.

The ladder exit is a common technique when diving from dive boats. Keep your mask on and breathe from your regulator until you're all the way aboard.

Confined Water Dive Two

- ☐ Briefing and dive planning
- ☐ Air awareness and management
- ☐ Assemble, put on and adjust equipment, predive safety check
- ☐ Entry – giant stride (suggested)
- ☐ Proper weighting and weight check
- ☐ Snorkel clearing
- ☐ Snorkel-to-regulator, regulator-to-snorkel exchange
- ☐ Swimming on the surface – good surface habits
- ☐ Five point descent with reference
- ☐ Neutral buoyancy – fin pivot (suggested)
- ☐ Loose cylinder band (suggested – dive flexible)

- ☐ Clearing a fully flooded mask
- ☐ Mask removal and replacement; no mask breathing
- ☐ Disconnect freeflowing LP inflator (suggested – dive flexible)
- ☐ Gas depletion exercise
- ☐ Five point ascent with reference
- ☐ Free time for skill practice and fun
- ☐ Exit – ladder exit (suggested)
- ☐ Debrief
- ☐ Post dive equipment care (dive flexible)

Note: *Your instructor may modify this to some extent to meet class and logistical requirements.*

Knowledge Review Two

Some questions may have more than one correct answer. Choose all that apply.

1. I take a colorful fish identification slate with me while diving. Looking at the slate underwater at 12 metres/40 feet, I would expect the slate to look
   - ☐ a. smaller/farther away.
   - ☐ b. more colorful.
   - ☑ c. less colorful.
   - ☑ d. larger/closer.

2. While underwater, I want to move efficiently by
   - ☐ a. moving as quickly as possible.
   - ☑ b. being streamlined.
   - ☐ c. having just a little more weight than I actually need.
   - ☑ d. swimming slowly and steadily.
   - ☑ e. maintaining proper trim.

3. During a dive, I can't stop shivering. The proper response would be to
   - ☑ a. exit the water immediately, dry off and seek warmth.
   - ☐ b. exit the water as planned, but wear more exposure protection next time.
   - ☐ c. exit the water when convenient, and swim rapidly to warm up.

4. During a dive, my buddy and I have to swim hard because of an unexpected current. If I were to begin to feel fatigued, have labored breathing, experience a feeling of suffocation or air starvation, and perhaps feel like I may panic, I should
   - ☒ a. signal "up" and head to the surface.
   - ☐ b. switch to an alternate air source.
   - ☑ c. stop all activity, signal my buddy and rest.

5. When planning our dive, my two buddies and I agreed that the general procedure for buddy separation would be adequate. If during the dive I find I am with one buddy but can't see the other, which of the following applies?
   - ☑ a. This is a buddy separation. Stay with the remaining buddy and search for no more than a minute, then reunite on the surface.
   - ☐ b. This is a buddy separation. Stay with the remaining buddy, return to where the missing buddy was last seen and wait.
   - ☑ c. This is a buddy separation. The remaining buddy and I should split up and look for the missing buddy.
   - ☐ d. This is not a buddy separation for the remaining buddy and me. Stay with the remaining buddy and continue the dive while the one who is missing looks for us.

6. The buddy system is _____ responsibility.
   - ☐ a. my buddy's
   - ☐ b. the divemaster's
   - ☑ c. my
   - ☐ d. no one's

7. My buddy and I are planning a shore dive. We're descending onto a very gradual slope that begins at 5 metres/15 feet, so our descent and ascent will be a gradual part of swimming out and back underwater. We have similar cylinders filled to 200 bar/3000 psi. We plan:
   - • 50 bar/500 psi reserve.
   - • 20 bar/300 psi for our safety stop.
   - • To turn the dive when we've used one-third of the air available to use on the dive.

   This means we should head back when either of our SPGs read
   - ☒ a. 70 bar/800 psi
   - ☐ b. 145 bar/1900 psi
   - ☑ c. 157 bar/2270 psi
   - ☐ d. 170 bar/2500 psi

8. My fin strap comes loose (later I discover that I didn't buckle it properly) while swimming at the surface in choppy waves. Which of the following habits would help me as I handle this problem?
   - ☑ a. Having my mask on and a mouthpiece in my mouth.
   - ☑ b. Having enough air in my BCD for adequate buoyancy.
   - ☑ c. Staying close to and signaling my buddy.

9. I'm about to begin a descent with my buddy. Which of the following steps should I take before actually beginning my descent?
   - ☐ a. equalize my ears
   - ☑ b. orient myself to something at the surface
   - ☑ c. check that my computer is active
   - ☑ d. confirm that my buddy is ready
   - ☐ e. add air to my BCD

10. My buddies and I are wearing wet suits for exposure protection. As I descend, my buoyancy will _____, so I should _____ to control my buoyancy.
   - ☐ a. remain constant, do nothing
   - ☐ b. increase, release air infrequently from my BCD in large amounts
   - ☒ c. increase, release air frequently from my BCD in small amounts
   - ☐ d. decrease, add air infrequently to my BCD in large amounts
   - ☑ e. decrease, add air frequently to my BCD in small amounts

11. I should never descend or ascend without a reference that I can follow or make contact with.
   - ☒ True
   - ☑ False

12. As a prudent, conservative diver, the following are normal parts of my ascents:
   - ☑ a. ascending at 18 m/60 ft per minute (or slower if specified by my computer)
   - ☐ b. inflating my BCD to begin my ascent
   - ☑ c. stopping for 3 minutes at approximately 5 metres/15 feet
   - ☑ d. adjusting my buoyancy in small amounts frequently

13. While boat diving, my buddy and I finish our safety stop and ascend to the surface. When I reach the surface, I should
   - ☐ a. switch to my snorkel, inflate my BCD and signal "okay" to the divemaster.
   - ☐ b. signal "okay" to the divemaster, switch to my snorkel and inflate my BCD.
   - ☑ c. inflate my BCD, switch to my snorkel and signal "okay" to the divemaster.

14. Match the letter with the characteristics of the exposure suit type.
   a. insulation provided by layer of air and undergarment
   b. proper fit is important to keep water trapped against your body
   c. little or no insulation
   - __ab__ wet suit
   - __a__ dry suit
   - __c__ skin suit

15. Which of the following can be a problem before the dive when diving on a warm day in a wet or dry suit?
   - ☐ a. proper weighting
   - ☒ b. entering the water
   - ☑ c. overheating
   - ☐ d. hypothermia

16. If I have only one cutting tool, the recommendation is that I wear it where _____ hand can reach it
   - ☐ a. my right
   - ☒ b. my left
   - ☐ c. my dominant
   - ☑ d. either

Student Diver Statement: I've completed this Knowledge Review to the best of my ability and any questions I answered incorrectly or incompletely, I have had explained to me and I understand what I missed.

_____   _____
                    Name   Date

section

three

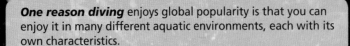

One reason diving enjoys global popularity is that you can enjoy it in many different aquatic environments, each with its own characteristics.

LEARNING OBJECTIVES

By the end of this section, I should be able to answer these questions:

1. What types of environments might I dive in?

2. What six general environmental conditions can affect me while diving?

3. How can I expect depth to affect water temperature?

4. How do I measure (define) visibility as a diver?

5. What four principal factors affect visibility?

6. In what three ways can reduced visibility affect me while diving? What do I do about them?

7. How do I avoid the potential problems of diving in clear water?

Being a Diver III

Dive Environments and Conditions

Part of dive planning includes recognizing what to expect in different dive environments and how conditions can affect dive plans. This section starts by looking at these, followed by assessing conditions, setting personal limits, aquatic life and some of the techniques you use when diving in different areas.

Types of Dive Environments

One reason diving is popular worldwide is that you can enjoy it in many different aquatic environments, each with its own characteristics. Common popular dive environments include:

- coral reefs
- temperate water oceans
- lakes and reservoirs
- rivers
- springs
- flooded quarries
- human-made dive environments (purpose-built sites, aquariums, etc.)

In all these environments, six general conditions can affect you. The degree to which each condition varies and affects you depends on the environment. Some environments have little temperature change, whereas others have significant changes. Some places never have water movement, others always do and yet others may or may not, depending upon different factors. The six general conditions are:

- temperature
- visibility
- water movement
- bottom composition
- aquatic life
- sunlight

Temperature

Diving takes place in water as cool as near freezing (-2°C/28°F – requires special training and equipment) to above 30°C/85°F. Most diving takes place in water on the warm end of this range, but thanks to modern exposure suits, often in water much cooler than would otherwise be comfortable.

8. What two types of water movement primarily affect me as a diver?

9. When diving in a mild current, in what direction would I normally go? Why?

10. What do I do if I'm caught in a current and am carried downstream from where I planned to dive or exit the water?

11. What should I do if I get caught in a surface current while diving from a boat and find myself unable to swim to the boat?

12. What are five types of bottom compositions I'm likely to find while diving?

13. How do I avoid contact with the bottom? What are three reasons why it is beneficial to avoid bottom contact?

14. How does sunlight affect me as a diver? How can I avoid sunburn?

15. What differences can I expect between diving in fresh water and in salt water?

In many environments, water temperature changes with the season, affecting how much exposure protection you need. Even most tropical environments call for more exposure protection during the winter months. A PADI dive operator where you plan to dive can usually tell you what to expect and suggest appropriate exposure suit choices. Similarly, the web and fellow divers on ScubaEarth® and other social sites often have information about popular dive destinations, including temperature.

Besides season, depth may affect temperature. In most environments, water gets colder as you go deeper. Water tends to form distinct layers based on temperature. The boundary between a warmer upper layer and a cooler deeper layer is called a *thermocline*. In still water, like a lake or quarry, it is so distinct that you can stick your hand into noticeably cooler water below while swimming in warmer water.

The depth at which you find a temperature difference depends upon the season and water motion. Some environments, however, like many rivers and springs, are the same temperature at all depths.

When planning your dive, it is important to base your exposure protection on the temperature at the deepest part of the dive. This is important to avoid hypothermia, but also so you're comfortable and enjoy the dive. If you find you don't have enough exposure protection, ascend to shallower, warmer water or abort the dive and return wearing more insulation.

Water tends to form distinct layers based on temperature. The boundary between a warmer upper layer and a cooler deeper layer is called a *thermocline*.

If you find you don't have enough exposure protection during a dive, ascend to shallower, warmer water or abort the dive and return wearing more insulation.

Visibility

Visibility underwater ranges from 0 to more than 60 metres/200 feet and influences your dive significantly. You want to learn how to adjust your dive based on the visibility, how to keep from reducing the visibility by your actions and when visibility is too poor to dive.

You measure visibility as the distance you can see horizontally underwater. This can be subjective – you may be able to recognize the silhouette of a diver 12 metres/40 feet away, and some would call this 12 metre/40 foot visibility. Others would use a shorter distance at which they can make out the details.

Factors Affecting Visibility

Four principal factors affect visibility at a dive site: water movement, weather, plankton and bottom composition. Each of these affects visibility by increasing or decreasing the amount of suspended particles. Like a dust storm in air, lots of particles in the water means less visibility.

Water movement – waves, current and diver fin kicks – can stir sediment up from the bottom, reducing visibility. Current can improve visibility by carrying away low-visibility water and replacing it with clearer water – or vice versa.

The weather can reduce or improve visibility. Wind creates waves (water movement) that stir up the bottom, or rain can cause sediment on land to run off into water. Prolonged offshore wind can push upper water seaward, replacing it with clearer (and cooler) deep water.

Plankton (microscopic organisms suspended in water) can, under some conditions, reproduce rapidly, clouding the water. Sunny weather can accelerate how fast these organisms reproduce.

The nature and composition of particles in the water affects visibility. Whether put in the water by careless fin kicks or natural forces, large, heavy material – like from gravel and rock bottoms – settles out of the water quickly, restoring visibility quickly. Small, light particles – like from mud and clay bottoms – can remain suspended for very long periods.

Diving in Reduced Visibility

Reduced visibility can affect your dive in many ways, but there are three effects in particular to be aware of. The first is that it's more difficult to stay with your buddy(ies). So, stay close together, take your time and watch each other. Second, lower visibility may make it harder to track where you are or where you're going. Use your compass and other navigation references (you'll learn about navigation in Section Five) to stay oriented. Third, when descending and ascending, reduced visibility can make you feel disoriented, especially when you can't see either the bottom or the surface. Avoid this by following a reference down and up (a sloping bottom, mooring line, etc.). If you must descend or ascend without a reference, as you've learned, use your dive computer to help you stay attuned to your depth and descent/ascent rate.

An important point is that reduced visibility *doesn't* mean you won't have a good dive. *What* you see is more important than *how far* you see. As you gain experience, you become more comfortable with lower visibility.

❶ *Reduced visibility* can make you feel disoriented when descending and ascending, especially when you can't see the bottom and the surface. Following a reference line on the way down and back up avoids this, though you can use your dive computer to guide descents and ascents without a reference.

❷ *In clear water* the bottom can seem closer than it really is, so monitor your computer so you don't exceed your planned depth. Keep in mind that you can see your buddy from farther apart than you should be. A good rule of thumb is to be able to reach each other within two seconds.

Also, the skills you learn in the PADI Underwater Navigator and Search and Recovery Diver courses help you find your way more easily in reduced visibility. But, there is a limit. If the visibility is so poor that you don't enjoy yourself, can't accomplish what you want to on the dive or makes diving hazardous in any way, it is best to not dive, or abort if already started.

Diving in Clear Water

Perhaps surprisingly, clear water can also present visibility-related problems. The bottom may seem closer than it really is, so monitor your dive computer as you descend so you don't exceed your planned depth. Also, because the bottom and the surface may seem closer than they really are, you can experience disorientation and vertigo when descending or ascending without a reference.

Perhaps the most common problem in clear water is getting too far from your buddy(ies), because you can still see each other. A good rule of thumb is to be able to reach each other within two seconds.

Water Movement

Two types of water motion primarily affect you while diving: waves and current. Waves result primarily from wind blowing over the water's surface. The stronger the wind and the longer the distance it passes over, the larger waves can grow. Waves affect swimming at the surface, as well as the techniques you use for entering and exiting the water. Small waves (up to 1 metre/3 feet) seldom restrict diving. Larger waves may require more experience and/or training; but even with experience/training, very large waves normally prevent diving.

Currents result from waves, water heating and cooling, the Earth's rotation and tides. Those caused by waves vary with wind direction. And, because water rises or sinks as it heats or cools, respectively, currents are created that tend to be seasonal. Although such water motion is initially vertical, when it reaches the bottom or an obstacle, the flow can continue horizontally.

Major oceanic currents and countercurrents result from Earth's rotation. Although these are permanent currents, their paths and strength vary to a degree due to other influences. Tides, which result from the gravitational pull of the sun and moon, lift the oceans and cause water levels to rise and fall as the earth rotates. This process causes currents that flow to and from enclosed areas like bays and harbors.

Diving in Mild Current

You can't swim against anything but a very weak current without overexerting, so you must use appropriate techniques and avoid all but a mild current. Currents tend to be strongest at the surface and weakest near the bottom, so avoid long surface swims in a current – descend, then swim against the likely milder current on the bottom. Begin a dive in mild current swimming slowly *into* the current. Do this so that when you turn the dive, the current will push you back to your exit point rather than away from it.

Particularly at the surface, if you get carried past your exit point or planned destination, swim *across* (perpendicular to) the current to reach shore or a line trailed from a boat, or (in some environments) to get out of the current. Fighting a current by swimming directly into it can exhaust you. When

Stronger Current

Weaker Current

Because currents tend to be weaker near the bottom, swim against a current on the bottom.

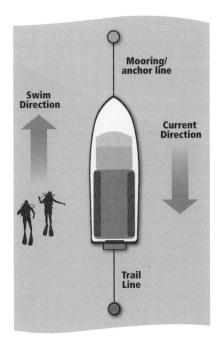

Mooring/anchor line

Swim Direction

Current Direction

Trail Line

Begin your dive swimming into a current, so that when you head back the current will assist your return instead of pushing you away from your exit.

If you get carried past your exit point or planned destination, swim across the current to reach shore or a line trailed from a boat, or to get out of the current where you're diving.

At a given dive site, the bottom may be entirely a single composition, or multiple types, such as sand bottom surrounding coral or rock. Regardless of type, there are at least three benefits to avoiding bottom contact as much as possible.

The first reason is that even with coarse bottoms, contact tends to reduce visibility. So, avoiding contact keeps the water clearer. Second, contact with some bottoms may present hazards. In environments like coral and rock, you can get cuts or scrapes if you're not careful. In most marine environments, bottom contact has some risk of stings or punctures from organisms like hydroids or sea urchins. Vegetation bottoms like kelp may have some entanglement risk. Avoiding contact reduces these risks. Third, many aquatic organisms that live on the bottom are fragile and sensitive. Resting or kneeling on them, or kicking them with your fin tips, can injure or destroy them. Staying off the bottom helps preserve the site's natural beauty.

The easiest way to avoid bottom contact is to stay neutrally buoyant and swim well above it. Being properly weighted and trimmed helps, as you've learned, because if you're overweighted you tend to swim with your feet low,

boat diving, if you can't get to the boat because you're exhausted (or better, because you're avoiding exhaustion), remain calm and inflate your BCD (or, drop your weights if you have a BCD problem). Signal the boat with your whistle/inflatable signal tube, etc. to pick you up.

Keep in mind that diving in anything stronger than a mild current requires special training, such as the PADI Drift Diver course.

Bottom Composition

You can divide the different types of bottom composition into five basic types:

Silt/mud – Clay, fine organic/inorganic material or mud.

Sand – Larger, coarser particles.

Rock – Gravel and larger rock.

Coral – Living and dead coral in tropical water.

Vegetation – Various plants and algae found in both fresh and salt water.

Avoiding bottom contact helps keep the water clear, reduces risk from possible bottom hazards, and helps preserve the underwater world.

which makes it much easier to kick or stir up the bottom. Similarly, on wrecks, avoid contact that would damage or deface them. If possible, rest only on your fin tips, or even with just light finger contact, if you need to make contact on insensitive bottom. Also, stay streamlined and don't allow your gear to drag.

If you must make bottom contact during a dive (there will be times when it's appropriate), choose an insensitive area (no fragile aquatic life) free of hazards and settle onto it gently. If possible, rest only on your fin tips. Remain aware of the bottom and watch where you put your hands and feet. Entries and exits that involve wading from shore make bottom contact unavoidable. Know what kind of bottom you'll wade through as you plan your dive. Be prepared for the effect on visibility, sinking into mud, etc. Stop wading and start swimming as soon as the water is deep enough, either by inflating your BCD and surface swimming, or by

If you must make bottom contact during a dive (there will be times when it's appropriate), choose an insensitive area and settle onto it gently. If possible, rest only on your fin tips. Sometimes, finger contact may be all you need.

Prevent sunburn by wearing sunscreen and protective clothing, and by staying in the shade as much as possible. Protect your eyes from long-term damage with good quality sunglasses.

submerging and swimming underwater. Wear wet suit boots to reduce the risk of aquatic life stings or scrapes/cuts from sharp rocks, etc.

Sunlight

Diving typically takes you into direct sunshine. Besides influencing how much light you have underwater and how warm (or potentially, overheated) you are before and after a dive, it can affect you by causing sunburn. Sunburn can ruin a dive vacation, but you can avoid it entirely.

To prevent sunburn, wear protective clothing and use sunscreen. Stay in the shade as much as possible. Be aware that overcast conditions do not protect you from burning, ultraviolet light. When choosing sunscreens, see your PADI Dive Center or Resort about types specifically designed for divers, with chemicals that won't affect aquatic life.

Besides sunburn, repeated long-term exposure to the sun can harm your eyes.

Like anyone who spends a lot of time outside, protect your eyes with good quality sunglasses.

Fresh Water and Salt Water

There's great diving in both fresh water (lakes, rivers, quarries) and salt water (all marine environments). In coastal areas, there are dive environments that are both fresh and salt – a shallow freshwater layer over a deeper seawater layer. The basic skills you learn as a diver apply to both environments, but there are some differences. Although there are exceptions, *generally:*

- Fresh water is less dense and therefore less buoyant than salt. Recheck your weight and trim when going from fresh water to salt or vice versa.

- Marine environments tend to have more types and amounts of aquatic life.

- Very distinct thermoclines (temperature changes) within the recreational diving depth range are more common in fresh water.

- Freshwater environments are more likely to have bottoms that you can stir up easily.

- Marine environments generally have more differences in water motion – currents and waves. For practical purposes, freshwater bodies don't have tides, whereas tides can significantly affect marine bodies.

On wrecks, avoid contact that would damage or deface them.

OVERHEAD ENVIRONMENTS

⚠ **Whether you dive in fresh or salt water, you may encounter places you can swim into that don't permit you to swim straight up to the surface.** Examples include inside shipwrecks, under ice and in caves or caverns. These are called overhead environments. They may appear deceptively safe and simple – *but they're not.* They can pose hazards that you may not recognize, nor realize are present, until it's too late.

Your training in this course prepares you for diving in *open water* – with direct access to the surface at any time. As soon as you lose the ability to ascend directly to the surface, your risk and the potential hazards go up dramatically. You can learn to dive in these environments safely – but it requires special training and special (often extensive) equipment to handle the added risks and complications.

For this reason, *until you have the training and equipment you need, do not enter a cavern, cave, wreck or any other overhead environment.* Doing so places you in an unnecessary and extremely hazardous situation. Many overhead environments may **seem** inviting and safe, but any time you can't swim directly up to the surface, you're in a special situation. A sobering thought: *One of the leading causes of diver fatalities is going into overhead environments without the proper training and equipment.*

Those with proper training and equipment have an excellent safety record in caves, wrecks, under ice and in other overhead environments – those without this training (including otherwise highly trained dive professionals), unfortunately do not.

Avoid this risk entirely. Enjoy the fun and adventure of diving outside the overhead environment. If you're interested in this type of diving, get the training you need – but stay out until then.

Exercise 3-1

1. I can enjoy diving in many different aquatic environments that include coral reefs, flooded quarries and human-made dive environments.
   - ☐ True
   - ☐ False

2. Conditions that may affect me while diving include (choose all that apply):
   - ☐ a. temperature.
   - ☐ b. water movement.
   - ☐ c. sunlight.
   - ☐ d. aquatic life.
   - ☐ e. bottom composition.

3. In most (but not all) environments, as I go deeper the water gets
   - ☐ a. warmer.
   - ☐ b. colder.
   - ☐ c. fresher.

4. Although somewhat subjective, I measure visibility as how far I can see _____ underwater.
   - ☐ a. horizontally
   - ☐ b. vertically upward
   - ☐ c. vertically downward

5. Particles made of fine material affect visibility by
   - ☐ a. remaining suspended for long periods.
   - ☐ b. settling out of the water relatively quickly.
   - ☐ c. being easily disturbed by fin kicks or natural forces.

6. When diving in reduced visibility, it's a good idea to descend and ascend with a reference.
   - ☐ True
   - ☐ False

7. When diving in clear water, I don't have to worry as much about staying close to my buddy.
   - ☐ True
   - ☐ False

8. The two types of water motion that most affect me as a diver are waves and current.
   - ☐ True
   - ☐ False

9. When diving in a mild current, normally I want to begin my dive _____ the current.
   - ☐ a. across
   - ☐ b. headed into
   - ☐ c. going with

10. If I were caught in a current and carried downstream past my planned exit, I should swim _____ the current.
    - ☐ a. across
    - ☐ b. headed into
    - ☐ c. going with

11. Due to a problem, my buddy and I had to surface away from the boat. There is a current, so we swam across it to reach the line trailed from the boat, but the current pushed us too quickly. To avoid overexertion, we should
    - ☐ a. establish positive buoyancy, signal the boat to pick us up and remain calm.
    - ☐ b. descend to the bottom and swim against the current there.
    - ☐ c. alternately fight the current and rest by towing each other.

12. When I'm diving, I want to avoid bottom contact because (choose all that apply):
    - ☐ a. it helps keep the water clearer.
    - ☐ b. there may be some hazard of cuts, scrapes or stings.
    - ☐ c. fragile aquatic life could be damaged.

13. The most common injury divers suffer may be
    - ☐ a. lung overexpansion.
    - ☐ b. aquatic animal bites.
    - ☐ c. sunburn.

14. Within the recreational depth range, very distinct temperature changes are most common in _____ water environments.
    - ☐ a. salt
    - ☐ b. fresh

How did you do?
1. True. 2. a, b, c, d, e. 3. b. 4. a. 5. a. 6. True. 7. False. In clear water, you may get too far from your buddy because you can still see each other. As a rule of thumb, stay within two seconds of each other. 8. True. 9. b. 10. a. 11. a. 12. a, b, c. 13. c. 14. b.

LEARNING OBJECTIVES

By the end of this section, I should be able to answer these questions:

1. How do I learn to assess conditions?

2. What should I do if any aspect of a dive, including my assessment of the environment, causes me significant concern and/or anxiety?

3. How do the different factors discussed in this section relate to the importance of getting an orientation when diving in unfamiliar environments?

Assessing Conditions

One of the skills you will develop as a diver is how to assess conditions. This is a skill you learn based upon what your instructor and other divers show you, and from your experiences as you go diving and continue your education. Through these, you will learn to assess the dive conditions at a site based on:

- The weather
- The season
- Water motion
- Water appearance
- Reports online and from other divers
- Dives made at similar sites in the area

 Your assessment should include the decision to dive or to not dive.
If your assessment (or any other aspect of the dive) causes you significant concern or anxiety, your first option is to get

Remember that ultimately, you decide to dive. You are responsible for your own safety, so only you can make the final decision to dive.

more information about the concern and how to handle it. If you can't reasonably address whatever the issue is, and you can't go to another dive site where you are comfortable, **do not dive.**

Remember that ultimately, *you* decide to dive. *You* are responsible for your own safety, so only *you* can make the final decision to dive.

Each environment has individual factors that differ from other dive environments. This is why it is important to get a local environmental orientation (Discover Local Diving) and gain experience when diving in an unfamiliar environment. Other options for getting oriented to a new environment are to take a course with a PADI Instructor, or to dive with someone familiar with the area.

An area orientation helps you learn how to address what's unique about the local diving and how to assess conditions, avoid hazards and identify points of interest. This can remove potential concerns that would cause you to cancel a dive due to insufficient information.

These orientations are important for both safety and for making your dives more enjoyable.

An orientation like Discover Local Diving
helps you learn to assess conditions, avoid hazards
and identify points of interest, which is important for
both safety and for making your dives more enjoyable.

By the end of this section, I should be able to answer these questions:

1. What is meant by "diving within my limits"? Why is it important to do so?

2. How does failure to dive within my limits raise my risk while diving?

3. How do I expand my limits?

4. What should I do if someone subjects me to peer pressure to make a dive that is beyond my limits or that makes me uncomfortable?

Exercise 3-2

1. I learn to assess dive conditions by reading dive magazines and online sources about diving.
   - ☐ True
   - ☐ False

2. If any aspect of a dive, including my assessment of the environment, causes me significant concern and/or anxiety, I should
   - ☐ a. be very cautious during the dive.
   - ☐ b. determine how to handle the concern, or not dive.
   - ☐ c. continue if my buddy has no concerns.

3. Local orientations are important for safety and for
   - ☐ a. making my dives more enjoyable.
   - ☐ b. letting me try out new gear.
   - ☐ c. meeting new buddies.

How did you do?
1. False. You learn to assess dive conditions based on what other divers and your instructor show you, and based on experience diving and continuing your education. 2. b. 3. a. You may sometimes get to use new gear and/or meet new buddies when diving in a new environment, but an orientation is always important for safety and enjoyment.

Diving Within Your Limits

Whether you're a new or experienced diver, dive within your personal limits – this means you do not exceed the limits of your training and/or experience. These limits apply to different dive environments and conditions, but also to many specialized dive activities and types of equipment. It also means you dive as you were trained, to the best of your ability.

Diving within your limits also applies to the limits of your *comfort*. Dives may be exciting and have some degree of challenge, but you should not have worries or any serious doubt about your ability to participate safely in the dive.

It is important to dive within your limits, because failure to do so contributes to incidents and accidents. Even if someone avoids an incident or accident when exceeding limits, the anxiety and uncertainty that result can take the fun out of the dive. Exceeding your personal limits raises your risk at least three ways.

Whether you're a new or experienced diver, dive within your personal limits – this means you do not exceed the limits of your training and/or experience. Dives may be exciting and have some degree of challenge, but you should not have worries or any serious doubt about your ability to participate safely in the dive.

The first is that some forms of diving have risks that may not be obvious. These require special training in recognizing and managing these risks, without which, incidents and accidents may become more likely – a diver may not know there's a danger until it's too late to do anything about it.

The second is that exceeding limits can cause false security. Divers may "get away with" diving beyond their limits (or having bad habits within their limits) *provided nothing goes wrong.* If this leads divers to think they can dive beyond their limits, they continue to do so. But the day something goes wrong, they may lack the skills and/or equipment to manage the situation and the result is an incident or accident.

The third way it raises your risk is indirectly. Some divers experience anxiety when diving outside their limits (which they should – it's not a safe way to dive), which can cause them to focus on some concerns so much that they neglect potential problems they would normally recognize and manage appropriately. Because the diver is distracted, an incident or accident may result.

Even in the same general environment, different divers may have different limits, training and equipment requirements. For example, rebreather divers don't typically wear snorkels for important performance reasons, and tec divers go far deeper than

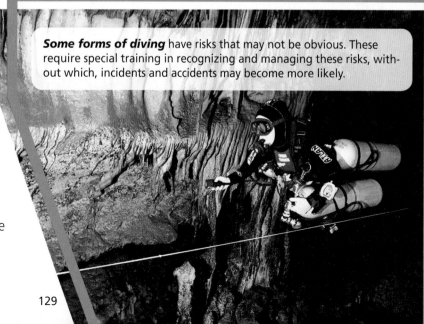

Some forms of diving have risks that may not be obvious. These require special training in recognizing and managing these risks, without which, incidents and accidents may become more likely.

129

recreational divers. These divers *do* have training, equipment requirements and limits that they're supposed to follow, but theirs differ from yours. Their gear requirements and limits do *not* change *your* gear requirements and limits.

To do more and gradually expand your personal limits as you gain experience, continue your training and dive with more experienced divers.

The PADI Advanced Open Water Diver course specifically gives you a structured path for learning new skills, trying new activities and visiting new dive sites while expanding your limits under instructor supervision. Continuing education is especially important for specialized diving like rebreather diving, or cave and other forms of tec diving, because they have unique potential hazards you have to learn to manage.

Diving with more experienced divers doesn't replace training for activities that require it, but it does help you gradually extend your limits. For example, suppose you have local

The PADI Advanced Open Water Diver course specifically gives you a structured path for learning new skills, trying new activities and visiting new dive sites while expanding your limits under instructor supervision.

Even in the same general environment, different divers have may have different limits, training and equipment requirements. Their gear requirements and limits do not change your gear requirements and limits.

diving experience but have always been diving with 5 metre/15 foot visibility or more. It may be reasonable to dive with 2 metre/6 foot visibility with a buddy who has local experience doing so.

You also gradually extend your personal limits as you gain experience (but again, this doesn't replace training). For example, suppose you have experience diving local sites in a wet suit, and you're also certified as a PADI Dry Suit Diver, but all your dry suit experience is in a different environment. You can extend your personal limits by making dry suit dives at local sites, starting with dives that are well within your capabilities.

Divers should not use peer pressure to get others to make a dive they're not comfortable with, or without equipment they know they should have. However, it does happen (not usually intentionally).

If pressured to make a dive beyond your limits or comfort, usually all you have to do is politely say "no." You can often suggest a more conservative dive or some other adjustment that keeps you within your limits and comfort. When you explain that you have concerns, most divers will respect them. At the same time, make a point of respecting concerns other divers might have.

The rule of thumb is that if a proposed dive plan exceeds your limits, *decline.* That keeps the dive within your limits. If a proposed dive plan adds something that is *more* conservative, *agree.* Doing so may be necessary to keep the dive within another diver's limits, or it may be based on a local need or practice.

For example, suppose a diver tells you that you don't need your snorkel, you politely say that you prefer to take it with you. On the other hand, suppose an experienced local diver says that in addition to a whistle and inflatable signal tube, local divers also carry a signal mirror to attract attention. Adding a signal mirror to your kit may be prudent.

Exercise 3-3

1. "Diving within my limits" simply means diving within the limits of my (choose all that apply):
   - ☐ a. training.
   - ☐ b. experience.
   - ☐ c. comfort.

2. One way exceeding my limits can increase my risk is by exposing me to hazards that I'm not prepared to handle or may not even recognize until it's too late.
   - ☐ True
   - ☐ False

3. Diving with an experienced diver and gaining dive experience are two ways to generally expand my limits, but they don't replace training for activities that require training.
   - ☐ True
   - ☐ False

4. While planning a dive, my buddy (who is not an instructor) suggests that we dive significantly deeper than I have either training or experience with. My best response is to
   - ☐ a. agree if my buddy has enough experience diving that deep.
   - ☐ b. make the dive but be prepared to abort at any time.
   - ☐ c. politely say "no" and propose a depth limit appropriate for my limits.

How did you do?
1. a, b, c. 2. True. 3. True. 4. c.

LEARNING OBJECTIVES

By the end of this section, I should be able to answer these questions:

1. What are the two basic types of interactions I can have with aquatic life? Which interaction should I generally have?

2. What are the different types of potentially hazardous aquatic organisms?

3. What causes nearly all injuries from aquatic life?

4. What nine steps should I follow to prevent and/or handle aquatic injuries caused by aquatic animals?

5. What should I do if I see a potentially aggressive animal underwater?

6. Why are there laws and regulations concerning aquatic life? Why is it important that I follow them?

7. What hazards may aquatic plants present?

8. What is Project AWARE? How can I participate in Project AWARE's mission?

Aquatic Life

Aquatic life is one of the attractions of diving. Many aquatic plants and animals have an appealing natural beauty, or are unusual and fascinating. For all their diversity, the vast majority of organisms pose no serious threat to divers. As you approach, organisms range from having no response, to fleeing, to watching you curiously. The ability to see and (when appropriate) interact with these organisms is one of the privileges of being a diver.

Passive and Active Interactions

You can have *passive* and/or *active* interactions with aquatic life. Passive interactions are those that leave aquatic life undisturbed: watching, photographing, etc. Active interactions are those that affect aquatic life directly, by altering their normal behaviors: feeding, hunting, touching, moving, chasing, scaring, etc.

Generally, you want to have passive interactions. Move slowly and smoothly and be sensitive to the natural rhythm of the underwater world. You will see more when you don't disturb aquatic organisms.

Aquatic life is one of the attractions of diving. It's the main reason many people become divers.

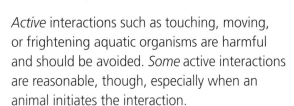

Active interactions such as touching, moving, or frightening aquatic organisms are harmful and should be avoided. *Some* active interactions are reasonable, though, especially when an animal initiates the interaction.

The goal for divers is to set good examples as the underwater world's advocates and ambassadors, helping preserve the aquatic environment for generations to come.

▶ Want to know more?
Visit: projectaware.org

PROJECT AWARE

Preventing and Managing Injuries from Hazardous Aquatic Organisms

Although most aquatic organisms are harmless, some can injure you. Potentially hazardous aquatic organisms are, broadly, those that sting and/or puncture, and those that bite.

Those that sting and/or puncture make up the largest group, which includes:

- Jellyfish ❶
- Portuguese man-o-war
- Lionfish and scorpion fish
- Stingrays ❷
- Sea urchins ❸
- Cone shells
- Fire coral and other hydroids
- Sea nettles

Aquatic organisms that bite include, but are not limited to:

- Moray eels ❹
- Trigger fish
- Crocodilians
- Some sharks (not all)
- Barracuda and other fish ❺
- Snakes (venomous bite)
- Octopuses (a few species have a venomous bite)
- Clawed lobsters/crab (pinchers, not a true bite) ❻

There are organisms not typically thought of as "hazardous" that can injure a diver who fails to use common sense. For example, sea lions are not considered hazardous, but males protect their harems (females) during mating season, and may be aggressive if they think a diver is a threat.

You can generally avoid aquatic life injuries by being alert and aware of where these organisms live and how they behave. Nearly all aquatic life injuries result from human carelessness.

Very few organisms are outwardly aggressive, and most injuries result from

Very few organisms are outwardly aggressive. Bites, which can seem aggressive, are most often defensive. For example, an eel may bite a hand put into the hole it lives in.

Exposure suits and gloves reduce the risk of accidental stings and punctures, but nonetheless, avoid contact with aquatic organisms. You can still be injured through suits and gloves, and contact can injure fragile organisms.

defensive responses by animals. Bites, which can *seem* aggressive, are most often defensive (e.g., an eel may bite a hand put into the hole it lives in). Despite what fictional television and cinema often depict, shark attacks are very rare. Among divers, attacks have been been associated most commonly with spearfishing, because injured or dead fish can stimulate feeding behavior.

There are at least nine steps you can follow to prevent and/or handle aquatic animal injuries.

1. Be familiar with potentially hazardous organisms that may be in the local environment, where you find them and how they could cause harm. (A local area orientation can help with this.)

2. Treat all organisms with respect. Don't touch, tease or intentionally disturb them.

3. Avoid wearing shiny, dangling jewelry, which may look like baitfish/small prey to some predators.

4. Watch where you put your feet, knees and hands. As you learned in Section Two, exposure suits and/or gloves may help protect you, but you can still be injured through them. And remember that exposure protection doesn't protect aquatic life *from* you – avoid contact that may injure fragile organisms.

5. Maintain neutral buoyancy, stay well above the bottom and move slowly and carefully.

6. Be cautious in murky water. It's easier to accidentally touch something you shouldn't. Also, potentially aggressive animals may mistake a diver for prey when visibility is poor; it may be best to avoid diving if such animals are known to be in the area.

7. You should generally avoid contact with all organisms, but *especially* avoid contact with unfamiliar ones. Some stinging organisms are very ugly or very pretty and don't attempt to escape from divers. If you don't know how to identify the potentially harmful ones, be cautious when you encounter these and other creatures.

8. Be cautious with apparently dead organisms or detached body parts. Jellyfish, in particular, still sting when dead as do their detached tentacles.

9. In case of an aquatic life injury, be prepared and apply basic first aid.

   - Assure the victim is breathing. Provide CPR or control bleeding if necessary.

   - If diving in salt water, rinse stings with salt water (not fresh). Don't rub stings – it makes them worse and spreads them.

- Use vinegar on jellyfish, fire coral and other hydroid stings.

- Immerse stings from fish spines, scorpion/lionfish and stingrays in hot water (not above 49°C/120°F) for 30 to 90 minutes.

- Remove spines from punctures (sea urchins) with forceps if you can do so without breaking them. Otherwise, leave this for medical personnel.

- Treat bites like any wound by controlling bleeding, and bandaging.

- Seek emergency medical care for bites (even small ones, to avoid infection), severe reactions, large injuries or those that don't respond to treatment.

- You can learn more about handling aquatic life injuries (and other emergencies) by completing the PADI Rescue Diver course and the Emergency First Response Primary Care (CPR) and Secondary Care (First Aid) courses.

Potentially Aggressive Animals

Most new divers want to know what they should do if they see a shark or other large, potentially aggressive animal. You should watch it and enjoy the experience. You don't see them often. Remain still and calm on or near the bottom, and don't swim toward the creature (doing so may cause defensive behavior). If it stays in the area longer than you're comfortable, calmly swim away along the bottom, keeping an eye on it, and exit the water if it seems overly curious or aggressive.

Aquatic Life Laws and Regulations

Most areas have laws and regulations concerning aquatic life. They exist to preserve and protect organisms, and also for human safety. Game laws/regulations exist to assure a continuing population of organisms in the future. However, in many areas the dive community does not take game, even where it is legal to do so.

In addition, some laws/regulations restrict access during breeding seasons. These keep people away to avoid interrupting breeding behaviors. Other laws/regulations have been instituted to reduce the potential that some species might become hazardous by associating humans with food. In many areas, regulations require that only professionals with appropriate training in animal behavior conduct special activities like shark feedings for tourist divers.

It is important to follow these laws and regulations to avoid legal consequences, to set a good example, and to help preserve the aquatic world.

Some stinging organisms are very ugly or very pretty and don't attempt to escape from you. These include the lionfish, which has spines that can inject a very painful venom.

If diving in salt water, rinse stings with salt water, not fresh, and don't rub them.

In many areas, regulations require that only professionals with appropriate training in animal behavior conduct special activities like shark feedings for tourist divers.

Aquatic Plant Hazards

Underwater plants do not typically pose significant hazards. They do, however, provide homes to other organisms, including some that sting, so again avoid unnecessary contact and watch what you touch.

You can get entangled in some plants and kelp, though you can deal with this potential problem easily.

- Keep your kit streamlined.

- Don't swim through dense growth areas.

- If you get snagged, stop. If you can, simply back up. Don't turn, which can make things worse.

- If necessary, release entanglement by bending and snapping the plant with your buddy's help. Don't struggle, pull or twist.

- Use your knife or cutting tool, if necessary.

Project AWARE

Project AWARE is a movement of scuba divers protecting our ocean planet – one dive at a time. You can be part of the AWARE movement and help keep our ocean clean, and full of healthy and abundant marine life. Project AWARE works in three ways:

1. Diver action and awareness – aquatic life surveys, aquatic debris removal and diver courses that teach you about the major challenges facing the ocean today.

2. Grassroots protection – Project AWARE supports and participates in local actions to protect the ocean. You can take part in local efforts, or start your own.

3. Policy change and advocacy – From marine park campaigns to improvements in species management, Project AWARE is making sure the highest levels of government and business hear the united voice of divers worldwide.

Project AWARE is a nonprofit organization. You can participate in Project AWARE actions directly as a volunteer, by making a donation or both. Ask your PADI dive operator about local Project AWARE activities and visit projectaware.org.

1. The type of interaction I should generally have with aquatic life is
   - ☐ a. active.
   - ☐ b. passive.

2. Potentially hazardous aquatic animals are, broadly, those that _____ and those that _____.
   - ☐ a. attack, flee
   - ☐ b. bite, strike
   - ☐ c. sting/puncture, bite
   - ☐ d. attack, sting/puncture

3. Nearly all injuries from aquatic life result from
   - ☐ a. human carelessness.
   - ☐ b. breeding behavior.
   - ☐ c. species aggression.
   - ☐ d. spearfishing.

4. I should be familiar with potentially hazardous organisms that may be in the local environment, where I would find them and how they could harm me.
   - ☐ True   ☐ False

5. I can learn more about handling aquatic life injuries (and other emergencies) in the PADI Rescue Diver and Emergency First Response Primary Care (CPR) and Secondary Care (First Aid) courses.
   - ☐ True   ☐ False

6. While underwater near a kelp forest, my buddy and I see a large shark approach. We should
   - ☐ a. use our cutting tools.
   - ☐ b. immediately surface and signal the boat.
   - ☐ c. swim rapidly toward it.
   - ☐ d. remain calm, near the bottom and watch it.

7. Laws and regulations about aquatic life exist to preserve and protect organisms, and also for human safety.
   - ☐ True   ☐ False

8. One potential hazard of some plants and kelp is
   - ☐ a. toxic spines.
   - ☐ b. entanglement.
   - ☐ c. poisoning the water.

9. Project AWARE involves me and other divers as part of a movement to help keep our ocean clean and full of healthy, abundant marine life.
   - ☐ True   ☐ False

How did you do?
1. b. 2. c. 3. a. 4. True. 5. True. 6. d. 7. True. 8. b. 9. True

LEARNING OBJECTIVES

By the end of this section, I should be able to answer these questions:

1. What are the procedures for entering and exiting the water when diving from shore? What are some of the considerations?

2. How does the environment affect the best way to wade as I walk through water shallow enough in which to stand?

3. What are typical methods I should use to descend and ascend when shore diving?

Diving from Shore

Entries and Exits

Most (but not all) environments offer diving from shore. There are some environments, however, that you can *only* dive from shore.

Begin by evaluating the environment and conditions, and planning the dive with your buddy(ies). Gear up, pacing yourselves so you're ready at the same time and remembering to put exposure suits on at the last moment in hot climates, especially if you have to walk some distance to the water.

Typically, you put on all your equipment except your mask, fins, snorkel and gloves, then conduct your predive safety check.

Put on your mask, snorkel and gloves just before you enter. When shore diving you may put your fins on in waist-to-chest deep water, depending upon the entry technique you use.

After entering, keep your mask on at the surface until you exit the water (in calm conditions, you can remove it momentarily to refresh the defog, adjust the strap, etc.), and breathe from your snorkel or regulator, unless you're talking to your buddy.

There are many ways you may enter and exit the water when diving from shore. You may use deep water entries and exits from a dock, or climb down and up a ladder or stairs. Often, you wade in and out from land, and where permitted, you may walk down and up a boat ramp.

Basic considerations when planning shore dive entries and exits include:

- bottom composition and hazardous or fragile aquatic life if you will be wading.

- wave, surge and current.

- the best entry and exit techniques for the situation.

- surface swim distance (surface swims when shore diving are commonly longer than when boat diving).

Wading to and from water too deep in which to stand are probably the most common entry and exit techniques. Generally, you walk into water deep enough for your BCD to support you (about chest deep), then put your fins on. When exiting, you remove your fins at about the same depth. With silty bottoms, though, you usually want to swim as soon as possible (typically about waist deep) to preserve the visibility. This is not usually as big an issue when you exit, though it may be for others divers still in or getting in.

Wading to and from water too deep in which to stand are probably the most common entry and exit techniques. Generally, you wade into water deep enough for your BCD to support you (about chest deep), then put your fins on. When exiting, you remove your fins at about the same depth.

Bottom composition and aquatic life generally determine the best way to wade in and out, or how soon you put your fins on. It's wise to have foot protection to reduce the risk of cuts, scrapes or aquatic life stings, and if stingrays are known to be in an area, it's common to shuffle your feet on the bottom as you walk. You're less likely to step on a ray, and this encourages them to flee the area.

Sometimes, it's best to have your fins on from the start of your entry. If so, walk backward looking over your shoulder. If it is impossible or difficult to wade in from shore due to deep mud, entangling plants, sharp rock, etc., walk down a dock, or make a boat dive.

For exits, remember to plan your dive so that you have your reserve remaining once you're back on land. If you need to use your regulator during your exit, plan that as part of your air management.

❶ Bottom composition and aquatic life determine the best way to wade in and out, or how soon you put your fins on. It's wise to have foot protection to reduce the risk of cuts, scrapes or aquatic life stings.

❷ At some shore dive sites, when you reach water too deep in which to stand, to conserve air, you remain buoyant and surface swim to where you want to dive, then descend.

Descents and Ascents

At some dive sites, you descend immediately or soon after reaching water too deep in which to stand, and follow the bottom contour downward. You ascend by following the contour back to shallower water.

At other dive sites, when you reach water too deep in which to stand, to conserve air, you remain buoyant and surface swim to where you want to dive, then descend. After the dive you ascend, inflate your BCD and return to the exit on the surface. In yet other locations, it is common to surface swim some distance to descend into deeper water, but to follow the bottom contour all the way back to water shallow enough in which to stand. When diving through mild surf (discussed shortly), you typically descend after passing through the surf area when entering, and ascend before returning through it when exiting. In all these situations, you may descend and ascend along a line from a surface float you tow (more about these later in this section).

Exercise 3-5

1. When wading into water while shore diving, the general procedure is to put my fins on in water about knee deep, then walk backward until I can swim.
   □ True
   □ False

2. _____ and _____ generally determine the best way to wade in and out or how soon I put my fins on.
   □ a. Equipment, water temperature
   □ b. Visibility, bottom composition
   □ c. Aquatic life, equipment
   □ d. Bottom composition, aquatic life

3. When shore diving, I always have a long surface swim before descending and after ascending.
   □ True
   □ False

How did you do?
1. False. The general procedure is to wade until your BCD can support you – about chest deep – then put your fins on. 2. d. 3. False. How far you swim before descending and/or after ascending varies with the dive site.

By the end of this section, I should be able to answer these questions:

1. In what depth water do waves break? Why should I avoid diving in anything larger than mild surf without special training?

2. What causes surge and undertow? How do they affect me as a diver and how should I adjust for them?

3. What causes currents to move parallel to shore, and how may they affect my dive plan?

4. What is a rip current and what causes it? What should I do if I get caught in one?

5. What can cause deeper water to rise toward the surface? How may it affect dive conditions?

6. What three environmental conditions do tides generally affect? When is generally the best time to shore dive with respect to the tide?

7. How should I enter and exit the water through mild surf?

Entering and exiting through mild surf on a gently sloping beach isn't difficult. Moderate to large surf requires special training.

section three

Shore Diving Through Mild Surf

Surf and the Surf Zone

Some shore diving involves entering and exiting through breaking waves – *surf*. Diving around breaking waves begins with a basic understanding of surf and the related shore environment. Entering and exiting through *mild* surf on a gently sloping beach isn't difficult, and it's what we'll cover here. However, moderate to large surf requires training in the special techniques required. **Avoid diving in large and rough surf. Not only can it be hazardous, but the dive conditions tend to be poor anyway.**

Surf or the *surf zone* is the area in which waves break. Waves break in water only slightly deeper than their height. This is because the bottom slows the bottom of the wave, making the faster top "tip over" and break. This means that by watching the waves, you can tell something about the depth. For example, waves breaking offshore indicate a shallow reef, sandbar, or wreck. If waves break, reform and break again, it tells you that the bottom rises again after a deep spot as you move seaward. And, if waves break along a continuous line but have a significant gap, it may indicate a channel, which can also be associated with rip currents (more about rip currents later).

Waves break in water only slightly deeper than their height. This is because the bottom slows the bottom of the wave, making the faster top "tip over" and break.

The waves can tell you something about the depth. Waves breaking offshore indicate a shallow reef, sandbar or wreck. A gap in a line of waves may indicate a channel, and waves breaking, reforming and breaking again tell you that the bottom rises again after a deep spot as you move seaward.

Surge and Undertow

Waves coming into shore create *surge* and *undertow.* Surge is a back-and-forth motion caused by waves passing overhead. The bigger the waves, the stronger the surge and the deeper it affects you. Strong surge can be hazardous because it can swing you against reef or rocks. Weak surge isn't usually as hazardous, but can cause moments of disorientation. You adjust for the effects of surge by diving deep enough that it has little effect, and by staying away from shallow, rock or reef areas. If surge is stronger than you expected, aborting the dive is always a prudent option.

Undertow (also called *backrush)* is the water of breaking waves flowing back to sea under incoming waves. The larger the waves and the steeper the beach, the stronger the undertow. In mild surf on a gently sloping beach, undertow usually isn't strong and dissipates at about 1 metre/3 feet of depth.

Undertow is the water of breaking waves flowing back to sea under the incoming waves. It pushes your feet seaward as waves push your upper body shoreward, so be cautious not to lose your balance.

Undertow isn't a current that carries things far out to sea, but it can cause you to lose your balance if you're not careful – waves push your upper body toward shore, and undertow pushes your feet and legs toward the sea. To avoid strong undertow, don't dive from steep shorelines unless there is little or no surf. With light undertow, be careful to keep your balance as you enter and exit.

Longshore Current

Waves usually approach shore from an angle. This causes a *longshore* current parallel to the shoreline. Even small waves do this if they come in quickly and close together. These currents tend to move you along the shoreline.

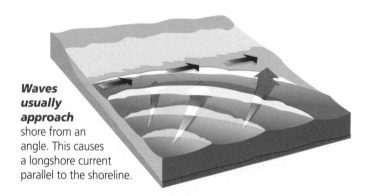

Waves usually approach shore from an angle. This causes a longshore current parallel to the shoreline.

Longshore currents can affect your dive plan in several ways, depending upon your location and its strength.

- One option is to enter up current and exit down current.

- You may plan to swim into a mild longshore current for the start of the dive, and let it help you return to the exit.

- The main point is to prepare for how the current will affect your exit. This is particularly important if there's a moderately strong current, and you must exit at a specific spot on the shoreline.

Rip Currents

Rip currents result when waves push water over a long obstruction (such as a reef or sandbar). The water can't flow back on the bottom, so it funnels back to sea through an available opening. Rip currents may have turbid water you can see moving away from shore, but not always. They usually create a break in the incoming waves.

Rip currents can be alarming, because they are strong and carry you away from shore rapidly. Beyond the obstruction, however, the current dissipates. You generally want to avoid rip currents, and you may see warnings posted. Most accidents associated with rip currents result from panic, not from the current itself. If accidentally caught in one, *don't* try to swim against it.

The *general* recommendation is to establish buoyancy and swim at a sustainable pace parallel to shore until clear of the rip. Then you can swim back to shore. In some locations divers intentionally use rip currents to carry them out to a dive site. These rip currents may make entries through mild surf or through a break in a fringing reef easier.

A local orientation can help you identify rips and brief you on the local procedures to follow if caught in one.

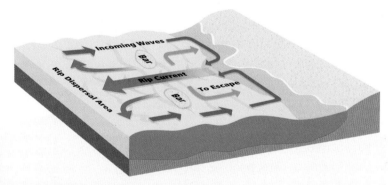

The general recommendation if caught in a rip is to establish buoyancy and swim at a sustainable pace parallel to shore until clear of the rip area. Don't try to swim against a rip.

Upwelling

Wind blowing from shore can push surface water away, causing cooler, deeper water to rise toward the surface to replace it. This is called an *upwelling*. Other causes can also create upwellings, but wind is the most common in diving circumstances.

Upwellings are most noted in the ocean, but also occur on large lakes. In many environments, upwellings are associated with excellent diving conditions because deeper water, while cooler, tends to be clearer. They may also bring up nutrients that support marine life.

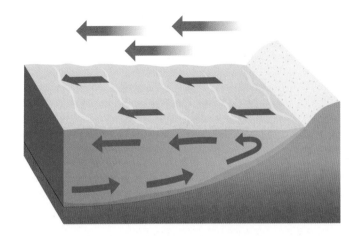

Wind blowing from shore can push surface water away, causing cooler, deeper water to rise up to replace it. Upwellings are generally associated with excellent dive conditions.

Tide

Tides result from the moon and sun's gravity pulling on the water of the oceans. This causes a regular rise and fall of water level throughout the day as the earth rotates. Geography and other influences cause some places to have two high tides and two low tides daily, and some only one each. Although large lakes have tides, the effect is too small to be noticeable.

The difference between high and low tides can be very extreme – more than 6 metres/20 feet in some areas – or almost unnoticeable, depending upon the location and the positions of the moon and the sun.

Tides are predictable for a given location. By using tide tables you can find the time and height for local tides. Tides affect three environmental conditions related to diving.

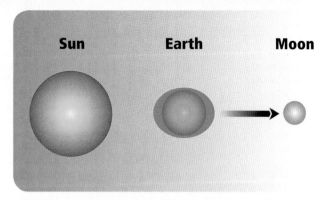

Sun   Earth   Moon

Tides result from the moon and the sun's gravity pulling on the water of the oceans. This causes a regular rise and fall of the water level throughout the day as the earth rotates.

Currents – Tides cause currents, particularly when water flows to and from enclosed areas like harbors and bays. Tidal currents change direction as the tides change. At slack tide (the midpoint at which high tide reverses to low tide, and vice versa), there is almost no current. Depending upon the location, currents can be very strong, or so mild as to be unnoticeable.

Depth – For a given site, depths will be deepest at high tide and shallowest at low tide. In some areas, the difference is enough to significantly affect your planned dive time.

Visibility – Tidal currents tend to carry sediment seaward as the tide goes out. This reduces visibility; the incoming high tide tends to bring in clearer water.

Because tides vary regionally, check with your local PADI dive operator if you're not familiar with local tides. You can also check printed or online tide tables.

Generally, the best time to dive is at high tide. If outgoing tidal currents are strong, plan to end the dive and exit the water when (or before) high tide peaks. A local orientation can help you learn how tides affect conditions. Tides affect boat dives as well, though tidal changes are, generally speaking, most notable when shore diving.

Entries Through Mild Surf

Here are the general steps for entering and exiting through mild surf (waves no higher than approximately waist level).

Start by watching the waves. Note where they're breaking and their pattern – you usually have periods when the waves are larger and more frequent, and lulls when waves are absent or smallest, which are when you want to enter.

When ready and during a lull, enter with all your equipment in place, except your fins. Have enough air in your BCD so you would float. Use your regulator so you can breathe in case a wave causes you to stumble.

Staying with your buddy(ies), wade quickly toward deeper water. Watch the waves. When a wave approaches, stand sideways to it for a steady balance, lean into it a bit and hold your mask and regulator as it washes around you. If you put your fins on before entering (some divers prefer this), walk backward looking over your shoulder. If you're towing a float, keep it between you and the shore so a wave can't push it into you.

When you reach water deep enough in which to swim (waist to chest deep for most people), put

Enter mild surf with all your equipment in place except your fins. Have enough air in your BCD to float, and breathe from your regulator.

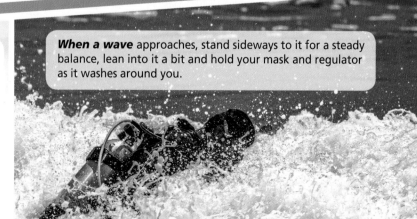

When a wave approaches, stand sideways to it for a steady balance, lean into it a bit and hold your mask and regulator as it washes around you.

When exiting through mild surf, when you reach water shallow enough in which to stand, deflate your BCD so you can stand and walk. Watch the waves as you remove your fins, then wade quickly toward shore.

on your fins and continue to swim out. The idea is to swim through the surf zone as quickly as possible.

Once clear of the surf zone, switch to your snorkel to conserve air if you will continue to swim on the surface. You and your buddy(ies) may descend immediately once past the surf zone, or you may continue on the surface to a specific place where you want to descend.

You use your regulator during your exit, so save enough air for this, in addition to your reserve. When exiting, surface outside the surf zone. Watch the waves and their pattern in case it changed somewhat during your dive. Discuss any changes as necessary with your buddy(ies), and try to time your exit for a lull.

When ready, switch to your regulator and swim quickly toward shore while staying with your buddy. If you're towing a float, push it ahead of you as you go through the surf. When you reach water shallow enough in which to stand and wade (waist-to-chest deep), deflate your BCD enough to be able to stand, keep your balance and walk.

Watching the waves, remove your fins. Handle waves as you did entering – hold your mask and regulator, stand sideways and lean into them. Wade quickly toward shore. Some divers walk out backward with their fins on.

If you stumble and find it hard to get up, you don't need to. Just crawl until you're almost out and get your buddy to help you up. Crawling out is also an option if you are very tired.

Exercise 3-6

1. My buddy and I are assessing conditions for a shore dive. The waves are breaking when they are about 1 metre/3 feet tall. About how deep is the water where they break?
   - ☐ a. 0.5 metres/1.5 feet
   - ☐ b. 1 metre/3 feet
   - ☐ c. 2 metres/6 feet
   - ☐ d. 3 metres/10 feet

2. Diving in moderate to large surf requires special training. Diving in large and rough surf can be hazardous.
   - ☐ True
   - ☐ False

3. My buddy and I experience mild surge after entering the water. We may be able to adjust for this by diving
   - ☐ a. shallower.
   - ☐ b. deeper.
   - ☐ c. facing the shore.
   - ☐ d. facing away from shore.

4. While assessing conditions, my buddy and I note that there are waves approaching shore from an angle. Our dive plan should account for having
   - ☐ a. a current that moves us parallel to shore.
   - ☐ b. a current that moves us perpendicular to shore.
   - ☐ c. no noticeable current.

5. By accident, I find myself in a strong current rushing rapidly away from shore. Generally, I should inflate my BCD and swim
   - ☐ a. with the current.
   - ☐ b. against the current.
   - ☐ c. parallel to shore.

6. The wind has been blowing from shore for several days. During a dive, it is likely I will find _____ water.
   - ☐ a. cooler, clearer
   - ☐ b. warmer, clearer

7. Tides affect conditions related to diving including (choose all that apply):
   - ☐ a. currents.
   - ☐ b. depth.
   - ☐ c. visibility.

8. While entering through mild surf, as a wave approaches I should stand
   - ☐ a. with my back toward it.
   - ☐ b. facing the sea.
   - ☐ c. behind my buddy.
   - ☐ d. sideways to it.

How did you do?
1. b. 2. True. 3. b. 4. a.
5. c. 6. a. 7. a, b, c. 8. d.

LEARNING OBJECTIVES

By the end of this section, I should be able to answer these questions:

1. How should I pack and prepare my gear for a boat dive?

2. How should I prepare myself for a boat dive?

3. How can I prevent seasickness? What should I do if I begin to feel seasick?

Diving from Boats – Preparation

You will almost certainly be diving from boats at some point. In many regions, most or all diving is from boats, because there's no desirable shore diving. Even where there is good shore diving, boats typically provide easier access. They can also reach sites you can't get to from shore.

Boat diving usually eliminates the need for long walks wearing gear and surface swims of any appreciable distance. You can dive from larger boats (typical dive charter boats) that carry six or more passengers and small runabouts – even kayaks are used at times.

Prepare your gear and yourself for boat dives. Start by inspecting your gear and making sure it's working. On a boat, you don't have many options if something is broken. Mark your gear so it doesn't get mixed up with someone else's (your PADI dive operator can show you different types of gear markers).

The usual precaution is to take seasickness medication. Read the instructions beforehand, and follow them – most medications have to be taken several hours before departure.

Use a proper gear bag for everything except your cylinder and weights. Pack what you need first on top. Space is often limited, so work in and out of your bag as much as possible. Know what you need to bring and have what you need on the boat – dry clothes, beverages, snacks, sunscreen and towels, etc. Arrive early and stow your gear as directed by the crew.

Make sure you're well rested and fed to make the most of the trip. Avoid alcohol and drink plenty of water, juices (but avoid particularly acidic ones), etc. so you're well hydrated.

Seasickness

Seasickness (motion sickness) can ruin a day on a boat, but for most people it is *preventable*. People do vary in how prone they are to seasickness, however.

BOAT TERMINOLOGY

The bow – The front of the boat. "Forward" means toward the bow.

The stern – The back of the boat. "Aft" means toward the stern.

Port – The left side of the boat as you face forward.

Starboard – The right side of the boat as you face forward.

"Port" and "starboard" reduce confusion because they are always relative to the bow.

Leeward – The side away from the wind. It is often pronounced "loo-erd."

Windward – The side toward the wind.

The bridge (wheelhouse) – The portion of the boat where the controls are; often elevated for visibility.

Head – The boat's toilet facilities or the boat's commode specifically.

Galley – The boat's kitchen/ cooking area (in some areas, most larger dive boats have galleys; in others, few do).

Swim step – A platform on the stern that is close to water level. You commonly enter and exit the water there.

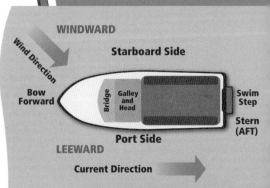

The usual precaution is to take seasickness medication. In most areas, you can get a suitable medication without a prescription, but if you have questions, ask your physician. Read the instructions beforehand, and follow them – most medications have to be taken several hours before departure.

Besides taking a seasickness medication, generally avoid greasy or hard to digest foods while underway. Many people find it helps to avoid complicated tasks and reading.

If you do feel motion sick, stay in open, fresh air and look at the horizon or close your eyes. Try to be as close to the water level and as near the center of the boat as possible while still in fresh air. Do not go into the head (that's the *worst* place you can go) and stay away from engine exhaust.

If you are going to vomit, go to the leeward rail (side of the boat with the wind coming toward your back). As a precaution, take someone with you so you don't fall over the side.

Exercise 3-7

1. While packing my gear bag for a boat dive, I want to pack it so
   □ a. what I need first is on top.
   □ b. what I need first is on the bottom.
   □ c. I can easily empty it while aboard.
   □ d. it carries my cylinder and weights.

2. It is recommended that I avoid excessive alcohol the night before a dive, or before any day of diving.
   □ True
   □ False

3. While on a boat, I begin to feel seasick, but I don't feel like I am going to be sick. The best place to go is
   □ a. into the head (toilet facilities).
   □ b. as high and far from the water as possible.
   □ c. the windward rail.
   □ d. into fresh air, close to the water level in the center of the boat.
   How did you do?
   1. a. 2. True. 3. d

By the end of this section, I should be able to answer these questions:

1. Why is a roll call important for my safety?

2. How should I gear up and move around on a dive boat? Why is it important to secure my equipment on a boat?

3. What are the general procedures and considerations for entering the water when diving from a boat?

4. What are typical methods I may use to descend and ascend when boat diving? Why is it important to stay well away from a dive boat's propeller?

5. Why should I avoid swimming just below the surface?

6. What are the general procedures and considerations for exiting the water when diving from a boat?

7. What are the general procedures for diving from a boat in a moderate current? How should I use a trail (tag) line, swim line and mooring/anchor line when diving from a boat in a moderate current?

8. What should I do if I surface from a boat dive and the boat is not in sight?

section three

Diving from Boats – Procedures
Roll Calls

Before leaving the dock, most dive vessels conduct a roll call of all passengers. Be sure your name is on the list.

 Follow the boat's procedures for knowing who is aboard. After each dive, the crew calls roll, or uses some other specific procedure (some dive boats

Follow the boat's procedures for knowing who is aboard. After each dive, the crew calls roll, or uses some other specific procedure to check that everyone is aboard.

You may set up your scuba kit, test its function and confirm a full cylinder some time before you dive. If so, when done, close the cylinder valve and purge the regulator.

◄ **Even in calm conditions** it's important to secure your equipment on a boat because equipment can fall and injure someone, break something or go over the side if the boat rocks for any reason.

use special marker boards or tags) to check that everyone is aboard. **This is important for your safety, because it greatly reduces the risk of accidentally leaving someone behind at the site.** Also, *do not answer for another diver during a roll call,* even if you're sure the person is aboard.

On small boats, or large ones with few passengers, there may not be a formal roll call. The crew will, however, still have an established method to verify that everyone is aboard before leaving each dive site.

Predive Preparation and Gearing Up for a Boat Dive

The ride to a dive site may take minutes or several hours. If it is only minutes, you may get into all your gear before the boat leaves the dock. More typically, though, you set up your kit, but wait until the boat nears or arrives at the dive site to put on your exposure suit and gear up.

If you set up your scuba kit in advance, test its function and confirm a full cylinder, then close the cylinder valve and purge the regulator. In most instances, you plan your dive with your buddy(ies) when you arrive at the site.

Be careful when moving around on a dive boat, especially when carrying or wearing gear. It is easy to lose your balance, especially when the water isn't calm.

You learned in Section One to secure your cylinder so it can't fall. Some boats have special racks that hold cylinders securely without any additional restraints; others have bungees you secure over the valves after placing cylinders in the rack; and sometimes, you secure cylinders by laying them down. If you lay your cylinder down, lay it BCD up, and block it so it can't slide or roll. However you do it, if you're working with your gear and must walk away for even a moment, be sure it is secure.

Briefings and Entries

While general procedures and considerations for boat entries vary, those discussed here apply to most charter dive boats.

The divemaster will usually give a dive site briefing. If it is the first briefing for the day, it may also cover general diving procedures, safety issues and other information that won't have to be repeated before every dive. The briefing may include information about the best sights underwater, possible hazards and the conditions. All of these affect your dive plan, so listen to the briefing. If you don't understand something, speak up and ask questions.

One safety consideration may be the boat's emergency recall signal and procedure. Generally, if you hear the recall signal (it may be an underwater alarm, repeated pounding on the boat ladder or other noise, etc.), the procedure is to carefully surface at a safe rate with your buddy(ies) where you are. At the surface, look to the boat for instructions. However, procedures vary depending upon the environment and conditions.

As part of dive planning, check how you'll get back aboard (usually covered in the briefing). While this is often obvious, sometimes it's not. Be sure you know the procedures for exiting before you get in. Check the conditions and note current direction (if there is one) so you can swim into the current while underwater (the boat usually points into the current, but may not if there is a strong wind).

On small boats, you may gear up seated and back roll into the water. Another common small boat method is to inflate your BCD, put your kit in the water and get into it after you enter.

On many large dive boats, you gear up while seated, though on some boats when diving in relatively calm water, you gear up while standing (unless you're physically unable to do so) with buddies helping each other. Put on everything except your fins.

When your buddy(ies) is ready, conduct your predive safety check seated or standing, depending upon the situation. Then, go to the entry area and let the divemaster know you're ready to get in. Put your fins on using a rail or buddy assistance for balance. Avoid walking with fins on any more than you must.

Most dive boats do everything reasonably possible to address special physical needs, including entry and exit techniques – let the crew know if you need assistance. If you will be taking special equipment (like a camera), ask the divemaster/crew to hand it to you after you enter the water.

For a given situation, the best entry technique is usually the easiest one. Procedures vary depending upon the boat design and the environment. The crew will usually recommend a technique appropriate for the boat, the conditions and your physical characteristics.

Descending and Ascending When Boat Diving

When boat diving, you commonly have a descent line (vertical weighted line) or the mooring/anchor line to use as a reference for at least the beginning of your descent. In some cases, it may be more convenient to simply use your dive computer and BCD (or dry suit) to monitor and control your descent without a line. After reaching the bottom, you may follow the bottom farther downward, and on some occasions you surface swim from the boat to a specific descent/ascent area that may or may not have a reference to follow.

Once on the bottom or at your planned depth, you normally swim into the current for the first part of your dive. In most situations, this means you swim generally in the direction the boat's pointed and stay in front of the boat (there are exceptions, such as drift diving – the crew will brief you accordingly).

When you reach your turn point based upon your planned time, air use or other limit, turn around and head back. You return to the mooring/anchor line or descent line, or in clear water with little or no current, to where you can see the

When boat diving, you commonly will have a vertical weighted descent line or the mooring/anchor line for a reference.

boat above you. If you have more air/time remaining than required for your ascent, safety stop and reserve, you and your buddy(ies) can explore the immediate area until it's time to go up.

You usually ascend following the same references you used to descend. That is, you may follow the bottom until you reach the mooring/anchor line, then follow it up. It is common to make your safety stop next to a line for reference, though you may do so on the bottom if the boat is moored/anchored in 6 metres/20 feet to 5 metres/15 feet of water. Sometimes you make the stop without a reference using your dive computer to monitor depth, and many dive boats hang a bar or line as a convenient place to make a safety stop.

⚠️ **Stay *well away* from the dive boat's propeller(s). Do not approach it or get near it, even when the boat engine is not running.** A boat propeller can inflict *catastrophic* injuries with little warning. Boat propeller injuries are commonly fatal; those that aren't usually leave permanent disabilities. Treat propellers as though they will start turning with full force at any time without warning – because they can do so. If you see something that requires attention relating to the propeller (e.g. a rope entangling it), do not attempt to clear it. Inform the crew; they will deal with it appropriately.

Surface Swimming When Boat Diving

In most circumstances, you surface near the boat in front of or next to it. Signal to the crew that you're okay (assuming you are). If there is no current, you can also surface just behind the boat. In all cases, stay where you're visible to the crew.

Sometimes, you may have a surface swim when boat diving. It may be planned to reach a descent/ascent area some distance from the boat. Or, it may be unplanned, because you may have to surface away from the boat due to running low on air. If you get disoriented, surfacing may be the easiest way to relocate and return to the boat.

When on the surface (whether diving from boat or shore) and there is boat traffic, watch for approaching vessels. If necessary, use your surface signaling devices so they know you're present. **Do not swim just below the surface, because you are not visible to boats, and you could be struck.** Either be fully visible at the surface, or stay deep enough to be safely below boats.

Boat Diving Exit Procedures

General procedures and considerations for exiting when boat diving depend upon the vessel and the conditions. On larger dive boats, you commonly board with all your gear on, except fins, by climbing a ladder. When doing this:

- Stay out from underneath divers climbing the ladder, just in case they fall back or some of their gear slips.

- If there is a current, you normally hang onto a rope with a buoy attached to the boat for that purpose.

- When it's your turn, switch from your snorkel back to your regulator and swim (or pull yourself via the trail line) to the ladder.

- Hand up specialized equipment (e.g. a camera) if carrying any.

Stay well away from the dive boat's propeller(s). Do not approach it or get near it, even when the boat engine is not running. A boat propeller can inflict catastrophic injuries with little warning.

Do not swim just below the surface, because you are not visible to boats and you could be struck. Either be fully visible at the surface, or stay deep enough to be safely below boats.

Keep hold of the ladder while you remove your fins. You may hand them up or slide your hands through heel straps and wrist-carry them.

After exiting, sit as soon as possible, especially if the boat is rocking. Alternatively, have someone help you take your gear off immediately.

On small boats, a common technique is to inflate your BCD and slip out of your kit while in the water at the surface.

- Keep hold of the ladder while you remove your fins. You may hand them up, or slide your hands through heel straps and wrist-carry them (that way you still have them if you lose grip and need them to swim against the current).

- Breathe from your regulator and keep your mask on until you're all the way aboard.

- Especially if the boat is rocking, sit as soon as possible and/or have someone help you out of your gear. Secure your kit immediately.

- If physical limitations keep you from climbing a ladder with your kit on, you may get out of your scuba gear, then climb the ladder.

On small boats, a common technique is to inflate your BCD and slip out of your kit while in the water at the surface. If your weight system isn't integrated, you usually hand it up first. Someone aboard may lift your kit aboard, or you may secure it to a line to retrieve yourself after you're out. If there's no ladder, keep your fins on if they will help you lift yourself from the water.

Boat Diving with a Moderate Current

In many popular dive locations, it's normal to have a mild to moderate current. To keep from having to fight the current, you may use lines during descents and ascents so the current doesn't carry you away from the boat, and you reduce the risk of overexertion. (Strong currents require special training.) The following procedures (with variation) apply:

You typically use three lines:

- The trail line (also known as a tag line or current line) as previously discussed.

- The swim line, which runs from the stern along the side of the boat to the mooring/anchor line. It is typically within reach of the trail line.

- The mooring or anchor line, which secures the boat in place to the dive site.

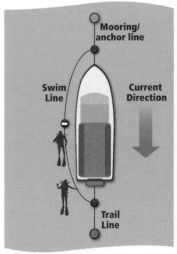
When boat diving with mild to moderate current, you may use lines during descents and ascents so the current doesn't carry you away from the boat.

After you enter the water using an appropriate technique, you and your buddy(ies) pull yourselves single file along the swim line to the mooring/anchor line, then continue hand over hand down it to the bottom.

The current is typically weaker when you reach the bottom. Swim into the current for the first part of the dive as you would normally, and stay up current of the boat for the entire dive. Turn the dive as planned (air used, time, etc.) and return to the mooring/anchor line with ample air for a safe ascent and safety stop. If you arrive with more air/dive time remaining than you need (which is likely on a well planned, conservative dive), you can explore within sight of the mooring/anchor line until you need to head up.

When it's time, ascend the mooring/anchor line. As needed, use the line to keep from drifting downstream. Depending on the current strength, you may ascend hand over hand to maintain contact. Make your safety stop holding on to the mooring/anchor line. Complete your ascent up the mooring/anchor line and follow the swim line to the trail line. Wait on the trail line until it's your turn to exit.

If you lose contact with a line and cannot regain hold in the current, surface if you haven't already. Don't try to fight the current. Swim *across* the current to intercept the trail line. The more current there is, the longer the trail line will usually be. If you miss the trail line, inflate your BCD and signal the crew that you need them to pick you up. Relax and use your surface signaling devices if you're away from the boat. It may be a while before the boat comes for you if they're still picking up divers. The crew may advise you of other procedures they use with moderate to mild current in their local environment.

Dive Boat Not In Sight

It's not likely, but if you surface and don't see the boat, stay calm and get buoyant. Relax, use your surface signaling devices so it will be easier for the crew to spot you when the boat returns and wait to get

picked up. The boat may have slipped anchor, or the captain may have had to leave in an emergency (to pick up other divers). If there is a mooring or anchored float in place, hang on to it. If the shore and a reasonable exit area are close (you can realistically expect to reach it without becoming exhausted) and in sight, swim slowly toward it.

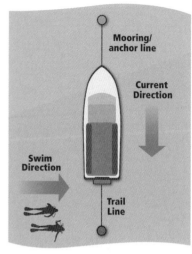

If you lose contact with a line and cannot regain hold in the current, surface if you haven't already. Don't try to fight the current. Swim across the current to intercept the trail line.

Exercise 3-8

1. A roll call (or other method to verify everyone is aboard before leaving each dive site) is important for my safety.
   ☐ True
   ☐ False

2. It is important to secure my equipment on a boat in rough conditions, but it is not important in calm conditions.
   ☐ True
   ☐ False

3. Generally, if I hear the dive boat's recall signal, I should
   ☐ a. return to the mooring/anchor line and wait for further instructions.
   ☐ b. return to the boat and surface.
   ☐ c. surface with my buddy where we are and look to the boat for instructions.

4. It's a good idea to avoid walking with fins on any more than I must.
   ☐ True
   ☐ False

5. My buddy and I are diving and there is a slight current. When we reach the bottom, we want to swim _____ the current for the first part of the dive.
   ☐ a. into
   ☐ b. with
   ☐ c. across

6. While making a safety stop at the end of a dive, I notice that some loose line has snagged on the boat propeller, and could severely entangle it when the engine starts. I should
   - ☐ a. disentangle the line from the propeller.
   - ☐ b. use a cutting tool to clear the line from the propeller.
   - ☐ c. stay away from the propeller and report the problem to the crew.

7. I don't want to swim just below the surface because
   - ☐ a. it is hard to navigate well.
   - ☐ b. boats can't see me, and could hit me.
   - ☐ c. the risk of aquatic animal bites is higher.

8. I have just exited the water onto a boat by climbing a ladder with all my gear on except fins. Once aboard, first I should
   - ☐ a. check my remaining air supply, or have my buddy check it for me.
   - ☐ b. write down data from my dive computer, or ask the divemaster do so.
   - ☐ c. sit down as soon as possible, or have someone help me out of my kit.

9. My buddy and I are boat diving with a mild current. After entering, we would use the _____ line to pull ourselves to the _____ line, which we will descend along to the bottom.
   - ☐ a. trail, swim
   - ☐ b. swim, mooring/anchor
   - ☐ c. trail, mooring/anchor
   - ☐ d. mooring/anchor, swim

10. During a boat dive in mild to moderate current, my buddy and I lose our grips on the mooring line as we are coming up. We should
    - ☐ a. surface and swim across the current to reach the trail line.
    - ☐ b. swim against the current to return to the mooring line.
    - ☐ c. surface and swim against the current back to the boat.
    - ☐ d. descend and swim with the current.

11. My buddy and I surface and discover that the boat is nowhere in sight. We are beyond sight of shore and there is no mooring buoy or anchored float. We should
    - ☐ a. swim perpendicular to the current, if there is one.
    - ☐ b. use our compasses to swim toward land.
    - ☐ c. swim against the current, if there is one.
    - ☐ d. inflate our BCDs, use our surface signaling devices and wait for pick up.

How did you do?
1. True. 2. False. Secure your equipment even in calm conditions because an unexpected wave (a passing boat's wake, for example) may cause it to fall and injure someone, break something or fall overboard. 3. c. 4. True. 5. a. 6. c. 7. b. 8. c. 9. b. 10. a. 11. d.

By the end of this section, I should be able to answer these questions:

1. What are the four stages of dive planning?
2. What should I do during the advance planning stage?
3. What should I do during the preparation planning stage?
4. What five steps should I follow during the last-minute preparation planning stage?
5. What seven steps should I follow during the predive planning stage?
6. What considerations should I have when I plan extended dive travel?

Dive Planning

Let's expand on what you've already learned about dive planning. We can divide planning in to four stages, each with its own characteristics: advance planning, preparation planning, last-minute preparation, and predive planning.

Dive planning doesn't have to be a long, drawn-out process; these planning stages provide a way to think about what you need to do before a dive. In practice you'll find they often overlap somewhat, and that you accomplish them quickly.

Advance Planning

Advance planning begins with the decision to go diving. What you do at this point typically includes:

- Deciding on which buddy(ies) and/or dive operator (boat, resort, etc.) to dive with.
- Choosing a dive site.
  - Initially, this may be general, with a specific site chosen later.

section three

- It may also be very specific if required for your dive objective.

- Agreeing on an objective (i.e., what you want to do on the dive).

- Scheduling logistics – where and when you will meet, get in the water, etc.

- Checking dive conditions, as well as weather, wave and surf information, conditions, etc., at ScubaEarth® and other online sources, as well as a local dive operator.

Preparation Planning

Preparation planning usually begins several days before the dive. Typically, you inspect your gear to be sure it's all working properly and together – this gives you time to have something serviced or replaced if necessary. Have your scuba cylinder filled if you need to, and recheck the weather and conditions as necessary to see if they're still acceptable, especially if it's been several days since you checked. You may also want to reconfirm with your buddy.

Often, you start packing your gear bag at this stage. You may put some things in it right before you go, but you can stow most of it after you confirm it's working okay. Many active divers stay "permanently prepared" by always having their gear ready and by regularly checking conditions.

Last-Minute Preparation

Last-minute preparation is what you do a few hours before, right up to when you leave for the dive site. Typically, you'll include these five steps:

1. Recheck the weather, surf and/or dive conditions as appropriate. In some areas, this may not be necessary, but in others with quickly changeable conditions, this is a good idea.

2. Let someone know where you're going, when you expect to be back and what to do if you're delayed. Give that person your mobile number.

3. Gather personal items you'll want, such as a jacket, your certification card (or eCard), sunscreen, ice chest, bever-

ages, lunch, etc. These items vary depending upon the dive.

4. Pack any remaining items into your gear bag. When boat diving, remember to put what you need first in last, so it's on top.

5. Double check that you're not forgetting anything. Showing up at the dive site with only one fin can keep you out of the water if no one has an extra you can borrow.

Predive Planning

Predive planning is the actual dive plan. You do this to settle on details and make decisions based upon what you find at the dive site. The idea is to foresee, discuss and plan for as much as reasonably possible before the dive. The PADI Skill Practice and Dive Planning Slate lists reminders:

- Evaluate the conditions. Take the time you need to do this properly.

- Decide whether the conditions are acceptable for diving. If not, go to an alternate site or cancel diving altogether. Diving is supposed to be fun and rewarding; if it won't be, do something else.

- Agree on techniques, including where/how to enter, the course to follow, techniques you'll use during the dive and where/how to exit.

- Review signals and communications as necessary.
    - You may need little or no review with buddies you dive with often.
    - Spend time on it with new buddies, or if you'll need special signals.

- Agree on buddy separation procedures.

- Agree on time, depth and air supply limits.

- Discuss what to do if an emergency arises.

Extended Dive Travel

Planning extended dive travel – that is, a dive trip to a remote destination, typically involving staying one or more nights – has some extra considerations.

The first is to determine what gear to take. When traveling by air, you usually rent cylinders and weights at your destination. Confirm anything else you may choose to rent at the destination before you go. Check with the airline regarding baggage allowances. Weigh your bags to avoid surprises when you check in.

Take your logbook and certification card to document your experience and qualifications (PADI eLog and eCards reduce what you need to carry and help if you forget). PADI Members have access to the Dive Chek system, which allows an operator to confirm your certification if you forgot it. If you lose your certification card (it happens), you can replace it through the **PADI Mobile App** or **padi.com** or see your PADI Dive Center or Resort.

If you're new to dive travel, it helps to make your first trips with experienced dive travelers. Go on a trip led by your PADI Dive Center or other dive group. Even with experience, you may find you prefer group travel because it provides social activities and a way to make new friends.

Research the destination so you know any special requirements, the weather to expect, the types of diving available, ground transportation, local customs, etc. Most destinations have websites, and ScubaEarth® has destination information. Social networking sites with dive groups can give you personal insights. If you're making a group trip with a PADI dive operation, they can help you with this.

Plan to learn something new. Dive travel often lets you try new dive activities. For example, if there are no wrecks in your local area, traveling to an area known for wreck diving is a good reason to take the PADI Wreck Diver course. If diving on the wrecks also requires using a dry suit, you can complete the PADI Dry Suit Diver course, too. Taking courses and learning special activities add to the fun of dive travel, and expand the locations you're qualified to visit.

Finally, the diving lifestyle involves more than diving; it includes sightseeing, other sports and getting a glimpse of new parts of the world above water as well as underwater. Even dive trips that are primarily dive-focused (like on most live-aboard dive vessels) usually offer these opportunities.

Exercise 3-9

1. The four stages of dive planning are advance planning, preparation planning, last-minute preparation and predive planning.
   - ☐ True
   - ☐ False

2. Typically, I decide on a dive buddy(ies) or dive operator (boat or resort) during_____.
   - ☐ a. advance planning
   - ☐ b. preparation planning
   - ☐ c. last-minute preparation
   - ☐ d. predive planning

3. _____ is what I do a few hours before, to right up to when I leave for the dive site.
   - ☐ a. Advance planning
   - ☐ b. Preparation planning
   - ☐ c. Last-minute preparation
   - ☐ d. Predive planning

4. I want to begin _____ at least a day or two before the dive.
   - ☐ a. advance planning
   - ☐ b. preparation planning
   - ☐ c. last-minute preparation
   - ☐ d. predive planning

5. During _____, my buddy and I settle on details and make decisions based upon what we find at the dive site.
   - ☐ a. advance planning
   - ☐ b. preparation planning
   - ☐ c. last-minute preparation
   - ☐ d. predive planning

6. Considerations for extended dive travel may include (choose all that apply):
   - ☐ a. what gear to take.
   - ☐ b. having my logbook and certification with me.
   - ☐ c. researching the destination.
   - ☐ d. planning activities other than diving.

How did you do?
1. True. 2. a. 3. c. 4. b. 5. d. 6. a, b, c, d.

Problem Management

Prevention

The Approach to Diving that Helps Prevent Problems

Diving has a better safety record than many other sports and activities, but you still face hazards and risks. It is common sense that being in and under water presents some of this risk. You have also learned that breathing compressed air (or other gases) underwater also has potential risks, and you've learned how to manage and avoid the problems.

The guidelines and procedures you learn help you reduce and control the risks of diving, but you can never completely eliminate risk. Diving within your limitations, planning your dives, staying physically fit, maintaining your dive skills and following safe diving practices will help you avoid problem situations. You can also adopt an approach to diving that can help prevent problems: To the best of your ability, always follow safe diving guidelines, have the recommended equipment and do as you've been trained, *even when it doesn't seem necessary.* For example, on a calm day without a current, you may expect to ascend and surface right next to the boat, and, as a result, consider leaving your snorkel behind. But conditions can change and you can get lost. If you unexpectedly surface away from the boat due to low air and find that choppy waves had come up, you'd be very glad you had your snorkel.

There are several reasons this approach helps you reduce risk and manage problems. As previously discussed, under stress you tend to do what you do by habit, so maintain habits that prevent problems and help you when one arises. Unfortunately, problems don't announce themselves in advance. And, because you are human, you *will* make mistakes. The procedures and

LEARNING OBJECTIVES

By the end of this section, I should be able to answer these questions:

1. What approach to diving can help me prevent and manage problems?

2. How does continuing my diver education improve my ability to manage problems? Which four courses are recommended?

The more you stick with proper habits and equipment, the fewer problems you'll have and the better prepared you'll be to deal with them.

equipment requirements you learn help address this by providing a margin for error. When you don't follow your training, you reduce this margin.

Continuing Education and Managing Problems

Along with a well-stocked first-aid kit and emergency oxygen, continuing your diver education improves your ability to manage problems by learning, extending and refining emergency skills and giving you practice under guidance. While this benefits you regardless of where you dive, if you plan to dive where secondary professional assistance (paramedic, lifeguard, divemaster, instructor, etc.) is either remote (due to time or distance) or unavailable, you should have additional training and emergency equipment.

If you plan to dive where secondary professional assistance (paramedic, lifeguard, divemaster, instructor, etc.) is either remote (due to time or distance) or unavailable, you should have additional training in preventing and managing emergencies.

Continuing your education through these four courses is recommended:

- The PADI Advanced Open Water Diver course broadens your experience in (among other things) planning dives and evaluating conditions under instructor supervision.

- The PADI Rescue Diver course expands on your dive emergency training with extensive skill development and hands-on practice. It provides an environment for learning techniques best suited to you.

- The Emergency First Response Primary and Secondary Care courses teach you CPR and first aid. These emergency skills have application outside of diving.

- The PADI Emergency Oxygen Provider course qualifies you to provide oxygen in diving emergencies. This is a primary first-aid step for serious medical emergencies in diving.

Ask your instructor or PADI Dive Center or Resort for more information about these programs.

Exercise 3-10

1. My buddy and I have surfaced from a dive. The water is completely calm and there is no clear need to keep my mask on. Following the approach to diving that helps prevent problems, I would
   - ☐ a. remove my mask if I want.
   - ☐ b. keep my mask on.
   - ☐ c. partially remove my mask.

2. Under stress, I tend to do what I do by habit.
   - ☐ True
   - ☐ False

3. Continuing my diver education can extend and refine the emergency skills I learn in this course.
   - ☐ True
   - ☐ False

   How did you do?
   1. b. 2. True. 3. True.

LEARNING OBJECTIVES

By the end of this section, I should be able to answer these questions:

1. In what three ways can I prevent or control most dive problems that occur at the surface?

2. What should I do if a diving-related problem occurs at the surface?

3. How do the appearance and actions of a diver who needs help and is in control (not panicked) differ from a diver who needs help and is out of control (panicked)?

4. What are the four basic steps for assisting a responsive diver at the surface?

Surface Problem Management – Responsive Diver

Most diver-in-distress situations occur at the surface. You can control or prevent having a surface problem yourself by diving within your limits, relaxing while you dive, and establishing and maintaining positive buoyancy on the surface.

Regardless of the cause, if a diving-related problem occurs at the surface, *immediately* establish buoyancy by inflating your BCD or dropping your weights. Stay at the surface using the least energy possible – by *floating,* not by kicking. Don't hesitate to drop your weights. Be cautious about divers who may be below, but it is never wrong to drop your weights (they can *usually* be recovered).

You can control or prevent having a surface problem yourself by diving within your limits, relaxing while you dive, and establishing and maintaining positive buoyancy on the surface.

Stop, think and *then* act. If you need help, ask. Asking for help when you have a small problem often avoids a big problem and makes everything easier for you, your buddies and the divemaster/crew. Use your surface signaling devices to whistle, wave or otherwise attract attention if necessary when you need assistance.

Common surface problems include overexertion, leg muscle cramps and choking on inhaled water. As you learned, avoid overexertion by staying relaxed. If you start to overexert, be sure you're buoyant, stop all activity and rest. Signal your buddy or instructor, and don't hesitate to ask for assistance. Leg cramps results from involuntary muscle contractions, and tend to be more common if you have not been diving for a while because your muscles aren't used to swimming with fins. You've learned that airway control helps prevent choking on inhaled water, as does keeping your mask on and your regulator or snorkel in your mouth. If you do choke on a bit of water at the surface, be sure you float, and cough into your regulator or snorkel while you hold it. Swallowing may help, too.

Assisting a Responsive Diver at the Surface

A diver who is breathing, alert and active is considered responsive. There are two types of responsive divers at the surface: in control (not panicked) and out of control (panicked). Divers who are in control (not panicked) and need help usually signal or ask for assistance. They appear *relatively* relaxed and move with controlled, deliberate (purposeful) actions. If able, they typically respond to and follow instructions. Divers in control keep their gear in place (except weights, which they may drop) and establish buoyancy.

Divers who are out of control (panicked) have been overcome by unreasoned fear that displaces purposeful, controlled actions for instinctive, inappropriate and often repetitive actions. Fearing drowning, they struggle violently and expend tremendous energy to stay at the surface, often to the point they become exhausted.

Divers who have panicked typically fail to establish buoyancy. They may climb upon anything or anyone they think will

keep them from sinking. They often have their masks on their foreheads or gone altogether, and don't use their breathing equipment. They usually have wide, unseeing eyes, quick and jerky movements, and do not follow instructions. In this state of mind, they respond only to their fear and pay little attention to anything else. They need immediate help because they may continue to struggle until exhausted, at which point they are at risk of sinking and drowning.

There are four basic steps for assisting a responsive diver – in control or panicked – at the surface.

1 Establish buoyancy for *yourself* and the diver. Always begin with buoyancy. You greatly reduce the immediate risk by assuring neither of you will sink. The ideal way to do this is to throw or extend flotation to the diver. If you must make contact to help, make yourself buoyant before doing so, then inflate the victim's BCD and/or drop weights after you make contact.

2 Calm the diver by reassuring, offering encouragement and asking the person to relax. A diver who is in control stays in control with reassurance. A panicked diver usually begins to regain control once buoyant. Reassurance usually helps.

3 Help the diver reestablish breathing control. Often, dealing with a problem leads to strenuous exertion, so have the diver take slow, deep breaths to relax and restore self-control. If appropriate in the circumstances, give the diver a chance to rest and recover before any further action.

4 As necessary, assist the diver to the boat or shore. Even divers who don't panic may need assistance due to leg cramps or being overly tired.

Exercise 3-11

1. I can prevent or control most dive problems that occur at the surface by diving within my limits, relaxing while I dive and
   - ☐ a. becoming and staying buoyant.
   - ☐ b. reserving 50 bar/500 psi in my cylinder.
   - ☐ c. diving with a buddy.
   - ☐ d. carrying a cutting tool.

2. If a diving related problem occurs at the surface, I should immediately switch from my snorkel to my regulator.
   - ☐ True
   - ☐ False

3. I can tell if my buddy is in control (not panicked) with a problem at the surface if my buddy (choose all that apply):
   - ☐ a. has no mask on.
   - ☐ b. appears relatively relaxed.
   - ☐ c. asks for help.
   - ☐ d. has not established buoyancy.
   - ☐ e. follows instructions.
   - ☐ f. breathes from the snorkel or regulator.
   - ☐ g. struggles violently.

4. When assisting a responsive diver at the surface, I always begin by
   - ☐ a. calming the diver.
   - ☐ b. helping the diver establish breathing control.
   - ☐ c. swimming to the diver.
   - ☐ d. establishing buoyancy for myself and the diver.

How did you do?
1. a. The other choices are important safe diving practices, becoming and staying buoyant is specific to preventing and controlling dive problems on the surface. 2. False. You should immediately establish buoyancy by inflating your BCD and/or dropping your weights. 3. b, c, e, f. 4. d.

Surface Problem Management – Unresponsive Diver

An *unresponsive* (unconscious) diver at the surface needs immediate help. The diver may be unresponsive due to inhaling water, extreme fatigue, heart attack or lung overexpansion injuries, among other causes. Panic, inefficient breathing, throat blockage and exhaustion can also contribute.

The primary concerns are to check for breathing and to begin rescue breathing if the diver isn't breathing. Do this after making sure that you and the diver both have adequate positive buoyancy.

An unresponsive diver does not move and does not respond when tapped or spoken to. The diver's equipment may be in place, but the diver may have no mask or not have a mouthpiece in. Commonly, an unresponsive diver will not have significant

buoyancy and will barely float, or even may have begun to sink. If there's a current, the diver will drift with it.

Alternatively, an unresponsive diver may not be *obviously* unresponsive. An unresponsive diver floating face down may appear to be resting or watching something underwater. Confirm responsiveness if a diver floats without moving. Assume that a diver who is floating in an odd position (e.g., legs at the surface, bent at the torso with the head at the deepest point) and not moving needs help until you confirm otherwise. A diver who surfaces alone, calls for help or shows signs of panic, then stops moving, should also be considered unresponsive until you confirm otherwise.

Assisting an Unresponsive Diver at the Surface

Follow these four basic steps to assist an unresponsive diver at the surface.

❶ Establish buoyancy for the victim and for yourself. Inflate both BCDs and/or drop weights as necessary.

❷ Call for help to the boat or shore. Depending upon the circumstances, others can assist with the rescue by helping with towing the

With an unresponsive diver at the surface, the primary concerns are to check for breathing and to begin rescue breathing if necessary.

Confirm responsiveness if a diver floats without moving. Assume that a diver who is floating in an odd position and not moving needs help until you confirm otherwise.

victim, preparing emergency equipment, alerting emergency medical services and so on.

❸ Check for breathing. Begin providing rescue breaths if the victim isn't breathing as you tow the diver to the boat or shore.

❹ Continue rescue breathing (if needed) during the tow, and help get the victim out of the water. Rescue procedures continue out of the water; we'll look at those shortly.

Exercise 3-12

1. After establishing buoyancy for both of us, the primary concerns with an unresponsive diver at the surface are _____ and _____.
   - ☐ a. determining what happened, ensuring buddy safety
   - ☐ b. equipment function, confirming air supply
   - ☐ c. air supply, check for a pulse
   - ☐ d. checking for breathing, providing rescue breaths if needed

2. My buddy doesn't move while floating at the surface, so I tap my buddy's shoulder. My buddy signals "okay." I should disregard this signal and assume my buddy is unresponsive.
   - ☐ True
   - ☐ False

3. When assisting an unresponsive diver at the surface, if I find the victim isn't breathing, I should
   - ☐ a. provide rescue breaths.
   - ☐ b. signal the divemaster to provide rescue breaths.
   - ☐ c. check the diver's regulator for proper function.

   How did you do?
   1. d. 2. False. A diver who responds to communication is not unresponsive. 3. a.

By the end of this section, I should be able to answer these questions:

1. In what three ways can I prevent or control most dive problems that may occur underwater?

2. How should I prevent and respond to overexertion underwater?

3. How should I breathe from a freeflowing regulator?

4. What should I do if I become entangled underwater?

5. How should I prevent running low on or out of air underwater?

6. In order of priority, what are my four options if I run out of air underwater?

7. How should I assist an unresponsive diver underwater? What is the priority?

Underwater Problem Management

Preventing and Controlling Underwater Problems

Much of what you learn in this course teaches you to prevent and control underwater problems, so the following ways to prevent or control underwater problems should sound familiar:

1. Relax while you dive.

2. Plan your air use with your buddy(ies) and watch it closely.

3. Dive within the limits of your experience and training.

Overexertion

Overexertion is one of the most common underwater problems so it's worth repeating that you want to dive relaxed to prevent overexertion. Breathe slowly, deeply and continuously, and pace yourself.

Overexertion may create a feeling of air starvation because breathing resistance increases with depth. The problem is

section three

Overexertion may create a feeling of air starvation, because breathing resistance increases with depth. The problem is overexertion, though it may feel like the regulator doesn't deliver enough air.

▲ **You can breathe** from a freeflowing regulator, but begin your ascent promptly. A freeflow will exhaust your air supply quickly.

overexertion, though it may feel like the regulator doesn't deliver enough air. What's actually happening is that you're demanding more air than it can supply. Avoid this by avoiding strenuous activity.

If you start to feel overexerted – air-starved and unable to catch your breath – stop all activity. *Do not ignore the feeling.* Rest, relax and breathe slowly until you breathe normally again.

- Signal "stop" or "hold" and indicate that you need to rest.

- Continue at a reduced pace after you recover.

- If you can't return to a relaxed state, end the dive.

- If conditions are adding to overexertion, it may be best to abort the dive.

Freeflowing Regulator

Modern regulators are highly reliable and designed so that if they fail, they release air continuously (called a *freeflow*). This keeps a failure from cutting off your air, because you can breathe from a freeflowing regulator.

To breathe from a freeflowing regulator, do *not* seal your mouth on the mouthpiece. There is some risk of lung overexpansion injury if the flow is high, but the main reason is because flowing air may make it hard to keep the regulator in your mouth. Also, it may flood your mask. Instead, hold the second stage in your hand and press the mouthpiece outside your lips. Let the excess air escape freely. You may insert only one end of the mouthpiece into your mouth if it helps.

Breathe the air you need by "sipping" it, somewhat like drinking from a water fountain. Begin your ascent promptly,

because freeflow will exhaust your air supply quickly. Obviously, a regulator that freeflows needs professional servicing by your PADI Dive Center or Resort before using it again.

Entanglement

Entanglement is rare, but fishing line, loose line from a reel, and old fishing nets may cause it. Some aquatic plants have entanglement potential.

Prevent entanglement by moving slowly, watching where you're going and keeping your equipment streamlined. If you do get entangled, it's *not* usually an emergency if you have enough air.

- Stop, think and work slowly and calmly to free yourself.

- Get your buddy(ies) to help.

- Avoid turning or twisting, because this tends to wrap what's entangling you around you.

- If severely tangled or low on air, you may need to use a cutting tool. If so, be careful – don't cut yourself or your gear. With tough line, disentangling may be faster than cutting.

- In extreme cases, you may have to slip out of your scuba kit, free yourself and put it back on (this is one reason you practice removing and replacing your scuba rig underwater).

Running Low On/Out of Air Underwater

Running out of air is one of the easiest problems to avoid, and stoppage due to malfunction is highly unlikely due to regulator design. Plan your air use, including a reserve, during dive planning. During the dive, check your SPG often.

If you run low on air before you reach your planned ascent point, ascend where you are while you still have adequate air. It is better to have a long surface swim than to run out of air underwater. Ascending with enough air allows you to control your ascent and to make a safety stop.

Although you should avoid becoming very low on air or running out, you should know the four options to consider, and when to apply each. Remain calm, quickly consider each and then act intelligently based on your training.

Option ❶ : Make a normal ascent.

- Do this if you're very low on air (you feel some breathing resistance), but your cylinder isn't completely empty.

- As you ascend, you can get more air from your cylinder, because the surrounding water pressure decreases.

- Breathe lightly (but continuously) and make a controlled, continuous ascent to the surface.

- Do not attempt a safety stop.

Option ❷ : Ascend using an alternate air source.

- Think of this as your best, all around choice when you have an alternate air source immediately available.

- During your predive safety check, confirm what alternate air sources your buddies have and how to secure them. Test breathe your alternate air source(s).

- To use an alternate air source supplied by a buddy, you need to stay close to your buddy(ies).

Option ❸ : Make a Controlled Emergency Swimming Ascent (sometimes called CESA).

- This is the best choice if you were completely out of air, no deeper than approximately 6 to 9 metres/20 to 30 feet, the surface is closer than your buddy(ies) or another diver, and you have no other alternate air source.

- Simply look up and swim to the surface making a continuous "ahhhhh" sound into your regulator. The "ahhhhh" sound assures that you exhale expanding gas, which is necessary to avoid lung overexpansion injury.

- Leave all your gear in place and keep the regulator in your mouth. Do not drop your weights to start your ascent.

- Ascend at a safe rate. The ascent gets easier as you ascend because air expanding in your BCD increases your buoyancy. Vent air as needed to maintain a proper rate.

Option ❹ : Make a buoyant emergency ascent.

- Use this option when you are too far from your buddy(ies) or another diver, have no other alternate air source and are so deep that you doubt you can reach the surface any other way.

- You make a buoyant emergency ascent exactly like a Controlled Emergency Swimming Ascent, except you ditch your weights and exceed a safe rate.

- Again, look up and make the "ahhhhh" sound as you ascend.

- Because you exceed a safe rate, this method has more risk than the other options (which is why it is your last choice), but is obviously better than staying on the bottom without air.

- As you near the surface, you can flare out your arms and legs to create drag and slow your ascent.

If the situation calls for it, you can use more than one of these options. For example, suppose in an emergency you determine that the controlled emergency ascent is your best option. As you head up, another diver reaches you and offers an alternate air source. You could switch to the alternate and complete the ascent breathing normally from it.

After reaching the surface in an out-of-air emergency, make yourself buoyant, but remember that you can't inflate your BCD by using the low-pressure inflator, because you have an empty cylinder. Instead, inflate your BCD orally and/or drop your weights. (You practice BCD oral inflation and emergency weight drop during your confined and open water dives.)

section three

161

Assisting an Unresponsive Diver Underwater

An unresponsive diver underwater is a serious emergency situation. The priority is to get the diver to the surface.

Assist an unresponsive diver following these procedures:

1. Swim the diver to the surface. If necessary, use the diver's BCD and/or drop weights to make the victim buoyant.

2. If the diver's regulator is in the mouth, hold it there. If it is not, don't waste time trying to replace it.

3. Ascend at a safe rate. If the diver's buoyancy becomes too great for a safe ascent rate, let the victim go. Finish a safe ascent and resume the rescue at the surface. *Keep yourself safe.* You can't help someone else if you have troubles of your own.

4. At the surface, follow the priorities and procedures for an unresponsive diver at the surface.

Exercise 3-13

1. To prevent and control underwater problems, I should (choose all that apply):
   - ☐ a. relax while I dive.
   - ☐ b. plan my air use.
   - ☐ c. dive within my limits.

2. While diving, I begin to feel air-starved because I have been swimming hard. I should
   - ☐ a. signal "stop" and rest.
   - ☐ b. immediately ascend.
   - ☐ c. descend slightly.
   - ☐ d. switch to an alternate air source.

3. To breathe from a freeflowing regulator, I should hold the second stage
   - ☐ a. firmly in my mouth.
   - ☐ b. about .3 metres/1 foot from my mouth.
   - ☐ c. with the mouthpiece pressed against my lips.

4. If I were to become entangled underwater, I should
   - ☐ a. stop, think and work to free myself.
   - ☐ b. turn side to side until free.
   - ☐ c. wait for someone to rescue me.

5. During a dive, I find I am running low on air sooner than expected. My buddy and I are still several minutes from our planned ascent point, but I am almost at reserve pressure. We should
   - ☐ a. use the reserve to continue to our planned ascent point.
   - ☐ b. ascend immediately where we are.

6. Although it shouldn't have happened, on a dive I fail to watch my SPG and run out of air. I don't have a pony bottle or self-contained ascent bottle. My buddy is close at hand – less than two seconds away, and has an alternate second stage. My best option is probably to
   - ☐ a. make a normal ascent.
   - ☐ b. ascend using an alternate air source.
   - ☐ c. make a Controlled Emergency Swimming Ascent.
   - ☐ d. make a buoyant emergency ascent.

7. If I am bringing an unresponsive diver to the surface and the victim becomes too buoyant to control, I should stay with the victim even if our ascent is too fast.

   ☐ True   ☐ False

How did you do?
1. a, b, c. 2. a. 3. c. 4. a. 5. b. 6. b. 7. False. You should let the victim go, complete your ascent at a safe rate, and resume the rescue at the surface.

LEARNING OBJECTIVES

By the end of this section, I should be able to answer these questions:

1. What signs and symptoms may be present with a diver who is or was unresponsive?

2. What are my priorities when assisting someone who is or was unresponsive?

3. What are the general steps to follow when giving aid to a diver who is or was unresponsive?

First Responder Care for Diving-Related Emergencies

Signs and Symptoms

A diver who is or was unresponsive in water or underwater should be considered a serious medical emergency. Being unresponsive is being unconscious, or unable to respond or act coherently.

Near-drowning or otherwise becoming unresponsive underwater, pressure-related injuries and medical conditions not directly related to diving (like heart attack) can cause these signs (what you observe) and symptoms (what the victim feels):

- difficulty breathing
- unconsciousness
- unclear thinking
- visual problems

- paralysis
- chest pain
- lowered alertness
- cardiac and respiratory arrest

Assisting the Unresponsive Diver Out of the Water

After removing the diver from the water, your priorities when assisting someone who is or was unresponsive are to make sure the diver is breathing (by providing rescue breathing and/or CPR if necessary), and to contact emergency medical care.

Your first contact is usually to the appropriate local emergency medical care. If a diver emergency service like DAN (Divers Alert Network) serves the area, contact it next. This service coordinates with local emergency personnel to provide specialized medical guidance for diving accidents, and helps the diver reach specialized medical care. You'll learn more about this in Knowledge Development Section Four.

Follow these general steps when giving aid to a diver who is or was unresponsive:

1. Keep the diver's airway open and check for breathing.

2. Provide rescue breathing or CPR as necessary.

   - Do not use abdominal thrusts unless you are unable to provide rescue breathing due to a suspected obstruction.

   - Inhaled water, if present, does not prevent rescue breaths. You don't have to try to clear it.

3. If the diver is unresponsive but breathing, keep the diver lying level on the left side (recovery position). This position is *not* more important than transporting the diver to safety or providing rescue breaths or CPR if necessary.

4. Check the diver's breathing frequently.

5. If the diver has regained responsiveness, keep the diver lying down comfortably.

6. Administer emergency oxygen as soon as possible.

7. Keep the diver still and maintain a normal body temperature by protecting from heat or cold.

8. Continue to provide care until emergency medical care arrives.

9. If you can't accompany the diver to medical care, write down as much background information as possible about the individual and the dive, and attach it to the diver in a conspicuous place.

- Provide only information relevant to care, such as the dive profile, emergency care provided, emergency contact information, and any known medical conditions.

- Write only facts. Do not speculate or guess – bad information is worse than no information.

Any diver who has been unresponsive in or under water *requires* medical examination, even if the person seems fully recovered. Some conditions, such as near-drowning, can have delayed serious, potentially fatal, consequences hours after the incident. Post-incident medical examination can identify these problems and provide appropriate treatment.

You practice these steps in the PADI Rescue Diver course, applying CPR/first aid that you learn in the Emergency First Response Primary and Secondary Care courses. The PADI Emergency Oxygen Provider course gives you hands-on practice with emergency oxygen system use.

Exercise 3-14

1. A diver who is or was unresponsive may have which of the following signs and symptoms? (choose all that apply):
   - ☐ a. difficulty breathing
   - ☐ b. elevated body temperature
   - ☐ c. unconsciousness
   - ☐ d. cardiac and respiratory arrest
   - ☐ e. chest pain
   - ☐ f. hyperactivity
   - ☐ g. inappropriate humor

2. My first priority when assisting someone who is or was unresponsive is to contact emergency medical care and to
   - ☐ a. keep the victim warm.
   - ☐ b. administer emergency oxygen.
   - ☐ c. write down background information.
   - ☐ d. be sure the person is breathing.

3. A diver who was unresponsive is breathing. Nonetheless, I should check breathing frequently while waiting for emergency medical care.

   ☐ True   ☐ False

4. A diver who was unresponsive underwater has become fully responsive, is fully alert and shows no apparent further problems. The diver still requires medical examination.

   ☐ True   ☐ False

How did you do?
1. a, c, d, e. 2. d. 3. True. 4. True.

Signaling devices, floats and dive flags are important tools in many diving situations. Let's look at the basics; your PADI Dive Center or Resort can guide you in choosing the best ones for you.

Surface Signaling Devices

You have already learned that at times, you want to have *surface signaling devices* to help you get attention and be visible in the water. Let's look at these devices in more detail, and be sure to check out your options at your PADI dive shop.

Typically, you should have at least *two* surface signaling devices with you on a dive. The easiest way to be sure you always have them is to make them a standard part of your scuba kit. Of the two devices, you should have an audible device that allows you to attract attention with sound, and a visual device that makes you easier to see at a distance, especially amid waves. In an emergency, you may use both – the audible signal to alert help from the boat or shore, and the visual signal so responders can see where you are.

Divers commonly use the following devices, from which you'll choose two or more:

* *Whistles* are the most common audible devices. You normally attach them to the BCD inflator where you can get them quickly, but they're out of the way.

* *Low-pressure horns* use air from your cylinder. They are much louder than whistles. They usually attach to the BCD inflator; you probably want a standard whistle, too, to use if your cylinder is empty.

* *Inflatable signal tubes* are brightly colored (usually orange) plastic/fabric tubes that you inflate at the surface. They stand more than 1 metre/3 feet above the surface, helping make

DSMBs are similar to inflatable signal tubes, except you can deploy them from the bottom, from midwater or at the surface.

Signal lights and flashers are the best visual signaling devices when night diving.

you visible even in rough conditions. They roll up compactly and fit in your pocket when not in use.

- *Delayed Surface Marker Buoys (DSMBs)* do the same job as inflatable signal tubes. The main difference is that you can attach them to a line and reel and deploy them from the bottom, from midwater or at the surface. For some types of diving, like rebreather diving, DSMBs are standard equipment. They've become standard equipment for all divers in some areas; if this applies to your area, your instructor will introduce you to DSMB use during the course, and may have you practice using one.

- *Signal mirrors* allow you to reflect sunlight to attract attention. Besides signaling boats, you can signal aircraft. They are compact and fit in your pocket.

- *Signal lights and flashers* designed specifically for diving are the best visual signaling devices when night diving. They fit in a pocket, or may strap to an arm or wrist.

Exercise 3-15

1. At a minimum, I should have _____ visual and _____ audible surface signaling devices.
   - ☐ a. 1, 1
   - ☐ b. 2, 1
   - ☐ c. 1, 2
   - ☐ d. 2, 2

2. The visual signaling device that I might use to signal aircraft is a(n)
   - ☐ a. inflatable signal tube.
   - ☐ b. signal mirror.
   - ☐ c. DSMB.
   - ☐ d. aircraft flag.

   How did you do?
   1. a. 2. b.

LEARNING OBJECTIVES

By the end of this section, I should be able to answer these questions:

1. What are five uses for a surface float?

2. How should I carry line used for a surface float?

3. Why should I use a dive flag?

4. What are the two types of dive flags? Under what conditions should I use each?

5. How close am I supposed to stay to a dive flag, and how far away are boaters supposed to stay from a dive flag?

Dive Floats and Flags

Surface Floats

You may use a surface float when diving from shore, or if diving some distance from a dive boat. A surface float is any small float that you use for:

1. resting

2. marking a dive site location

3. carrying accessories or other items

4. assisting another diver (as a flotation aid)

5. supporting a dive flag

section three

There are many sizes and styles ranging from just large enough to hold up a dive flag, to big enough for several people to hang on to at once. Among these, tire inner tubes with special covers are one of the most popular types. Ask your instructor or a professional at your dive center or resort what type divers in your area favor.

Depending upon the dive plan and the site, you may tow a float the entire dive, or anchor it. Either way, you will need line (usually nylon or other synthetic suitable for aquatic use) at least 15 metres/50 feet long. Trying to carry that much line loose can cause entanglement, so use a reel or line caddy.

Do *not* attach the float to your gear; tow it by hand. If it gets entangled on something or snagged by a boat, you can simply let go.

Dive Flags

Underwater, boaters and other watercraft can't see you. You use a dive flag to alert them that you're there. This reduces the risk of being run over. In many areas, you are required by law to use a dive flag, but it's a wise practice any time you're diving where boats are, required or not. The flag may fly from a dive boat, or from a surface float.

There are two recognized dive flags. Where you use each depends upon the circumstances, but you should fly either high enough, and have one big enough to be visible from 100 metres/yards. Both versions usually have a wire extender to make them visible even without wind.

The traditional dive flag is a red rectangle with a white diagonal stripe. It indicates there are divers below and boats

should keep clear. Many areas require this flag when diving in navigable waters.

The Alpha flag is a blue-white pennant, and indicates that the vessel flying it has divers in the water and can't maneuver. Generally, only boats have to use the Alpha flag when people dive from them, and it is not used on diver-towed floats. But some areas use the Alpha flag for all diving activities. Your instructor will tell you the practices in your area.

Regional regulations and practices tell you which flag to use. In some situations, you may need to use both flags. However, don't display either flag unless divers are actually in the water.

Local law often regulates how close you must stay to your dive flag and how far away boaters must stay. If there are no specific laws, the rule of thumb is to stay within 15 metres/50 feet of the flag. Boats should stay 30 to 60 metres/100 to 200 feet away. But don't assume boats know what the flags mean. If a boat sounds like it is close, stay down, deep enough to be safe until it clears the area. For your part, stay close to the flag or you can't expect boats to avoid you.

15m/50ft   30-60m/100-200ft

1. One possible use for a surface float is to use it to assist another diver.
   - ☐ True
   - ☐ False

2. My buddy and I are using a surface float. We should carry the line with which we will tow it
   - ☐ a. coiled up in one hand.
   - ☐ b. clipped to my BCD.
   - ☐ c. wrapped around the float.
   - ☐ d. attached to a line caddy or reel.

3. I use a dive flag so that boaters and other watercraft know that I'm underwater and should keep clear.
   - ☐ True
   - ☐ False

4. The _____ flag indicates that a vessel has divers in the water and can't maneuver.
   - ☐ a. Alpha
   - ☐ b. traditional dive

5. If there are no specific laws, the rule of thumb is that I should stay within _____ of my dive flag.
   - ☐ a. 60 metres/200 feet
   - ☐ b. 30 metres/100 feet
   - ☐ c. 15 metres/50 feet
   - ☐ d. 8 metres/25 feet

How did you do?
1. True. 2. d. 3. True. 4. a. 5. c.

Your Skills as a Diver III

Let's look at some more skills you'll learn during this course. As previously mentioned, your instructor may demonstrate a method that differs from what you learn here.

Deep Water Entry – Seated Back Roll

Your instructor may have you practice the *seated back roll* entry. This is used when you're relatively close to the water, and is useful when diving from small boats as well as from platforms like low docks. It's also sometimes used by people who cannot stand while wearing scuba equipment.

- Enter with your BCD partially inflated, holding your mask and breathing from your regulator.

- Tuck your chin toward your chest.

- Lean backward until your weight rolls you in.

- After you're stable on the surface, signal you're okay (assuming you are) and clear the area so your buddy(ies) can enter.

Remove and Replace Weights at the Surface

You have learned the emergency weight drop, which allows you to become buoyant in an emergency. You need to learn to remove and replace your weights at the surface so you can adjust your weighting in the water, and for some entries and exits.

- The technique varies with equipment – your instructor will help you.

- Be careful not to drop the weights.

- Give your weights to someone, put them on a platform or secure them to a line.

- Be sure you have enough buoyancy and breathe from your regulator before taking weights handed to you.

- It is best if buddies put weights on one at a time, so they can assist each other if necessary.

- With most integrated weight systems, you remove the weights as you would in an emergency weight drop. You replace them the same way you install them when setting up your kit, but with some types you may have to remove and replace the entire kit.

- With many systems, it helps to tilt back in the water, almost face up, so the weight pockets tend to slide into place.

- When removing a standard nylon web belt, be sure to hold the free end and release the buckle end so the weights can't slide off.

Cramp Releases

Cramps are painful, involuntary muscle contractions, which in diving are most common in the leg or foot muscles. They don't cause emergencies if you know how to respond. You will practice the skills both at the surface and underwater.

- If you have or start to have a cramp, signal your buddy and stop.

- Allow the muscle to rest. It may help to gently stretch and massage the cramped muscle.

- After relieving a cramp, rest for a few minutes before continuing at a slower pace. Cramped muscles usually recover better if you resume using them at a slower pace after a brief stop, than if you stop using them completely.

- Dehydration, cold, restricted circulation and working a muscle beyond its fitness level can all cause cramping.

Neutral Buoyancy – Hovering

When you are neutrally buoyant, you can hover in midwater without using hands or fins to maintain your depth.

- Become neutrally buoyant.
- Push gently off the bottom – about 1 metre/3 feet – and maintain your depth without using your hands or fins.
- Use breath control to fine-tune your buoyancy. If you start to rise a bit, exhale and breathe with a slightly lower lung volume. If you start to sink, inhale and breathe with a slightly higher lung volume for a moment.
- Do not hold your breath!
- If you can't hover by adjusting with breathing, make small adjustments to your BCD.
- Practice until you can hover for at least 30 seconds.

Fine-Tuning Your Trim

After establishing neutral buoyancy, you can check your trim, which is important for streamlined, relaxed diving that helps you conserve energy and avoiding accidental contact with the environment.

- Relax in midwater to check your natural position.
- Usually, you want trim for a normal swimming position.
- You want to feel balanced and stable, both side to side and front to back.
- Your instructor will help you reposition gear and weight for good trim.
- You will learn to fine-tune your trim from one dive to the next.
- Ask your instructor about the PADI Peak Performance Buoyancy course to learn more about mastering buoyancy and trim.

Air Depletion/Alternate Air Source Combined Exercise

This exercise combines the air depletion exercise and alternate air source skills, simulating what you would feel and how you would respond in an out of air emergency.

- Your instructor closes your cylinder valve. When it becomes hard to breathe, signal "out-of-air" and "share air," then secure your buddy's alternate air source and begin breathing from it.
- Your instructor will reopen your cylinder valve as soon as you begin using your buddy's alternate air source, so it is available if necessary.

- After taking a few breaths and getting settled, you and your buddy will swim for at least a minute sharing air.
- In an actual out-of-air emergency you wouldn't usually swim around, but ascend to the surface. Because your confined water dives are much shallower than open water dives, you practice the swim to experience sharing air while in motion for a similar amount of time as it might take to reach the surface on an open water dive.
- Your instructor will have you finish the swim by ascending to the surface. Because you're simulating not having air, don't use the low-pressure inflator on your BCD to attain buoyancy at the surface. Instead, inflate it orally. Keep using the alternate air source until you're buoyant.

Controlled Emergency Swimming Ascent

During Confined Water Dive Three you will practice the Controlled Emergency Swimming Ascent.

- In a real emergency, you would swim to the surface. To cover the same distance in confined water, your instructor will have you practice the skill swimming *horizontally*.
- Imagine moving vertically, and that ahead of you is *up*.
- Reach out holding your BCD deflator and look ahead (in the position that would have you reaching *up* and looking *up* if you were vertical, swimming up to the surface).
- Your instructor will be beneath you, face up, or beside you, holding on to your BCD.
- On your instructor's signal, take a breath and exhale it continuously making a loud "ahhhhh" sound as you swim no faster than 18 metres/60 feet per minute for at least 9 metres/30 feet (a 30-second swim).
- Keep all your equipment in place.
- By making an "ahhhhhh" sound, you should be able to complete the swim in a single breath.
- Your instructor will have you practice diagonally to the surface (deep to shallow) after successfully performing the skill horizontally.

During your open water training dives, you'll get to practice a Controlled Emergency Swimming Ascent vertically under your instructor's supervision.

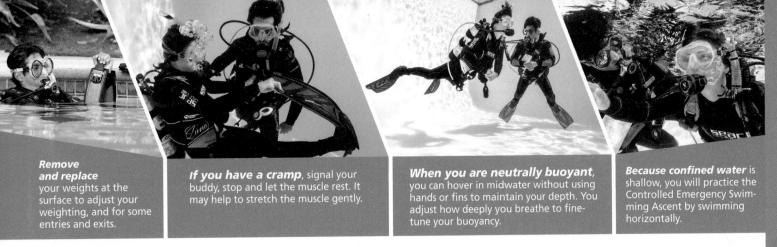

Remove and replace your weights at the surface to adjust your weighting, and for some entries and exits.

If you have a cramp, signal your buddy, stop and let the muscle rest. It may help to stretch the muscle gently.

When you are neutrally buoyant, you can hover in midwater without using hands or fins to maintain your depth. You adjust how deeply you breathe to fine-tune your buoyancy.

Because confined water is shallow, you will practice the Controlled Emergency Swimming Ascent by swimming horizontally.

Confined Water Dive Three

- ☐ Briefing
- ☐ Equipment assembly, dive planning, gearing up and predive safety check
- ☐ Deep water entry
- ☐ Weight and trim check and adjustment
- ☐ Remove and replace weights at surface (dive flexible)
- ☐ Cramp release at surface
- ☐ Five point descent with visual reference
- ☐ Neutral buoyancy
- ☐ Trim and weight positioning
- ☐ Air depletion and alternate air source combined exercise
- ☐ Controlled Emergency Swimming Ascent (CESA)
- ☐ Cramp release underwater
- ☐ Free time for skill practice and fun
- ☐ Debrief

Note: *Your instructor may modify this to some extent to meet class and logistical requirements.*

Open Water Dive One

- ☐ Briefing – signals introduction/review
- ☐ Assemble, put on and adjust equipment
- ☐ Predive safety check
- ☐ Inflate BCD at surface
- ☐ Entry
- ☐ Buoyancy/weight check
- ☐ Controlled descent
- ☐ Trim check
- ☐ Clearing a partially flooded mask
- ☐ Regulator recovery and clearing
- ☐ Underwater exploration
- ☐ Five point ascent
- ☐ Exit
- ☐ Debrief and log dive
- ☐ Post dive equipment care

Note: *Your instructor may modify this to meet class and logistical requirements.*

Open Water Dive Two

- ☐ Briefing and dive planning
- ☐ Assemble, put on and adjust equipment
- ☐ Predive safety check
- ☐ Entry
- ☐ Weight and trim check, adjustment
- ☐ Orally inflate BCD at surface
- ☐ Controlled five point descent (max depth 12 metres/40 feet)
- ☐ Fully flood and clear mask
- ☐ Buoyancy control – establish neutral buoyancy
- ☐ Alternate air source stationary
- ☐ Underwater exploration
- ☐ Alternate air source ascent – switch roles from stationary
- ☐ Exit
- ☐ Debrief and log dive
- ☐ Post dive equipment care

Note: *Your instructor may modify this to meet class and logistical requirements.*

section three

Knowledge Review Three

Some questions may have more than one correct answer. Choose all that apply.

1. One way to avoid disorientation while descending and ascending is to
   - ☐ a. close my eyes.
   - ☐ b. stay away from any objects.
   - ☑ c. follow a reference.
   - ☐ d. monitor my air supply closely.

2. My buddy and I are diving from a boat and there's a mild current. In most circumstances, we would _____ for the first part of the dive.
   - ☑ a. swim into the current
   - ☐ b. let the current carry us
   - ☐ c. not try to go anywhere

3. My buddy and I get disoriented while boat diving. There is a mild current, and we surface away from the boat. We should _____. If unable to reach the boat or too tired, we should _____.
   - ☑ a. swim into the current to get ahead of the boat, redescend and return on the bottom.
   - ☑ b. swim across the current to reach the trail line, become buoyant and signal the boat to pick us up.
   - ☐ c. signal that we are okay, swim for shore.
   - ☐ d. swim with the current until rested, swim to the bottom and swim into the current.

4. My buddy and I remain neutrally buoyant and stay above the bottom enough to avoid contact. We do this because bottom contact
   - ☑ a. may injure or kill fragile aquatic life.
   - ☑ b. tends to disturb the bottom and reduce the visibility.
   - ☑ c. increases the risk of accidental cuts, scrapes or stings.

5. When assessing conditions, if there is anything that causes me significant anxiety or concern, if I can't address it, I should not dive. Ultimately, I am responsible for my own safety, so only I can make the final decision to dive.
   - ☑ True
   - ☐ False

6. When planning to dive in an environment that is new to me, it is recommended that I get a local orientation from an experienced diver or professional who knows the procedures, hazards, points of interest and other factors unique to the environment.
   - ☑ True
   - ☐ False

7. Risks of diving beyond my training and experience limits include that
   - ☑ a. in some forms of diving, the hazards are not obvious.
   - ☑ b. it can cause me to have a false sense of security.
   - ☑ c. anxiety from doing so can distract me from noticing other problems.

8. While planning a shore dive, my dive buddy says it will be "no problem" diving in high surf that I've never been trained in nor have experience with. Looking at the surf, I don't think I am prepared for diving in it. My best response is to
   - ☐ a. agree to dive, but be ready to back out at any moment.
   - ☐ b. make the dive using the techniques I've learned for little to mild surf.
   - ☑ c. politely refuse to dive and suggest an alternate location with no significant surf.

9. To prevent and/or handle injuries caused by aquatic life, I should
   - ☐ a. generally touch animals if I want, but only if I am familiar with them.
   - ☑ b. watch where I put my feet, hands and knees.
   - ☑ c. wear an exposure suit.
   - ☑ d. treat all organisms with respect.
   - ☑ e. be familiar with potentially hazardous animals where I'm diving.
   - ☑ f. be prepared to provide first aid for aquatic life injuries.
   - ☐ g. touch only dead stinging organisms.

10. My buddy and I accidentally find ourselves in a rip current. There are no special, local procedures, so we follow the generally recommended action of
    - ☐ a. inflating our BCDs and swimming against the current.
    - ☐ b. deflating our BCDs and swimming against it on the bottom.
    - ☐ c. deflating our BCDs and swimming parallel to shore.
    - ☑ d. inflating our BCDs and swimming parallel to shore.

11. Depending upon my location, tides can cause significant changes to depth, currents and visibility, or they may have hardly any effect.
    - ☑ True
    - ☐ False

12. When boarding a dive boat, the divemaster asks me to fill my name in on the roll. The reason for this is to
    - ☐ a. make sure I paid.
    - ☐ b. check my certification number.
    - ☐ c. see if I have a buddy.
    - ☑ d. make sure everyone's aboard after each dive.

13. The best entry is usually the
    - ☐ a. giant stride.
    - ☐ b. seated back roll.
    - ☑ c. easiest one.

14. I should stay well away from the boat propeller at all times, even when the engine isn't running.
- ☑ True
- ☐ False

15. My buddy and I are diving from a boat in mild to moderate current. There is a line from the back of the boat where we'll enter, which leads to the mooring line at the front of the boat. The purpose of the line leading to the mooring line is to
- ☐ a. provide a backup to the mooring line.
- ☒ b. allow us to swim to it if we surface away from the boat.
- ☐ c. guide our descent to the bottom.
- ☑ d. let us pull ourselves to the mooring line.

16. My buddy and I surface and the boat is not in sight, nor is there a float and we are beyond sight of shore. We should inflate our BCDs, deploy our surface signaling devices and stay together.
- ☑ True
- ☐ False

17. Training that expands and develops my skills in preventing and managing problems include:
- ☐ a. PADI Digital Underwater Photographer.
- ☑ b. PADI Rescue Diver.
- ☑ c. PADI Emergency Oxygen Provider.
- ☑ d. Emergency First Response Primary and Secondary Care courses.

18. At the surface, I have a problem. If I have not already done so, the first thing I should do is
- ☑ a. make myself buoyant (inflate BCD and/or drop weights).
- ☒ b. ask for help.
- ☐ c. relax and avoid overexertion.

19. A diver at the surface begins to struggle. He has wide, unseeing eyes and he has pushed off his mask. His BCD isn't inflated and he doesn't inflate it when the divemaster calls for him to do so. This diver is _____. To help, I should first _____.
- ☐ a. in control; encourage the diver to relax
- ☐ b. in control; tow the diver
- ☐ c. out of control; provide encouragement
- ☑ d. out of control; make myself and the diver buoyant (inflate BCD/ drop weights)

20. With an unresponsive diver underwater, the primary concern is _____. Once at the surface, besides establishing buoyancy and calling for help, the primary concern is _____.
- ☐ a. replacing the mouthpiece, towing to safety rapidly
- ☑ b. getting the victim to the surface, checking for breathing and providing rescue breaths if the victim isn't breathing
- ☐ c. compressing the torso, providing emergency oxygen

21. While diving, I begin to feel exhausted and air-starved because I have been swimming strenuously. I should
- ☐ a. descend slightly.
- ☑ b. signal "stop" and rest.
- ☐ c. immediately ascend.
- ☐ d. switch to an alternate air source.

22. In helping an unresponsive diver, after you check for breathing and provide CPR as needed (once out of the water), which of the following has the highest priority?
- ☑ a. Contact emergency medical care. ✓
- ☑ b. Give the diver emergency oxygen.
- ☑ c. Keep the diver warm.
- ☑ d. Write down what happened.

23. Although it shouldn't have happened, on a dive at 10 metres/30 feet, I fail to watch my SPG and run out of air. I don't have a pony bottle or self-contained ascent bottle. My buddy is about 12 metres/40 feet away, and has an alternate second stage. My best option is probably to
- ☑ a. make a normal ascent.
- ☑ b. ascend using an alternate air source.
- ☑ c. make a Controlled Emergency Swimming Ascent. ✓
- ☐ d. make a buoyant emergency ascent.

24. Any diver who has been unresponsive in or under water requires medical examination, even if the person seems fully recovered.
- ☑ True
- ☐ False

25. At a minimum, I should have ____ visual and ____ audible signaling devices.
- ☑ a. 1, 1
- ☐ b. 2, 1
- ☐ c. 1, 2
- ☐ d. 2, 2

26. My buddy and I are underwater within 6 metres/20 feet of our float with a locally-recognized dive flag. We hear a boat, and it sounds close and is getting closer.
- ☐ a. This isn't an issue. The flag will keep the boat at a safe distance.
- ☑ b. We should stay deep enough to be safe. The boater may not see or recognize the flag.

Student Diver Statement: I've completed this Knowledge Review to the best of my ability and any questions I answered incorrectly or incompletely, I have had explained to me and I understand what I missed.

Name_____

Date_____

section

four

A mesh utility bag is a heavy-duty bag made from nylon mesh (so it drains) or other water-resistant synthetic. Think of these as all-purpose containers for bulky or hard-to-carry items.

LEARNING OBJECTIVES

By the end of this section, I should be able to answer these questions:

1. What would I use a mesh utility bag for?

2. What options can I choose from when selecting mesh utility bags?

3. Why should I be cautious about attaching a mesh utility bag to my gear while diving?

Equipment IV

Let's look at a few more pieces of equipment your PADI dive shop can help you choose to best meet your personal needs.

Mesh Utility Bag

Besides your gear bag, you may want one or more mesh utility bags. A mesh utility bag is a heavy-duty bag made from nylon mesh (so it drains) or other water-resistant synthetic. Think of these as all-purpose containers for bulky or hard-to-carry items. Depending upon the size, common uses include:

- Holding litter during an underwater cleanup.
- Carrying small accessories.
- Transporting gear to and from the dive boat.

You can choose mesh utility bags for many purposes with different options. Many divers have several.

Style. Some bags are all mesh with a drawstring closure. Others have wire or plastic frames that allow you to hold them open with one hand and lock closed.

Material. Many mesh utility bags are entirely mesh; others have an upper portion that is solid so they last longer.

Size. Mesh bags range from hand sized to large enough to hold almost all your gear. Choose the size for the job you have in mind.

Straps or handles. Larger mesh bags, especially those intended for carrying gear, usually have handles and straps.

Be cautious about attaching a mesh utility bag to your gear while diving. In an emergency, you need to be able to quickly discard anything that may weigh you down or add a lot of drag. You also don't want to create potential entanglement/snagging problems.

Exercise 4-1

1. For an Underwater Naturalist dive, I want to carry several small slates and some measuring tools. A mesh utility bag may be an appropriate way to do this.
   - ☐ True
   - ☐ False

2. Mesh bags range in size and options. I would probably choose a larger one for carrying a wet exposure suit.
   - ☐ True
   - ☐ False

3. During an underwater cleanup, my buddy and I fill a large mesh utility bag with several kilograms/pounds of garbage. We should
   - ☐ a. attach the bag to our gear.
   - ☐ b. carry the bag in our hands.

How did you do?
1. True. 2. True. 3. b.

LEARNING OBJECTIVES

By the end of this section, I should be able to answer these questions:

1. For what four purposes might I carry a slate or wet book?

2. What options can I choose from when choosing slates and wet books?

Carry a slate or wet book for communication, limits and backup information, recording dive information and unexpected writing needs.

Slates and Wet Books

It is recommended that you carry a slate or a wet book that you can write on during a dive. One purpose is communication. You can use signals most of the time, but sometimes it's more effective to write down what you're trying to tell your buddy(ies).

A second purpose is for your limits and backup information. Many divers like to note the dive plan limits for reference rather than rely on memory. The more complex the dive, the more helpful this can be. A third purpose is to record information during a dive, such as where you found something you want to revisit, how much air you used to reach a site, etc. A fourth purpose is the unexpected. You don't always know what you'll need to write before the moment arrives. Make a slate or a wet book a standard part of your kit and you're always prepared.

Slates come in different sizes while wet books have many pages for ample room to write.

Slates, Wet Books and Options

A slate is a piece of rigid plastic upon which you write with an attached pencil or marker. Its main advantage is that you can reuse it (you erase it after the dive). A wet book is a compact notebook with waterproof pages that you also write on with an attached pencil. You don't reuse wet book pages – you remove them, so you have to replace wet books from time to time. Its main advantages are that you have much more writing space, and the pages can be kept.

The main option you consider is size. Slates come in many different sizes – a larger slate offers more writing room, but is harder to stow. Choose one that fits easily into one of your pockets.

Most wet books are about the same size (around 20 cm/8 in X 10 cm/4 in). They flex and fit comfortably in your exposure suit thigh pocket. Since they have many pages, one wet book gives you more room to write than a large slate.

Slates and wet books usually have an attached pencil as a standard feature.

Exercise 4-2

1. Which of the following are purposes for which I would carry a slate or a wet book? (choose all that apply):
   - ☐ a. communication
   - ☐ b. noting limits and backup information
   - ☐ c. recording information
   - ☐ d. the unexpected

2. When choosing a slate, the main option I usually consider is
   - ☐ a. weight.
   - ☐ b. size.
   - ☐ c. color.
   - ☐ d. pencil type.

How did you do?
1. a, b, c, d. 2. b.

TALKING UNDERWATER

Underwater communication systems that let divers talk to each other, as well as to people at the surface, have been around for decades. Military, commercial, scientific and public safety diving use these systems. Although applicable for recreational diving, cost, size, design, effectiveness and the need for special masks or mouthpieces have limited their use.

More recently, new underwater communication systems are emerging that are less costly and much simpler to use. Some systems don't even require special masks or mouthpieces, and there are even dive computers that send and/or receive text messages between buddies, or between the boat and divers.

Slates, wet books and hand signals will remain important communication tools, but as technology advances you may find yourself talking or texting more.

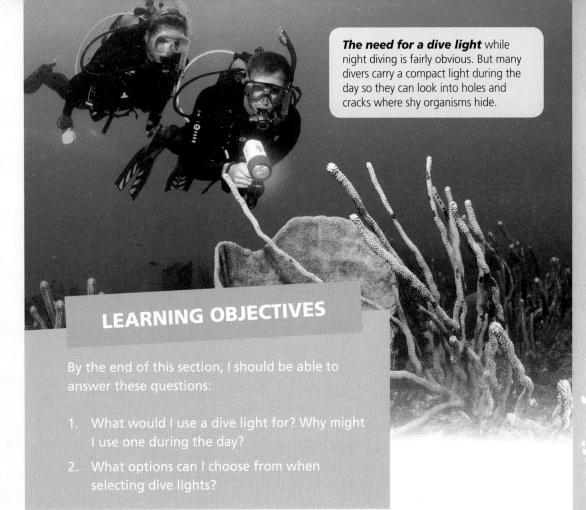

The need for a dive light while night diving is fairly obvious. But many divers carry a compact light during the day so they can look into holes and cracks where shy organisms hide.

LEARNING OBJECTIVES

By the end of this section, I should be able to answer these questions:

1. What would I use a dive light for? Why might I use one during the day?

2. What options can I choose from when selecting dive lights?

Dive Lights

Dive lights are designed specifically to be both watertight and to withstand pressure. As a recreational diver, you will use a dive light if you go night diving, but you also might use one during the day.

When you take the PADI Night Diver course, you learn night diving techniques, including handling and using a dive light (two, actually). But many divers carry a compact light during the day so they can look into holes and cracks where shy organisms hide.

Dive Light Options and Accessories

Your main choices in choosing dive lights are size, brightness and power source.

Size and brightness. There's a trade between brightness, beam width, and size. Compact lights stow easily, making them good choices for day use, and as spare lights when night diving. But they are not as bright and have narrower beams than larger lights, used as main lights for night diving, which are brighter and cover a wider area.

Compact lights have narrow beams but are easy to stow; they're good choices for day use and night backup lights. Larger lights are harder to put in a pocket, but have broad beams that make them your main choice for night diving.

There are also specialized lights used in technical diving, lighting underwater video, etc. Your dive retailer can provide guidance in choosing lights. As technology advances, size versus brightness/beam width is becoming less and less of an issue. Modern LED lights are making powerful, wide beam lights available in smaller packages. Today's "large" lights are smaller than many of the "compact" dive lights available 10 years ago.

Power source. Larger, more powerful lights usually have dedicated rechargeable battery systems, though many use disposables. Compact lights usually take disposables, with AA cells the most common. You can also use rechargeable NiMH AAs in most newer lights that take disposable AAs (check the manufacturer literature).

Accessories for your light. Most divers attach a clip on their light to secure it when not in use. Especially for larger lights, a wrist lanyard helps avoid loss, plus allows you to release the light without losing it.

LEARNING OBJECTIVES

By the end of this section, I should be able to answer these questions:

1. Why do I log my dives?

2. What options can I choose from when selecting a dive log? What information do I typically record, at a minimum, regardless of which I choose?

Logbooks and eLogs

As part of your diver training, your instructor has you log your dives and signs your log. This is important for validating the training you receive. It's recommended that you continue your log after you're certified, for several reasons.

Reference – Logged dives provide information to make planning subsequent dives easier. You can reference notes about dive sites, as well as your equipment. For example, if it has been a while since you wore your exposure suit in fresh water, you can check your logbook instead of having to figure out your required weight again.

Documentation – Upper training levels often require documentation of certain types and numbers of dives. Your log provides this record.

Onsite experience reference – Some dive operators want to know where you've been diving, how often and so on, so they can assist you better with the diving they offer. It's easier to provide complete information with a log.

To share – At ScubaEarth® and in other online communities, divers inform each other about dive sites. Posting your logged information helps other divers, and their information helps you, when choosing future dive sites.

Related information – Besides recording your dives, use your log to keep other information you may want when diving, including local emergency contact information for sites you dive frequently, as well as phone numbers and websites for dive buddies, gear manufacturers, dive resorts, your instructor, etc. Many divers also log GPS coordinates or addresses for dive boats or shore dive sites, and their equipment serial numbers and service dates.

eLogs and Printed Logbooks

You can choose from electronic logs (eLogs) or printed logbooks to record your dive information. There are many types of eLogs available, most of which use click boxes and few type-in fields. You can fill them out quickly, and many divers like having their information "in the cloud" where they can access it anywhere. You can choose from eLog programs or apps for your PC or tablet. See "Using your PADI eLog" in the PADI Mobile App, which allows you to log dives on the spot using your smart phone or tablet, and provides you with options to note the significant points of your dive as well as to keep track of your personal equipment, servicing dates and other useful features. Moreover, the PADI eLog allows you to instantaneously share your dive experiences with dive buddies all over the world.

Printed logbooks range in size and in the information you record, so compare different log pages for blank space, tick boxes, etc. The PADI Diver's log has special pages for logging training dives separately from nontraining dives. Choose a log that matches how you'll use it – with space for lots of details, or a smaller log with check boxes and fill-in blanks.

Some dive computers have special software that allows you to download dive information. With these, you may only

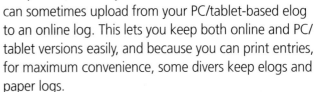

need to enter the dive site name and interest notes – the dive data upload automatically. These programs have become more standardized and compatible, so that you can sometimes upload from your PC/tablet-based elog to an online log. This lets you keep both online and PC/tablet versions easily, and because you can print entries, for maximum convenience, some divers keep elogs and paper logs.

It is recommended that at a *minimum,* for each dive you log the:

- Date
- Dive site (name or location)
- Dive buddy(ies)
- Dive depth and duration
- Objective/description

Exercise 4-4

1. I log my dives (choose all that apply):
   - ☐ a. to document training.
   - ☐ b. as a reference tool.
   - ☐ c. to share information.
   - ☐ d. keep related information.

2. The minimum information I would typically log includes (choose all that apply):
   - ☐ a. dive site name.
   - ☐ b. the depth.
   - ☐ c. dive time.
   - ☐ d. my buddy's name.

   How did you do?
   1. a, b, c, d. 2. a, b, c, d.

Dive Planning Software

A growing number of divers use computer programs or apps to help plan dives. This is common practice in technical diving, but as a recreational diver you will find two common uses.

The first is to estimate how long your air supply will last on a dive. By telling the program your air use (it's something you learn over time, and you learn more about this in the PADI Deep Diver course), the app or software can help you estimate how long your air will last (but you still turn the dive based on your actual use and plan a reserve, of course).

The second use of dive planning software is to estimate the time your dive computer will allow on a dive. This is based on how much nitrogen your body absorbs; you will learn more about nitrogen absorption and computer limits later in this section.

Options

You can choose dive planning software for desktop/laptop computers, though tablet apps are the most popular. Some of the software that interfaces with dive computers has a planning function (and may have an eLog function, too).

You can choose from very basic software intended only for planning recreational dives, as well as software designed for much more complex (technical) diving.

A growing number of divers use computer programs or apps to help plan dives.

Exercise 4-5

1. Dive planning software can help me estimate and plan (choose all that apply):

    ☐ a. my air use.

    ☐ b. computer dive time.

    ☐ c. the water temperature.

2. I can choose from very basic software intended only for planning recreational dives, as well as software designed for much more complex diving.

    ☐ True

    ☐ False

    How did you do?
    1. a, b.   2. True

180

By the end of this section, I should be able to answer these questions:

1. Why is it important to have a spare parts kit?

2. What items might I have in a spare parts kit?

You can miss a dive simply because you lose an o-ring or break a strap, so it is important to have a spare parts kit.

Spare Parts Kit

You can miss a dive simply because you lose an o-ring or break a strap. For this reason it is important to have a spare parts kit (some call it a save-a-dive kit). A spare parts kit is simply a collection of user-replaceable items in a compact, sturdy box (or other suitable container). Keep the spare parts kit in your gear bag so you're always prepared for a last-minute replacement.

A typical spare parts kit might have these items:

- Spare mask strap, fin strap and snorkel keeper (Tip: The Velcro™-type mask straps make good spares, because they're easy to put in place and fit almost any mask.)

- Harness/weight belt buckle

- Cable (pull) ties

- Adjustable wrench (spanner), pliers, screw drivers, hex wrenches (allen keys) or scuba tool

- Regulator mouthpiece

- Accessory clip

- Slate/wet book pencil

- Various sized cylinder valve/DIN valve o-rings

- Cement or glue appropriate for exposure suit repair

- Sunscreen and spare sunglasses (not really dive parts, but can come in handy)

Your PADI professional can usually suggest spare parts specific to your equipment as well. Choose a storage box or container somewhat larger than you actually need; you tend to add to it, so you'll want room to grow.

section four

Exercise 4-6

1. A spare parts kit contains
   - ☐ a. user-replaceable items.
   - ☐ b. parts that require professional installation.

2. Which of the following might I have in a spare parts kit? (choose all that apply):
   - ☐ a. spare mask strap, fin straps
   - ☐ b. harness/weight belt buckle
   - ☐ c. cable (pull) ties
   - ☐ d. adjustable wrench (spanner), pliers, screw drivers, hex wrenches (allen keys)
   - ☐ e. regulator mouthpiece
   - ☐ f. accessory clip
   - ☐ g. various sized cylinder valve/DIN valve o-rings

How did you do?
1. a. 2. a, b, c, d, e, f, g.

Maintain a reasonable level of physical fitness. Participate in a regular exercise program, but see your doctor before starting one.

LEARNING OBJECTIVES

By the end of this section, I should be able to answer these questions:

1. What general recommendations apply to my fitness as a diver?

2. How often is it recommended that I have a complete physical examination for diving?

3. What factors in diving can strain my heart and cardiovascular system?

4. What should I do as a diver if I am or may be predisposed to heart disease?

5. What are the two most common substances that I should refrain from using before diving, and why?

6. What are the recommendations for using prescribed or over-the-counter medications before diving?

7. What effect does menstruation have on diving?

8. Why is it recommended that pregnant women not dive?

9. What should I do if I feel ill before a dive?

Being a Diver IV

Your Health and Fitness

Diving is relaxing and you try to dive relaxed, but it is not always slow moving, even if you plan it to be, so you need to be in good health and reasonably fit. Strenuous activity can arise, including handling gear, currents, an emergency or unanticipated physical demands. Being in good health helps assure you can meet these demands and dive safely.

General Recommendations

Some general recommendations apply to your health and fitness as a diver.

- Maintain a reasonable level of physical fitness. This means that you have adequate fitness, plus a physical reserve, for the type of diving you do. Participate in a regular exercise program (see your physician before starting one, however). You don't have to be a professional athlete – just in good average health.

- Keep your immunizations current, especially tetanus and typhoid.

- Eat a well-balanced diet and get adequate rest, especially before diving.

- It's a good idea to have a physical examination when you start diving, and regularly thereafter. Ideally, have a medical doctor knowledgeable in dive medicine conduct the examination. However, the RSTC Medical Statement provides guidelines developed by dive medical experts that any physician can use to conduct dive physicals. Your instructor will give you this form, or you can download it from padi.com.

Like any activity that can cause physical exertion and stress, diving can strain your heart and cardiovascular system. Factors that can do this include exertion from swimming hard, carrying equipment, climbing a ladder, long walks wearing gear, and heat stress from wearing an exposure suit in a hot climate.

Heart Health

Like any activity that can cause physical exertion and stress, diving can strain your heart and cardiovascular system. Factors that can do this include exertion from swimming hard, carrying equipment, climbing a ladder, long walks wearing gear, and heat stress from wearing an exposure suit in a hot climate.

 These factors can cause heart attack in predisposed individuals. They can also be issues for other cardiovascular conditions.

If you have or may have risk factors that make it more likely to have heart disease due to your age, lifestyle, body composition, family history or any other factors, be sure to discuss them with your doctor. Your physician can help you assess the risk, and how you can manage that risk as a diver.

Alcohol, Tobacco and Drugs

Never use alcohol or tobacco before diving. Alcohol affects your judgment, and its effects may increase with depth. It also accelerates body heat loss, which can be an issue on cooler dives. Be moderate if drinking the night before diving, because it tends to dehydrate you, which some physiologists think can contribute to decompression sickness risk.

Smoking is undeniably harmful to your health, and not a good choice for anyone. If you do smoke, avoid doing so for several hours before and after diving.

Smoking is undeniably harmful to your health, and not a good choice for anyone, but particularly if you live an active lifestyle. If you do smoke, avoid doing so for several hours before and after diving, because it significantly decreases the efficiency of your circulatory and respiratory systems. Smoking theoretically raises the risk of lung overexpansion injury by causing air trapping within your lungs – even when you breathe normally. Nonsmoking tobacco use, including e-cigarettes, seems to pose less immediate risk, though it's still better to simply avoid nicotine.

Drugs can create problems when diving. It's obvious

Drugs can create problems when diving, so use prescription drugs and over-the-counter medications with caution. Consult your physician about any particular drug prior to diving.

that you should not be using illegal drugs. However, you also need to use prescription drugs and over-the-counter medications with caution. Any drug that affects your judgment, thinking and/or reactions should generally not be used, but many drugs have no effects that interfere with diving. Always consult your physician. If still in doubt, discontinue diving until you no longer use the medication.

Menstruation and Pregnancy

If menstruation doesn't normally keep you from doing other active recreations, it's not likely to affect diving either.

Pregnancy differs, and it's broadly recommended that pregnant women not dive. This isn't because of a known risk, but rather because there's not enough known about how diving could affect a developing fetus. It is generally agreed that it's not worth the risk, and you should not dive while pregnant or trying to become pregnant.

Day-to-Day Health

You want to be in good physical and mental health when diving so you can avoid problems and handle them if they occur. So if you feel ill before a dive, cancel the dive. Even a cold can cause problems by trapping air, making it difficult to equalize and in some cases, increasing the risk of lung overexpansion injuries.

Don't use medication to get rid of symptoms just so you can dive while unhealthy. Get well, then resume diving.

You want to be in good physical and mental health when diving. If you feel ill, get well, then resume diving.

Exercise 4-7

1. Diving can be physically demanding, so I should be in good health and reasonably fit.
   - ☐ True
   - ☐ False

2. It is recommended that I have a complete physical examination when I start diving and regularly thereafter.
   - ☐ a. True
   - ☐ b. False

3. Factors that can strain my heart in diving include (choose all that apply):
   - ☐ a. swimming hard.
   - ☐ b. carrying equipment.
   - ☐ c. climbing a ladder.
   - ☐ d. heat stress.

4. If I may be predisposed to heart disease, I should consult my doctor so I can assess and manage the risk as a diver.
   - ☐ True
   - ☐ False

5. Before diving, I should refrain using _____ and _____. (choose two):
   - ☐ a. alcohol
   - ☐ b. prescription drugs
   - ☐ c. seasickness medication
   - ☐ d. tobacco

6. Before using prescribed or over-the-counter medication, if I am not sure how they will affect me diving, I should consult my physician.
   - ☐ True
   - ☐ False

How did you do?
1. True. 2. True. 3. a, b, c, d. 4. True. 5. a, d. 6. True.

The best way to keep your knowledge and skills current and refreshed is to use them – dive regularly. If you can't get to open water, scuba dive in a pool with a buddy to keep your skills polished.

By the end of this section, I should be able to answer these questions:

1. How do I keep my dive skills and knowledge current and refreshed?

2. How do I refresh my dive skills and knowledge after a period of inactivity? As a new PADI Open Water Diver, after what interval of inactivity is this recommended?

3. How does continuing my diver training help keep my skills refreshed?

Staying Current and Active as a Diver

Like any specialized set of skills and knowledge, your dive skills and knowledge stay sharp if you use them often. But you start to lose them if you go an extended period without diving. The best way to keep your knowledge and skills current and refreshed is to use them – dive regularly. If you can't get to open water, scuba dive in a pool with a buddy to keep your skills sharp. The PADI Skill Practice and Dive Planning Slate is useful for this, as it lists the water skills you learn in the PADI Open Water Diver course, and prompts you to self-assess whether you're comfortable with each skill, or want more practice.

Besides going diving, involve yourself with the dive community in person (on dive outings, as part of a club, etc.) and online (ScubaEarth®, forums, other social sites, etc.). Interacting with other divers helps you keep up with the latest practices and trends.

Visit ScubaEarth®, padi.com and other dive websites regularly, and subscribe to dive magazines to keep up with new recommendations, new gear, the hottest dive travel destinations and the like.

Refreshing Your Knowledge and Skills

Although the ideal is to dive regularly, periods of inactivity are normal. If you don't go diving for six months or longer, it is recommended that you refresh your knowledge and skills. Your instructor can do this with the PADI ReActivate program (you can do the Knowledge Review on your tablet or online – check out ReActivate on the PADI App).

The Role of Continuing Education

One of the best ways to keep your skills refreshed is to continue your diver training. You keep diving and learn new things at the same time. In the PADI Advanced Open Water Diver course and most PADI specialties and upper level

After six months or longer without diving, it is recommended that you refresh your knowledge and skills. Your instructor can do this with the PADI ReActivate program.

courses, you will not only learn new skills and expand your capabilities, but use your existing skills as well.

Because you usually also make new friends, visit new dive sites and expand the types of diving you can do, continuing your training increases your opportunities to dive.

One of the best ways to keep your skills refreshed is to continue your diver training. You keep diving and learn new things at the same time.

Exercise 4-8

1. The *best* way to keep my dive knowledge and skills current and refreshed is to
   - ☐ a. visit online scuba forums.
   - ☐ b. join a dive club.
   - ☐ c. use them by diving regularly.

2. As a new PADI Open Water Diver, I should refresh my dive skills with a PADI ReActivate after _____ of inactivity?
   - ☐ a. one month
   - ☐ b. six months
   - ☐ c. one year
   - ☐ d. five years

3. Continuing my diver education helps keep my skills and knowledge sharp by (choose all that apply):
   - ☐ a. allowing me to visit new dive sites.
   - ☐ b. increasing my opportunities to dive.
   - ☐ c. expanding the types of diving I do.
   - ☐ d. introducing me to new buddies I can dive with.

   How did you do?
   1. c. 2. b. 3. a, b, c, d.

section four

LEARNING OBJECTIVES

By the end of this section, I should be able to answer these questions:

1. What component gases make up air?

2. For practical purposes, what percent of each of the component gases does air consist of?

3. To what four diving related issues does the makeup of air relate?

4. How does using enriched air nitrox affect the component gases that make up air?

The Air You Breathe

As a recreational diver underwater, you breathe air. Other than being specially filtered for scuba, it is the same as the air you're breathing now. Air is actually a *mix* of several gases. The nature of this mix is important for some of the ways diving can affect you, so let's begin by looking at the gases that make up air.

The component gases of air, in order of abundance, are nitrogen, oxygen and more than a dozen gases in very small amounts. These trace gases make up less than one percent of air, so for most *practical* purposes related to diving, we ignore them and consider air to be 79 percent nitrogen and 21 percent oxygen.

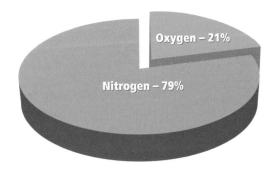

Oxygen – 21%

Nitrogen – 79%

For practical purposes, we can consider air 79 percent nitrogen and 21 percent oxygen.

Four Diving Issues That Relate to Component Gases

To review, air can be considered a single gas with respect to the depth-pressure-volume-density relationships you learned in Section One. As you recall, these relationships explain (among other things) why you need to equalize, why you use more air the deeper you dive, why buoyancy changes as you change depth, and why you must breathe continuously, never holding your breath to avoid lung overexpansion injuries. These apply identically in commercial and technical diving that involve breathing gases other than air.

However, there are four issues in diving that relate to the component gases in air:

- Oxygen toxicity
- Contaminated air
- Decompression sickness
- Gas narcosis

We'll look at oxygen toxicity, contaminated air and decompression sickness in this section. We'll look at gas narcosis in Section Five.

Enriched Air Nitrox

Enriched air nitrox (EANx) has the same component gases as air, but the proportions differ. EANx is any blend of oxygen and nitrogen with 22 percent or more oxygen. The rest is nitrogen. Common blends in recreational diving are 32 percent and 36 percent oxygen. Tec divers use EANx with even higher proportions of oxygen.

As you will see, increasing the oxygen content and decreasing the nitrogen content has advantages and disadvantages with respect to decompression sickness and oxygen toxicity problems. Many PADI Open Water Divers qualify to use EANx (enriched air nitrox) by taking the PADI Enriched Air Diver course shortly after completing this course. Or, at your instructor's discretion, you can start learning to use EANx during the PADI Open Water Diver course (ask your instructor for details).

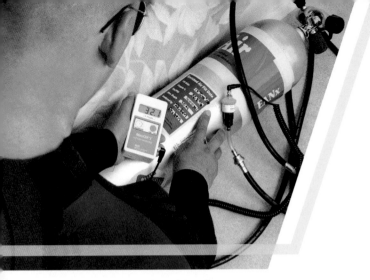

Enriched Air Nitrox (EANx) has the same component gases as air, but the percentage of oxygen is higher. This has advantages and disadvantages with respect to decompression sickness and oxygen toxicity problems.

By the end of this section, I should be able to answer these questions:

1. How do I prevent problems with oxygen when diving with air?

2. Why shouldn't I dive with a cylinder labeled "oxygen" or known to be filled with 100 percent oxygen?

3. Why is it important to be trained as a PADI Enriched Air Diver, or under the supervision of a PADI Enriched Air Instructor, before attempting to dive with enriched air?

Exercise 4-9

1. For *practical* purposes, air consists of oxygen and

   ☐ a. helium.

   ☐ b. hydrogen.

   ☐ c. argon.

   ☐ d. nitrogen.

2. For practical purposes, air is _____ percent oxygen.

   ☐ a. 11

   ☐ b. 21

   ☐ c. 51

   ☐ d. 100

3. Which of the following issues relate to the component gases of air? (choose all that apply):

   ☐ a. equalization

   ☐ b. lung overexpansion

   ☐ c. buoyancy changes with depth

   ☐ d. oxygen issues

   How did you do?

   1. d. 2. b. 3. d.

Oxygen Issues

Although we need oxygen to live, under high pressure, oxygen is toxic. If a gas has oxygen in it, oxygen toxicity can result from breathing it deeper than a specific depth. The higher the oxygen content, the shallower the limit for using it while diving. High oxygen percentages can also create some fire/combustion risks with respect to the equipment with which it must be used.

Fortunately, none of these are meaningful issues when breathing air within recreational depth limits.

• To avoid oxygen toxicity when diving with air, don't exceed the maximum depth for recreational diving (40 metres/130 feet).

• Fire/combustion problems aren't issues when using air with standard scuba equipment.

If a diver uses a breathing gas with *more* than 21 percent oxygen, then the oxygen in it can be toxic at shallower depths. The limit for pure (100 percent) oxygen is only 6 metres/20 feet – any deeper, it is toxic.

section four

Using air within recreational limits, oxygen doesn't pose meaningful issues with respect to being toxic or having fire/combustion problems.

Recreational divers don't use 100 percent oxygen, but tec divers often do (shallower than 6 metres/20 feet, as part of their ascent procedures). They are trained to do this, and also to use equipment that is oxygen service-rated when they do. As a recreational diver, never dive with a scuba cylinder labeled "oxygen" – these are used only by properly trained tec and rebreather divers (you can learn more about rebreather technology in the PADI Rebreather Diver course).

As you learned earlier, enriched air (EANx) has more than 21 percent oxygen. To avoid oxygen toxicity, the maximum depth at which you use enriched air is shallower than when diving with air. How much shallower depends upon how much oxygen the enriched air has.

Enriched air also has some equipment-related concerns associated with the higher oxygen content. It isn't difficult to avoid oxygen toxicity and equipment-related problems, but it's necessary to learn how to do so and become certified as a PADI Enriched Air Diver in the PADI Enriched Air Diver course, or to be under the supervision of a PADI Enriched Air Instructor, before diving with enriched air. Otherwise, never dive with a cylinder labeled "Nitrox," "EANx" or "Enriched Air Nitrox."

1. If I dive within recreational limits using air, I avoid the problems associated with oxygen being toxic or causing fire/combustion issues.
   ☐ True
   ☐ False

2. As a PADI Open Water Diver, I should not dive with a cylinder labeled "oxygen" or known to have 100 percent oxygen.
   ☐ True
   ☐ False

3. Enriched air nitrox can have oxygen issues. To avoid these, I should become qualified to dive with enriched air in the PADI Enriched Air Diver course, or be under the supervision of a PADI Enriched Air Instructor.
   ☐ True
   ☐ False

   How did you do?
   1. True. 2. True. 3. True.

Tec and rebreather divers use pure oxygen, which is toxic deeper than 6 metres/20 feet. Never dive with any scuba cylinder labeled "oxygen" – these are used only by properly trained tec and rebreather divers.

Scuba air must be especially pure, because small amounts of contaminants that might be harmless at the surface can be toxic when breathed under pressure. To prevent this, compressors for filling scuba cylinders use special filters and separators to keep contaminants out of breathing air.

LEARNING OBJECTIVES

By the end of this section, I should be able to answer these questions:

1. What are some possible causes of contaminated air?

2. What are five possible signs/symptoms of contaminated air?

3. What should I do for a diver who I suspect breathed contaminated air?

4. How do I avoid contaminated air problems?

Contaminated Air

Contaminated air contains unintended impurities. While this is actually very rare in scuba diving, scuba air must be especially pure, because trace contaminants (like carbon monoxide and oil vapor) that might be harmless at the surface can be toxic when breathed under pressure. To prevent this, compressors for filling scuba cylinders use special filters and separators to keep contaminants out of breathing air.

Possible causes of contaminated air include:

- Getting a cylinder filled at an improper source (i.e., some place other than a professional dive center, resort or dive boat).

- Improper maintenance of the filling system.

- Very high levels of a contaminant in the source gas – more than the filters can keep out.

Contaminated air may smell and taste bad, but sometimes can be odorless and tasteless. A diver breathing contaminated air may have these signs/symptoms:

- Headache
- Nausea
- Dizziness
- Unconsciousness/unresponsiveness
- Cherry-red lips/fingernail beds (though this is difficult to see underwater)

If you suspect a diver has breathed contaminated air, have the person breathe fresh air. Give emergency oxygen if available. Provide CPR if required. Contact emergency medical care. The diver should have medical attention in all cases.

Contaminated air is rare because it's not difficult to avoid: get your cylinder filled only at reputable scuba air sources – namely, professional dive operations. Professional dive operators know how serious air quality is. They take care of their fill systems and know the value of regular air testing.

Exercise 4-11

1. Possible causes of contaminated air in my scuba cylinder include high levels of contaminant in the source gas and
   - ☐ a. chemical reactions in the cylinder.
   - ☐ b. using the wrong type of regulator.
   - ☐ c. increasing the amount of oxygen.
   - ☐ d. getting it filled at an improper source.

2. During a dive, I begin to have a headache, feel ill and dizzy. Are these possible symptoms of contaminated air?
   - ☐ Yes
   - ☐ No

3. After a dive, my buddy feels ill and has cherry red lips and nail beds. After breathing oxygen, my buddy seems to be doing fine, so no other action is required.
   - ☐ True
   - ☐ False

4. To avoid contaminated air, I should have my cylinder filled only at reputable scuba air sources.
   - ☐ True
   - ☐ False

How did you do?
1. d. 2. Yes. 3. False. The diver should have medical attention in all cases of suspected contaminated air. 4. True.

By the end of this section, I should be able to answer these questions:

1. What two primary factors influence how much nitrogen dissolves into my body tissues during a dive?

2. What condition can result if I exceed established depth and time limits while diving, and then surface? What happens in the body that causes this condition?

3. What are nine signs/symptoms of decompression sickness? How soon do they occur after a dive?

4. Besides dive time and depth, what nine secondary factors are thought to influence how the body absorbs and releases dissolved nitrogen?

Decompression Sickness

Nitrogen Absorption

You've already learned that your time underwater has limits in addition to how long your air lasts, how warm you are or whether you're tired. These next limits relate to nitrogen gas that is in solution in your body.

During a dive, the increased pressure causes nitrogen from your breathing air to be absorbed, dissolving into your body tissues. The greater the pressure – that is the deeper you are – the faster nitrogen dissolves into your tissues. And, the longer you're underwater, the more time you give nitrogen to dissolve into your tissues. Therefore, the two primary factors that influence how much nitrogen you absorb during a dive are depth (pressure) and time.

Decompression Sickness

Your tissues don't use the nitrogen you absorb, so when you ascend and the pressure gets lower, there is more nitrogen than can remain dissolved in your body tissues. The excess nitrogen therefore dissolves out of your body tissues. Normal blood circulation carries the excess nitrogen to your lungs, which exits as you exhale.

If the amount of excess nitrogen is within accepted limits, your body normally gets rid of it harmlessly over the next several hours. You use your dive computer (or dive tables like the RDP or eRDPML) to stay within accepted nitrogen limits. You'll learn about doing this and about practices like safety stops that help you keep nitrogen levels within accepted limits.

If the excess nitrogen in your body tissues is too high, when you ascend and surface, the nitrogen may come out of solution faster than your body can eliminate it. This can cause nitrogen bubbles to form within your blood and body tissues, much like bubbles form when you open a soda bottle and release the pressure.

Bubbles forming in the body cause a very serious medical condition called

If the excess nitrogen in your body tissues is too high, when you ascend and surface the nitrogen may come out of solution faster than your body can eliminate it. This can cause bubbles to form in the body, which causes a very serious medical condition called *decompression sickness* (DCS).

decompression sickness (DCS for short). It is sometimes called "the bends." The signs and symptoms of DCS depend upon where bubbles form in the body. They include:

- Paralysis
- Dizziness
- Tingling
- Joint and limb pain
- Shock
- Numbness
- Difficulty breathing
- Weakness and prolonged fatigue
- In severe cases, unconsciousness and death

DCS signs and symptoms may be clear and obvious, but they may also be subtle, like a mild to moderate, dull ache (often, but not necessarily, in the joints), mild to moderate tingling or numbness, weakness and prolonged fatigue. They usually occur 15 minutes to 12 hours after a dive, though they can occur before surfacing, and they can occur after 12 hours. The signs and symptoms may be persistent or be intermittent. Treat all cases of suspected DCS as serious, no matter how serious or mild the signs/symptoms seem to be.

Secondary Factors

Although time and depth are the primary variables that affect whether bubbles will form in the body and cause decompression sickness, other factors influence how your body absorbs and releases excess nitrogen. Physiologists think that when present, the following secondary factors can contribute to developing DCS:

- Fatigue
- Cold
- Illness
- Age
- Dehydration
- Poor fitness/high body fat
- Injuries
- Alcohol consumption before or after a dive
- Vigorous exercise before, during or immediately after the dive

Section Five discusses how exposure to altitude (by flying, or driving through mountains) after diving can also contribute to getting DCS, and its first aid and treatment.

Exercise 4-12

1. The two primary factors that influence how much nitrogen dissolves into my body tissues during a dive are _____ and _____.
    - ☐ a. depth, time
    - ☐ b. temperature, time
    - ☐ c. depth, temperature

2. If I exceed established depth and time limits while diving and then surface, bubbles can form in my body tissues, causing decompression sickness.
    - ☐ True
    - ☐ False

3. After a dive, a diver has numbness, tingling and weakness in the arms. Are these possible signs/symptoms of DCS?
    - ☐ Yes
    - ☐ No

4. Secondary factors thought to contribute to DCS include (choose all that apply):
    - ☐ a. age.
    - ☐ b. cold.
    - ☐ c. injuries.
    - ☐ d. poor fitness/high body fat.

    How did you do?
    1. a. 2. True. 3. Yes. 4. a, b, c, d.

Physiologists think that when present, secondary factors, including being cold during a dive, can contribute to developing DCS.

To reduce DCS risk, you use a dive computer or dive tables like the Recreational Dive Planner (table or eRDPML electronic table versions) to estimate the theoretical changes in nitrogen in your body before, during and after a dive.

LEARNING OBJECTIVES

By the end of this section, I should be able to answer these questions:

1. How does a dive computer or dive table estimate the amount of nitrogen I absorb during a dive?

2. Does a dive computer or dive table directly assess anything going on inside a diver's body?

3. Why can no dive computer or table guarantee that decompression sickness will never occur, even within its limits? How do I address this concern?

Using Dive Computers and Tables I

How Dive Computers and Tables Work

In the last subsection, you learned that to avoid decompression sickness, you have to keep body nitrogen levels within accepted limits that it can tolerate without forming bubbles. At present, there is no way, during a dive, to measure the actual nitrogen absorbed by your body. To reduce DCS risk, physiologists and scientists created mathematical decompression models to estimate the theoretical changes in nitrogen in your body before, during and after a dive. As a diver, you use these models by using a dive computer or dive tables like the Recreational Dive Planner (table or eRDPML electronic table versions).

Dive computers and dive tables work by using your dive time and depth information to calculate the theoretical amount of nitrogen in your body. They compare these estimates against limits that resulted from experimental dives and human experience.

Dive computers measure depth and time throughout the dive and apply the information to the decompression model electronically. They constantly update the theoretical nitrogen in your body based on your dive depths and time, and compare it to the model.

Dive computers measure depth and time throughout a dive (and after) and apply the information to the decompression model electronically. A computer constantly updates the theoretical nitrogen in your body based on your dive depths and time, and compares it to the model. Dive computers have become the most common method of calculating decompression information.

Before dive computers, divers only used dive tables. With the Recreational Dive Planner (RDP) Table, you use the depth from a depth gauge and the time from a timer or watch to look up limit information on the RDP Table version. The eRDPML on the other hand, is a calculator-format electronic dive table. You enter your depth/time information, and it looks it up on the table for you.

No Direct Assessment

Dive computers and dive tables do not directly read anything going on inside a diver's body. They apply a mathematical decompression model that works for the vast majority of people most of the time. Decompression models are highly reliable, but they cannot account for

Because people vary in their susceptibility to decompression sickness, no dive computer or dive table can guarantee that decompression sickness will never occur, even when you dive within its limits. You must accept that there is always some risk of DCS when you go diving.

section four

Ascend slowly from every dive (18 metres/60 feet per minute, or slower as required by your computer) and make a three-minute safety stop at 5 metres/15 feet.

As a recreational diver, you plan your dive so that you can, if necessary, swim directly to the surface without unacceptable risk of decompression sickness. This is called no-stop diving.

individual variations in physiology, such as the secondary factors you learned in the last subsection.

Because people vary in their susceptibility to decompression sickness, no dive computer or dive table can guarantee that decompression sickness will never occur, even when you dive within its limits. **You must accept that there is always some risk of DCS when you go diving.**

Although dive computers and tables cannot account for individual variation, as a diver you can help further reduce risk by always following conservative dive practices.

⚠ **Always dive well within the limits of your dive computer or table. The more predisposing factors you have, the more conservative you want to be.**

Ascend slowly from every dive (18 metres/60 feet per minute, or slower as required by your computer) and make a three-minute safety stop at 5 metres/15 feet.

Exercise 4-13

1. Dive computers track the amount of theoretical nitrogen in my body by measuring the depth and time throughout the dive.
   - ☐ True
   - ☐ False

2. During a dive, my dive computer reads the nitrogen that is actually absorbed by my body.
   - ☐ True
   - ☐ False

3. Because dive computers and tables cannot account for individual variation, I should dive well within limits and
   - ☐ a. ascend rapidly.
   - ☐ b. ascend slowly.
   - ☐ c. descend rapidly.
   - ☐ d. descend slowly.

How did you do?
1. True. 2. False. Dive computers and tables do not directly access anything going on inside your body. 3. b. (Note: You should descend slowly so you can equalize, but doing so does not reduce your DCS risk.)

By the end of this section, I should be able to answer these questions:

1. What is no stop (no decompression) diving?

2. What is a no stop (no decompression) limit?

3. What do I have to do if I exceed a no stop limit?

4. What is the relationship between depth and my no stop limits?

5. What happens to my no stop limits as I ascend to a shallower depth during a dive?

6. Why is my ascent rate an important part of a no stop dive?

7. What is the difference between a decompression stop and a safety stop?

No Stop Diving

No Stop Limits

As a recreational diver, you plan your dive so that you can, if necessary, swim directly to the surface without unacceptable risk of decompression sickness. This is called *no stop diving.* (You sometimes hear it called "no decompression diving," but "no stop diving" is more technically accurate.)

You plan your dives so they are always well within the *no stop limits.* (You sometimes hear no stop limits called *no decompression limits – NDLs).* A no stop limit is the maximum time you can spend at a given depth and still ascend directly to the surface. If you exceed a no stop limit, to keep DCS risk within accepted limits, you must

make one or more emergency decompression stops. These are stops at specific depths for prescribed times to allow your body to release dissolved nitrogen before you ascend further. In recreational diving, decompression stops are emergency procedures only (you'll learn more about these in Section Five).

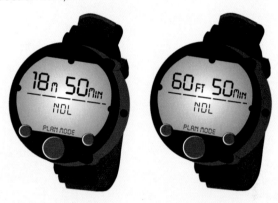

You can see the no stop limits for each depth in your dive computer's Dive Plan Mode.

Depth and No Stop Limits

As you've learned, the deeper you dive, the greater the pressure on your body. The greater the pressure, the faster nitrogen dissolves into your body tissues. This means the deeper you dive, the shorter your no stop limits.

You can see the no stop limits for each depth in your dive computer's Dive Plan Mode (your computer may use a different name for this; see the manufacturer literature, or ask your instructor to help you).

With most computers, you scroll depths in 3 metre/10 foot increments, displaying the maximum time allowed at each depth. You use this information to help plan your dive. Dive computers may have different decompression models. As a result, the no stop times for two different model computers may differ somewhat. You can also find no stop times on the RDP Table and eRDPML.

Depth (metres)	No Stop Time (minutes)
10	219
12	147
14	98
16	72
18	56
20	45
22	37
25	29
30	20
35	14
40	9

Depth (feet)	No Stop Time (minutes)
35	205
40	140
50	80
60	55
70	40
80	30
90	25
100	20
110	16
120	13
130	10

Note that your no stop time decreases significantly faster as your depth increases. Recall that you also use your air faster as go deeper. Therefore, the deeper you dive, the more frequently you should check your remaining air supply and your remaining no stop time.

You can see the relationship between depth and no stop time by comparing them. The times/depths shown are from the RDP Table, and are similar to many dive computers. Your computer may scroll in different depth steps, but the relationship is similar.

Note that your no stop time gets shorter *significantly* faster as your depth increases. Recall that you also use your air faster as go deeper. Therefore, the deeper you dive, the more frequently you should check your remaining air supply *and* your remaining no stop time (more about this shortly).

Here's an example: Suppose you and your buddy descend to 10 metres/30 feet, pause for a moment and then continue to 18 metres/60 feet. At 10 metres/30 feet, your computer would show you have more than three hours no stop time. When you arrive at 18 metres/60 feet, your computer now reads less than one hour no stop time remaining.

During the dive, your computer constantly updates your remaining no stop time based on your dive profile – your actual depths, and your times at each depth – and the limits set by the decompression model.

The no stop time you see when you scroll your computer during dive planning is the time you would have if you stayed at the depth the entire dive. Very commonly, however, you don't stay at the deepest depth the entire dive. You descend to a deepest point and then slowly ascend as you explore and tour along a sloping reef or bottom.

During the dive, your computer shows the no stop time you have remaining at your present depth. As you ascend, nitrogen absorption slows, so the remaining no stop time will increase. The remaining no stop time will, however, be less than you saw for that same depth during the predive scroll, because you have absorbed some nitrogen.

One of the advantages of dive computers is their ability to calculate more no stop dive time as you ascend. This is called *multilevel diving*. With dive tables, you must treat the dive as if you spend the entire dive at your deepest depth. This means you're limited to the no stop time of your deepest depth, even if you actually spend most of the dive shallower. (An exception is the eRDPML. Although not as versatile as a dive computer, the eRDPML allows you to plan multilevel dives that increase your no stop time as you ascend.)

Here's an example of the changing no stop times you might see on a typical dive: You and your buddy plan to descend to a reef to 18 metres/60 feet, explore a bit, then slowly ascend following the reef upward to shallower depths. You plan to keep the dive well within no stop times, and plan your air use so you will surface with 50 bar/500 psi.

For planning purposes, you scroll your computers and find that at 18 metres/60 feet, the no stop time is 55 minutes. You and your buddy agree to start up after 30 minutes if you have not already turned due to air use. You notice that the no stop time for 12 metres/40 feet is 140 minutes. The dive goes as planned. After exploring the reef for 30 minutes at 18 metres/60 feet, you and your buddy follow the reef upward. Just before you start up, your computer shows your remaining no stop time is 25 minutes.

As you ascend, the remaining no stop time increases. At 12 metres/40 feet, you see it showing a remaining no stop time of 83 minutes. This is much more time than you had remaining at 18 metres/60 feet, but less than the no stop time you noted predive. This reflects the nitrogen absorbed during your 30 minutes at 18 metres/60 feet. At this point, you have more no stop time available than the length of time your air supply will last. The dive will then need to end based on your air supply. At the appropriate point, you and your buddy ascend, make a safety stop and surface with 50 bar/500 psi in your cylinders based on your air supply, as you had planned.

Ascent Rates and Safety Stops

Most computers and dive tables have a required ascent rate. The no stop time assumes that you ascend at that rate. If you go faster than that rate, you may increase your risk of DCS. Ascending no faster than 18 metres/60 feet per minute, or the ascent rate of your computer (whichever is slower), also helps reduce the chance of lung overexpansion injury. Most computers have audible and/or visual warnings if you ascend too fast.

You've already learned that as you ascend from a dive, it is a good habit to make a safety stop for three minutes at 5 metres/15 feet before finishing the ascent and surfacing. A safety stop is *not* required to be within the limits of most dive computers' or tables' decompression models. You make the stop as a prudent, conservative diver to remain *well within* your dive computer or table limits. A few computers and tables have a "required" safety stop. With these, because you are nearing the limits, they call it "required" to put more importance on being conservative.

Recall that some problems, such as an out-of-air situation, may call for omitting the stop to reach the surface quickly. In such instances, it is more important to reach the surface safely than to make the safety stop.

Although not as versatile as a dive computer, the eRDPML allows you to plan multilevel dives that increase your no stop time as you ascend.

PADI Rebreather Diver teaches you to use Type R (recreational) rebreathers – scuba equipment that recycles your breathing gas – for recreational, no stop diving.

As mentioned before, a *decompression stop* is a stop in your ascent that is *required* because you exceeded the no stop limits. If you surface without making a decompression stop you would be outside model limits and theoretically have more nitrogen in your body tissues than acceptable. This creates a high risk of decompression sickness. In recreational diving, making a dive with required decompression stops is an emergency procedure only.

Exercise 4-14

1. A no stop dive means I can, if necessary, ascend directly to the surface without stopping _____ the dive.
   - ☐ a. for the first half of
   - ☐ b. for the last half of
   - ☐ c. at any time during

2. A no stop limit is the maximum time I can spend at a given depth and still ascend directly to the surface.
   - ☐ True
   - ☐ False

3. If I stay longer than a no stop limit, I must
   - ☐ a. ascend directly to the surface.
   - ☐ b. make a safety stop.
   - ☐ c. make an emergency decompression stop.

4. If I am planning a dive to 18 metres/60 feet, my no stop limits will be _____ than my no stop limits for a dive to 12 metres/40 feet.
   - ☐ a. longer
   - ☐ b. shorter

5. While at 18 metres/60 feet, my computer says I have 40 minutes no stop time remaining. My buddy and I ascend to 10 metres/30 feet. Our computers will show our no stop time is
   - ☐ a. longer.
   - ☐ b. shorter.
   - ☐ c. the same.

6. Ascending faster than the required ascent rate of my computer or table may increase my risk of DCS.
   - ☐ True
   - ☐ False

7. If I were to skip a(n) _____ stop, I would surface outside model limits and have a high risk of decompression sickness.
   - ☐ a. safety
   - ☐ b. emergency decompression

How did you do?
1. c. 2. True. 3. c. 4. b. 5. a. 6. True.
7. b.

By the end of this section, I should be able to answer these questions:

1. What is residual nitrogen? What is a repetitive dive?

2. How does residual nitrogen affect the no stop limits on a repetitive dive?

3. What is a surface interval?

4. What happens to the dissolved nitrogen in my body during a surface interval?

5. How does my dive computer calculate repetitive dives?

6. Why is it important that I dive with the same computer on every dive I make on a given day and not turn my computer off between dives?

7. How do dive tables address repetitive diving?

NDL before first dive

NDL before second dive

If you scroll your computer's no stop times after you've made a dive, you'll see that the times are shorter than they were before the dive. This is because after a dive, you still have excess nitrogen dissolved in your tissues.

section four

Repetitive Diving

Residual Nitrogen

If you scroll your computer's no stop times after you've made a dive, you'll see that the times are shorter than they were before the dive. This is because after a dive, you still have excess nitrogen dissolved in your body tissues. It takes quite a few hours after surfacing for all the excess nitrogen to dissolve out of your body. In theory, it can take longer than a day.

The nitrogen left in your body after a dive is called *residual nitrogen.* Residual nitrogen is important, because it shortens your no stop limits if you dive again. A dive made while you still have residual nitrogen is called a *repetitive dive.* When you make a repetitive dive, your dive computer gives you shorter no stop times to account for the nitrogen still in your body. If you stay at the surface long enough (usually 12 hours or more) for your body nitrogen levels to return to normal, the next dive is no longer considered a repetitive dive. You'll hear it called a "first" dive or a "clean" dive.

Surface Intervals

A *surface interval* is the time you spend at the surface between two dives. During a surface interval, the residual nitrogen in your body declines as it dissolves out of your tissues and leaves your body.

This means that the longer your surface interval is, the more no stop time you have on a repetitive dive, all else being the same. And, as just stated, if your surface interval is long enough (12 or more hours), residual nitrogen is zero (for practical purposes), so the next dive is a first dive.

Calculating Repetitive Dives

Your dive computer calculates repetitive dives the same way it calculates your first dive. Starting with the first dive, your computer tracks your depths and times. During the dive, it displays your remaining no stop time at your current depth.

After the dive, your computer continues to calculate. It "remembers" your residual nitrogen from the first dive. It calculates your time at the surface and how much theoretical residual nitrogen dissolves out of your body. If you scroll your no stop limits from time to time as you and your buddies relax during a surface interval, you will see no stop limits gradually lengthen as you spend time on the surface.

When you dive again, your computer "knows" the theoretical residual nitrogen remaining in your tissues. Your computer shortens your no stop times to account for the residual nitrogen. You will notice that at each depth, you have less no stop time than you did on your first dive. An important point is that a first dive deep enough to have been limited by your air supply might be limited by your no stop time as a repetitive dive.

⚠️ **Because your dive computer tracks *your* personal theoretical nitrogen levels *continuously* during all your dives and all your surface intervals, you *must* use the *same* computer the entire diving day, on *all* dives, and not share it with another diver.**

This is necessary in providing appropriate no stop times over multiple dives and surface intervals. Do not make a repetitive dive without the *same* computer you used on your previous dive or dives. If you were to use a different computer, it wouldn't have your previous dive information and your no stop times would be inaccurate. This could significantly increase the risk of decompression sickness.

Your dive computer continues to calculate the theoretical nitrogen in your body tissues until your surface interval has

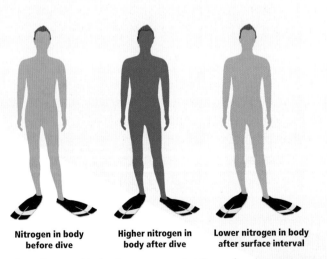

Nitrogen in body before dive — **Higher nitrogen in body after dive** — **Lower nitrogen in body after surface interval**

A surface interval is the time you spend at the surface between two dives. During a surface interval, the residual nitrogen in your body declines as it dissolves out of your tissues and leaves your body.

Because your dive computer tracks your personal theoretical nitrogen levels continuously during all your dives and all your surface intervals, you must use the same computer the entire diving day, on all dives, and not share it with another diver.

been long enough that the nitrogen levels have returned to normal (for practical purposes). During a day of diving, never turn off your dive computer (or remove the batteries), because it may lose all your repetitive dive information. This would make repetitive dive calculations inaccurate. Most modern computers won't let you turn them off for this reason, but some older models allowed it. Your computer may go to "sleep" to save power during a long surface interval, but it is still calculating. Follow any additional manufacturer recommendations regarding the use of a computer for repetitive diving.

Most modern computers also won't let you start diving with them if the battery power is too low. See the manufacturer literature/website and/or your instructor about powering off, sleep mode and battery replacement for your computer should it become necessary (batteries usually last a year or more).

When your computer calculates that nitrogen levels have returned to normal, it will turn itself off or go to sleep. Many dive computers – particularly those that are also watches – never turn off or go to sleep. This is normal. See your instructor if you have questions about the specifics for your dive computer.

Repetitive Diving with Tables

The RDP and other dive tables address repetitive diving by using three tables. The first table assigns a Pressure Group (as a letter) that represents the theoretical amount of residual nitrogen from your dive time and depth.

The second table gives you credit for nitrogen leaving your body during a surface interval. Taking the Pressure Group from the previous table, it assigns a new Pressure Group based on your surface interval time. This Pressure Group represents having less theoretical residual nitrogen in the body.

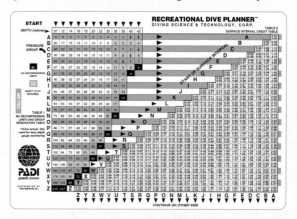

The third table shows you no stop times for each depth adjusted for your Pressure Group at the start of the dive.

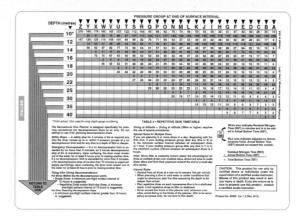

The RDP and other dive tables address repetitive diving by using three tables. The first table assigns a Pressure Group that represents the theoretical amount of residual nitrogen from your dive time and depth. The second table accounts for nitrogen leaving your body during a surface interval. The third table shows you no stop times for each depth adjusted for your Pressure Group at the start of the dive.

section four

The eRDPML uses these tables, but manages them electronically for user convenience. The RDP Table and eRDPML include detailed study guides on how to use them.

Exercise 4-15

1. A repetitive dive is a dive made while I still have theoretical residual nitrogen in my body.
   - ☐ True
   - ☐ False

2. On a repetitive dive, for a known depth my no stop limits will be _____ those of the first dive.
   - ☐ a. longer than
   - ☐ b. shorter than
   - ☐ c. the same as

3. A surface interval is the time it takes to reach the surface.
   - ☐ True
   - ☐ False

4. After a surface interval, the nitrogen dissolved in my body will
   - ☐ a. decline.
   - ☐ b. increase.
   - ☐ c. not change.

5. My dive computer only calculates while I am underwater. It doesn't do anything between dives.
   - ☐ True
   - ☐ False

6. I must use the same dive computer the entire day of diving, on all dives, and not share it with another diver.
   - ☐ True
   - ☐ False

7. Dive tables like the RDP and eRDPML use ___ tables to calculate repetitive dives.
   - ☐ a. 1
   - ☐ b. 2
   - ☐ c. 3
   - ☐ d. 4

How did you do?
1. True. 2. b. 3. False. A surface interval is the time you are at the surface between dives. 4. a. 5. False. Your dive computer continues to calculate until your theoretical nitrogen levels return to normal. 6. True. 7. c.

LEARNING OBJECTIVES

By the end of this section, I should be able to answer these questions:

1. What are four advantages of dive computers over dive tables?

2. What seven types of information do dive computers tell me before, during and/or between dives?

3. How do I set up and activate my dive computer? What is the first step?

4. How do I plan dives with my dive computer?

Planning Dives with Your Computer

Almost all active divers use dive computers, and they're considered standard equipment in most areas. Although dive tables are effective (diving has been around a lot longer than dive computers), there are four advantages that make dive computers far more popular.

1. *Dive computers are easier to use than tables.* Tables are not difficult to use, but dive computers are easier in that they do much of the work, but nonetheless allow you to control and stay aware of your depth and time limits.

2. *Dive computers help offset human error.* Your computer gives information based on the dive you actually make. Although it shouldn't happen, if you accidentally exceed your planned depth or time, your computer knows and adjusts its calculations. Dive computers also record your dive information, which allows you to put accurate details into your dive log later.

3. *Dive computers give you more time underwater.* Dive computers give you more no stop dive time on a multi-

Four advantages of dive computers include: they're easier to use than tables, help offset human error, give you more time underwater and have other features.

level dive. You'll notice more additional no stop time on a multilevel dive compared to a table-based dive, particularly on deeper dives. As mentioned, the eRDPML allows you to plan multilevel dives, too, but it is not as easy or as flexible as a dive computer.

4. *Besides the basic information you need while diving, most dive computers have other features.* These range from recording the water temperature to being able to download your dive information to an electronic dive log.

Dive Computer Information

Practically all dive computers provide the following information before, during and/or between dives (most of these have been discussed):

- ❶ *No stop (no decompression) limits.* You use these to plan your dives.

- ❷ *Depth.* During the dive, your computer always shows your current depth.

- ❸ *Elapsed time.* Underwater, your computer shows how long you've been down. Between dives, it shows the time since you surfaced from the previous dive.

- ❹ *No stop time remaining.* You always know how much time you have left at your present depth.

- ❺ *Ascent rate.* Ascent rate indicators range from visual "speedometers" to simple alarms that go off if you ascend too fast.

- ❻ *Emergency decompression.* If you exceed a no stop limit, your computer calculates the stops you have to make.

- ❼ *Previous dive information.* You can recall the maximum depth and total dive time for the last dive. Most computers will let you do this for several of the previous dives, in reverse order, and provide additional information.

Setting Up and Activating Your Dive Computer

Before you dive with a computer, you need to set it up and activate it. The first step is to *read the dive computer manual.* If you don't have it available, you can often download it from the manufacturer's website. Computers are very similar, but they have their individual characteristics. It is your responsibility to read and understand the manufacturer's instructions, because recommendations sometimes differ. As you learned in Section One, for example, some manufacturers recommend having a separate conventional SPG even when using their air-integrated computers.

Setup involves settings that you usually only make once. Following the manufacturer guidelines, these may include:

- Time and date
- Metric or imperial system measurements
- Ascent rate alarm (you usually leave this on)
- Maximum depth/time alarm (to warn you if you reach a limit)

If you're unsure about a setting even after checking the manufacturer literature, see your instructor. Usually, the best practice is to leave it at its default setting.

To activate your computer before diving (or to scroll the no stop limits) you usually press a button or touch some contacts. Check the time and date after activating it. You may want to reset these if you changed time zone, etc. Be sure there is not a low battery warning. Virtually all modern dive computers self-activate in the water if you forget to do so before you dive. However, best practice is to activate your computer.

Planning Dives

Planning with your computer is simple, whether making your first dive or a repetitive dive. Start by activating your computer and scrolling the no stop limits. Agree with your buddy(ies) on a maximum depth based on the no stop times displayed. Check the time for that depth.

If you plan to stay at your deepest depth for most of the dive, then your allowable dive time will be close to the time shown. If you plan to ascend and continue the dive shallower (multilevel dive), you will have more time than shown for the maximum depth. Repetitive dives have shorter no stop times than your first dive. If you want to dive longer than the no stop time shown for your planned maximum depth, make a multilevel dive, make a shallower dive or stay at the surface longer (if making a repetitive dive). On multilevel dives, it is generally recommended that you plan to descend relatively quickly to the maximum depth, then gradually work your way shallower. This gives you the most no stop time and makes most of the dive part of a long, slow, conservative ascent.

Plan your maximum time. On a shallow dive or multilevel dive, you usually have more no stop time available than the length of time your air supply will last. Agree with your buddy(ies) on a time to head back toward your exit, and to begin ascending to the surface.

The first step in setting up your dive computer is to read the dive computer manual.

Turn the dive based on what you reach first: time, air supply turn point or remaining no stop time. Many divers write these, as well as no stop times for the maximum and next deeper depths, on their slates for reference during the dive.

Plan your air management as you have already learned. Don't forget that your air supply commonly limits your dive – not your no stop time. Watch your SPG as well as your dive computer. Turn the dive based on which limit you reach first: time, air supply turn point or remaining no stop time. Note these, as well as no stop times for the maximum and next deeper depths, on the PADI Skill Practice and Dive Planning Slate for reference during the dive.

LEARNING OBJECTIVES

By the end of this section, I should be able to answer these questions:

1. What are six guidelines for diving with a computer?

2. What should I do if my dive computer fails during a dive or between dives?

Exercise 4-16

1. Advantages of a dive computer over dive tables include dive computers (choose all that apply):
   - ☐ a. are easier to use than tables.
   - ☐ b. help offset human error.
   - ☐ c. give me more time underwater.
   - ☐ d. read the actual nitrogen in my body.

2. Before, during and/or between dives, my computer will tell me (choose all that apply):
   - ☐ a. no stop limits.
   - ☐ b. the ascent rate.
   - ☐ c. emergency decompression information.
   - ☐ d. previous dive information.

3. The first step in setting up my dive computer is to
   - ☐ a. set the date.
   - ☐ b. put in the battery.
   - ☐ c. press the power button.
   - ☐ d. read the manufacturer instructions.

4. During a dive with my dive computer, my buddy and I will turn the dive based on the first limit we reach: remaining no stop time or air supply turn point.
   - ☐ True
   - ☐ False

How did you do?
1. a, b, c. 2. a, b, c, d. 3. d. 4. True.

Diving with Your Computer

Computer Diving Guidelines

There are six guidelines to follow when diving with a computer. You should be familiar with most of them:

1. *Dive the plan.* Don't exceed your planned depth or time just because your computer will let you. But never hesitate to make your dive shorter or shallower if appropriate.

2. *Stay well within your computer's limits.* Letting your no stop time get to or near 0 is "pushing" the limits – an unwise practice. Always have ample no stop time showing. Head shallower well before your computer nears 0 minutes remaining at your present depth.

When diving with your computer, dive the plan. Follow the most conservative computer and watch your SPG as well as your no stop time.

3. *Follow the most conservative computer – yours or a buddy's.* Your and your buddy's(ies') computers should have similar readings, but they won't be identical. Head shallower or end the dive (as needed) based on whom-ever's computer nears a limit first.

4. *Watch your SPG.* Check your air supply, not just your no stop time remaining. A good habit is to check both of them together. Air-integrated computers (computers with the SPG built into them) make it easy to check both together. Many of these track your air use and predict your time remaining based on how fast you've been breathing and your present depth.

5. *Start at your deepest point and go shallower.* When making more than one dive, plan to make the deepest dive first, with following dives to the same depth or shallower. Generally, avoid large increases in depths af-ter ascending to a shallower depth. Small increases and decreases aren't an issue. The principle of deep-to-shal-low gives you the most no stop time, and is considered more conservative because most test data are based on deep-to-shallow dives.

6. *Ascend slowly, well within your computer's ascent rate, and make a safety stop at 5 metres/15 feet for three minutes or longer.*

Computer Diving Simulators

One of the best ways to learn about computer diving is to use a computer-based simulator to see how a typical dive computer behaves before, during and between dives.

Computer diving simulators use a graph to show you what to expect from a generic dive computer in different situations. You can also experiment with your own depths and times.

⚠ **Many computer simulators are designed for training and learning only. Do not use them for planning actual dives unless otherwise specified by the manufacturer.**

Dive Computer Failure

Dive computers are highly reliable and failure is *very, very* rare. Most computers check themselves when you activate them and confirm adequate battery power for 12 to 24 hours (see the manufacturer's info on this). Failures generally cause a computer to display nothing, or display nonsense. Bad information is very rare. A failed computer may *appear* to be working later. This is rarely true; computers don't fix themselves. Have a faulty computer serviced before attempting to use it again, even if it seems fine.

If your computer fails during a dive, you have two options.

Option 1: Signal your buddy(ies), ascend, make a safety stop and end the dive. If you're remaining well within limits throughout the dive, you should surface within accepted limits. After surfacing, you must wait 12 or more hours (see the manufacturer recommendations) for your nitrogen levels to return to normal before diving again with a different computer. If you're writing down your dive depths and times (as you should), you *may* be able to continue to dive by applying all the information to dive tables. However, multilevel

If your computer fails during a dive and you're not wearing a backup, ascend, make a safety stop and end the dive.

no stop times commonly go over table limits, so this may not work.

Option 2: Continue the dive using a backup computer. Dive computers are inexpensive enough that more and more commonly, active divers have two. To use this option, you must dive with both computers at all times, and stay within the limits of the most conservative one. A double computer failure is highly unlikely; you can continue the dive and make repetitive dives with your backup. If your backup were to fail, though, use Option 1.

If your computer fails between dives during a surface interval and you have not been diving with a backup, you may be able to use tables to continue diving, as described above. Otherwise, wait 12 or more hours (see the manufacturer recommendations) for your nitrogen levels to return to normal before diving again with a different computer.

BE A SAFE DIVER

To reduce your risk of decompression sickness or lung over-expansion injuries, remember to be a SAFE Diver:

Slowly
Ascend
From
Every Dive

Make a safety stop at 5 metres/ 15 feet for at least three minutes.

THE RECREATIONAL DIVE PLANNER™

As part of your training, your PADI Instructor may have you learn to use the RDP Table or eRDPML. Although most divers use computers today, many still like the option of having tables to assist with dive planning, or as a backup to allow diving when a computer isn't available or has a problem. The RDP Table and eRDPML include study guides to assist your learning.

Exercise 4-17

1. During a dive, my dive computer allows more dive time than my buddy and I planned for a given depth. We have plenty of air, so it's okay to stay longer or go deeper than we planned.
   ☐ True
   ☐ False

2. During a dive, my dive computer fails and I'm not using a backup. I should
   ☐ a. continue the dive based on my buddy's computer.
   ☐ b. ascend, make a safety stop and end the dive.
   ☐ c. stay for the time we planned before the dive.

How did you do?
1. False. Don't exceed your planned depth or time just because your computer will let you. 2. b

The Underwater World's Ambassador

LEARNING OBJECTIVES

By the end of this section, I should be able to answer these questions:

1. Are divers a significant threat to the overall health of the underwater environment?

2. Why is it important to apply environmentally friendly dive skills and awareness while underwater?

3. What role do I have as a diver in the long-term survival and health of the world's aquatic ecosystems?

Poor dive techniques, and neglect, can damage fragile aquatic life. However, divers are not a significant threat to the overall health of the underwater environment. The *significant* threats are pollutants, climate change, dredging, the loss of mangroves and the spread of invasive species (among others).

The types of damage divers cause through poor technique are localized and do not threaten ecological survival. Injury and death of fragile organisms occur due to impacts and contact in nature without divers present. Even with diving's growth and popularity, it isn't expected that an underwater environment could be destroyed simply due to diving activity.

Intentional interactions by some divers can have serious environmental consequences, however. Underwater hunting without restraint and limits in the 1960s and 1970s showed that divers can reduce the population of important

species from large areas. Some of these species are only now recovering. Also, devastating effects result from using toxins to catch fish (once common for the aquarium trade) and similar actions. Damage to wrecks and other cultural resources, such as intentionally removing artifacts, can destroy the archaeological value and leave the site less desirable for other divers. Some countries have closed or greatly restricted diving due to such damage.

Although divers aren't a significant threat to the overall health of the aquatic environment, it is nonetheless very important to have environmentally friendly dive skills and awareness while underwater, for several reasons.

First, while diver damage may not (by itself) cause an ecosystem to collapse, it can destroy its natural beauty. Minimizing your effect on the environment is important to leave the places you visit beautiful for your next visit and for divers who follow.

Second, an ecosystem already under stress from pollution and other sources may struggle to recover from – or be *unable* to recover from – damage caused by divers (or any other sources). For example, a groove on a coral head caused by a dragging console would repair over a few months in healthy, pristine conditions. But in less than optimum conditions (increasingly widespread), the same injury could become a foothold for disease that eventually spreads and kills the entire coral head.

Third, dive skills and habits that are good for the environment are also good for you. You also cause less damage to your gear, save energy and reduce the risk of hazardous aquatic life injuries if you stay streamlined, control your buoyancy and swim well above the bottom.

Diving without damaging is also important to your influence as a role model and an ambassador for the underwater world. As society struggles to solve environmental problems, perspective and constructive insight become increasingly important.

Because you see it first hand, you can influence your nondiving peers to help preserve and protect the aquatic world. But, diving will lose this influence if people think diving is damaging. It would make divers appear hypocritical.

Your Role as a Diver

Your influence gives you a role in being part of the solution to the problems facing the long-term survival and health of the world's aquatic ecosystems. You can report your observations by taking part in environmental surveys and reporting online. Visit projectaware.org for more information.

You have credibility as the aquatic world's ambassador. Adding your voice and votes to those of other divers helps make positive changes. Diver support has already helped steer and advance initiatives to protect environments and preserve endangered species.

You also have the power to take direct action. Examples include:

• Underwater cleanups. Organized by PADI operators and other groups, these events remove, and document trash and litter to further efforts to reduce them at their sources.

• Invasive species removal. In some locations, divers may remove invasive species (organisms not native to the environment that have taken hold after being transferred there by human activity).

• Ecotourism and science. Several organizations rely on volunteer divers in gathering data. While some require substantial expertise, many do not.

To learn more about how you can help in preserving the underwater world, see your PADI operator and visit projectaware.org.

Exercise 4-18

1. Are divers a significant threat to the overall health of the underwater environment?
   ☐ Yes
   ☐ No

2. One reason it is important to apply environmentally friendly dive skills is to preserve the natural beauty for other divers.
   ☐ True
   ☐ False

3. My influence as a diver and ambassador for the underwater world allows me to be part of the solution to the problems the world's aquatic ecosystems face.
   ☐ True
   ☐ False

How did you do?
1. No. 2. True. 3. True.

Putting your scuba kit on at the surface in water too deep in which to stand is a useful technique when diving from small boats or if you're not physically able to wear scuba gear out of water.

Your Skills as a Diver IV

Let's look at some more skills you'll learn during this course. As previously mentioned, your instructor may demonstrate a method that differs from what you learn here.

Deep Water Entry – Put on Scuba Kit at the Surface, Controlled Seated Entry

One type of entry you may practice is the controlled seated entry followed by putting your scuba kit on at the surface in water too deep in which to stand. This is a useful technique when diving from small boats in which there is not enough room to kit up. It is also useful for entering the water from heights too great for a giant stride – you lower your kit on a line and descend to the water on a ladder. You may also use this technique if you're not physically able to wear scuba gear out of water.

- Completely assemble your gear, check your SPG for enough air and be sure the cylinder valve is open.

- Although you're not wearing your kit, you go through the steps of your predive safety check.

- If your BCD has integrated weights but will float adequately, then weights may be in place. For a separate weight system or if your gear won't float, you will put the weights on in the water after putting on your scuba kit. Don't enter the water without your BCD while wearing your weight system.

- After you and your buddy(ies) are in your gear, finish the F – Final Check – step of your predive safety check, making sure that all buckles are secure, no hoses are trapped, nothing dangles and everything is where it should be.

- In many instances, the controlled seated entry is suitable for getting into the water while wearing scuba gear.

Partially inflate your BCD and breathe from your regulator before entering. As you turn to ease into the water, be sure your cylinder has cleared the platform edge.

Helping a Tired Buddy

Sometimes divers find they can't swim to the boat or shore, because they have become too tired or have some other problem. Severe leg cramps may make swimming difficult as well. Tired-diver tows at the surface allow you to help.

- Begin by establishing buoyancy for yourself and the diver you're helping.

- Use the *cylinder valve tow,* with you and the diver floating face up, for short distances.

- Use the *tired-diver push* (modified tired-swimmer carry) for longer tows.

For both, swim at a slow, steady pace to the exit.

Neutral Buoyancy – Visual Reference Descents, Swimming and Ascents Near Sensitive Environments

You will practice descending and swimming as you would in an environment with sensitive aquatic organisms. These skills combine what you've already learned with respect to proper weighting, trim and buoyancy control.

- It is typical of how you dive near coral reefs and other fragile organisms, and over bottoms like mud that stir up easily, ruining the visibility.

- Although you can usually find insensitive areas where bottom contact is reasonable, for the purposes of this skill, your instructor will have you simulate that the entire bottom is sensitive, with no contact wanted.

No Mask Swim

If you were to lose your mask and not be able to locate it or retrieve it, you would have to end the dive without it. The no mask swim allows you to practice and demonstrate that you could.

- You may close your eyes if you have contacts, though you would keep them open if you really had to ascend without your mask.

- Otherwise, keep your eyes open because you can see enough to be useful.

- Swim with your buddy at least 15 metres/50 feet. Control your buoyancy, equalize your ears, etc. as you normally would. Your buddy will guide you (especially if you have your eyes closed).

- Concentrate on breathing through your mouth. Exhale through your nose if the water tickles it a bit.

- After the swim, replace your mask and clear it.

Freeflow Regulator Breathing

To simulate a freeflow, you or your instructor will depress the purge button.

- Hold the mouthpiece against your lips – don't seal your mouth on it.

- Allow excess air to escape; "sip" the air you need from the flow.

- It may help to insert just one side of the mouthpiece into your mouth, with the other side out.

- Practice for at least 30 seconds.

- Check your SPG after practicing. You may be surprised how much air you used. This emphasizes the need to start your ascent immediately when breathing from a freeflowing regulator.

BCD Oral Inflation Underwater

If you were to have a runaway low-pressure inflator (it becomes frozen or has a serious leak), as you've already learned, you would disconnect it. To maintain buoyancy control as you end the dive, you may need to orally inflate your BCD while underwater.

This is similar to orally inflating at the surface, except that you take each breath from your regulator and there is no need to kick up as you inhale.

- Blow a third to half your breath into the BCD by pressing the deflator (exhaust) button while you blow in (and only then). You won't put in as much air per breath as

Use the cylinder valve tow and the tired-diver push to assist a buddy who can't swim due to exhaustion, leg cramps or another problem.

You will practice descending and swimming as you would in an environment with sensitive aquatic organisms.

at the surface, because you're only adjusting to become neutrally buoyant.

• Let go of the deflator button while you're not blowing in, so the BCD does not deflate.

• Remember to blow a steady stream of bubbles when the regulator isn't in your mouth.

• Replace the regulator, clear it and resume breathing after blowing into your BCD. Wait a moment to see how your buoyancy has changed before making further adjustments.

• Do not continue a dive with a malfunctioning low-pressure inflator. Use oral inflation/normal deflation to maintain buoyancy control as you abort the dive.

• Once neutrally buoyant, hover for a least a minute using breath control and small adjustments.

Skin Diving Skills

Your instructor will demonstrate skin diving skills (diving with mask, fins and snorkel, but no scuba – sometimes called "free diving") and have you practice them. Skin diving skills are useful for scouting potential dive sites from the surface without wasting time and air (compared to scuba), diving in places where scuba equipment isn't

To maintain buoyancy control without a working low-pressure inflator, you may need to orally inflate your BCD while underwater.

available, and quickly going to someone's assistance in the water at the surface. You may also need to use skin diving to see some types of aquatic life, such as whales and whale sharks. And, being comfortable while skin diving can simply add to your enjoyment of the underwater world by giving you more opportunities to experience and explore. Proper breathing helps you hold your breath longer.

If you were to lose your mask and not be able to locate it or retrieve it, you would have to end the dive without it. The no mask swim allows you to practice and demonstrate that you could.

To simulate a freeflow, you or your instructor will hold the regulator purge button. Don't seal your lips on the mouthpiece. Allow excess air to escape as you "sip" the air you need from the flow.

When skin diving, your buddy remains on the surface when you dive down, and vice versa. The one-up, one-down technique allows your buddy to come to your aid if you need help.

- Breathe from your diaphragm before making a breath-hold dive. This is sometimes called "stomach breathing," because your diaphragm is the muscle over your stomach. To do this, breathe so your stomach area expands.

- Hyperventilation (breathing deeper and/or more rapidly than normal) is no longer preferred as a breath-hold technique because it can lower carbon dioxide levels so low that your body can run out of oxygen before you get the urge to breathe. If done improperly, it can cause you to lose consciousness and drown.

  Although some divers do this by limiting hyperventilation to only two or three deep breaths, it is better to breath-hold using relaxed diaphragm breathing, which allows you to hold your breath just as long (some evidence suggests longer).

- After returning to the surface, rest until your body restores normal oxygen and carbon dioxide levels.

- Breathe normally from your diaphragm – a strong exhalation after surfacing from a long breath-hold can cause you to become faint.

- If you feel dizzy or lightheaded, or feel tingling in your hands, arms or feet, stop diving down. Rest, relax and breathe at the surface.

Buddy Contact

- When skin diving, your buddy remains on the surface when you dive down, and vice versa.

- The one-up, one-down technique allows your buddy to come to your aid if you need help.

Besides practicing the previously learned blast snorkel clearing method, you'll learn and practice displacement snorkel clearing on ascents.

- When you ascend, look up and reach up as you come up. Rotate for a complete view as necessary.

- As you ascend, you can clear your snorkel by using displacement.

- While looking up, the tip of your snorkel is lower than the mouth-piece.

- Begin exhaling as you ascend through the last metre/few feet or so.

- Your exhalation displaces the water, pushing it out the tip.

While looking up as you ascend from a breath-hold dive, the tip of your snorkel is lower than the mouthpiece. Begin exhaling as you ascend through the last metre/few feet or so and your snorkel should be clear of water when you surface.

- Continue to exhale as you roll your head forward into a surface swimming position. Your snorkel should be free of water, but inhale cautiously as you've learned earlier just in case.

Some snorkels with self-drain valves may not clear well with this method. In this case, simply use the blast method that you learned in Confined Water Dive Two. Some divers just prefer the blast method.

These skin diving skills apply to casual breath-hold diving no deeper than approximately 10 metres/30 feet and for breath-holds of about a minute or less. Deeper, longer, more serious free dives involve more sophisticated techniques to avoid hazards and to improve performance. If skin diving deeper than 10 metres/30 feet and/or with breath-hold times longer than a minute interests you, see your instructor about specialized training.

Exit – Remove Scuba Kit in the Water

To exit on to a small boat, on to an unstable platform or on to vessels that don't have ladders, one technique is to slip out of your scuba kit while in the water. This is also useful for anyone who cannot wear a scuba kit out of water, or for exiting up a ladder without the weight of your gear.

- Begin by inflating your BCD to establish positive buoyancy.

- Remove and hand up your weights, or attach them to a line. This may not be necessary if your kit will float with integrated weights still in it.

- To exit the water without a ladder, push up and kick hard to lift your torso, then turn and sit on the swim step or boat side (as appropriate). Alternatively, lift yourself up, bend forward at the waist, and lower yourself so you're face down on the deck/boat, then roll face up.

- Sometimes you need to secure your kit to a gear line before exiting the water. This is especially true when there's a current.

To exit on to a small boat, unstable platform or other vessels that don't have ladders, one technique is to slip out of your scuba kit while in the water.

Confined Water Dive Four

- ☐ Briefing
- ☐ Equipment assembly, dive planning, gearing up and predive safety check
- ☐ Entry – Put scuba kit on in the water
- ☐ Weight and trim check and adjustment
- ☐ Tired-diver tows
- ☐ Neutral buoyancy – visual reference descents, swimming and ascents near sensitive environments
- ☐ No mask swim
- ☐ Freeflow regulator breathing
- ☐ Orally inflate BCD underwater – hover
- ☐ Skin diving skills (dive flexible)
- ☐ Free time for skill practice and fun
- ☐ Exit – Remove scuba kit in the water
- ☐ Post dive equipment care (dive flexible)

Note: *Your instructor may modify this to some extent to meet class and logistical requirements.*

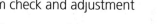

Knowledge Review Four

Some questions may have more than one correct answer. Choose all that apply.

1. During an underwater cleanup, my buddy and I fill a large mesh utility bag with several kilograms/pounds of garbage. We should
   - ☐ a. attach the bag to our gear.
   - ☐ b. carry the bag in our hands.

2. I have a bit of a cold but feel I can manage the dive well enough, so it is okay to dive.
   - ☐ True
   - ☐ False

3. Exertion from swimming hard, carrying equipment, climbing a ladder, long walks wearing gear, and heat stress from wearing an exposure suit in a hot climate can lead to heart attack in predisposed individuals. These factors can also cause problems for people with other cardiovascular conditions.
   - ☐ True
   - ☐ False

4. Before diving, I should refrain from using
   - ☐ a. alcohol.
   - ☐ b. tobacco.

5. Medications can create problems when diving, so I should use prescription drugs and over-the-counter medications with caution. Any drug that affects my judgment, thinking and/or reactions should generally not be used before diving.
   - ☐ True
   - ☐ False

6. It is recommended that pregnant women do not dive.
   - ☐ True
   - ☐ False

7. As a new PADI Open Water Diver, I should refresh my dive skills with a PADI Scuba Review after _____ of inactivity.
   - ☐ a. one month
   - ☐ b. six months
   - ☐ c. one year
   - ☐ d. five years

8. One reason it is important to be certified as a PADI Enriched Air Diver, or under the supervision of a PADI Enriched Air Instructor, before using enriched air nitrox is to avoid oxygen toxicity problems.
   - ☐ True
   - ☐ False

9. During a dive, I begin to have a headache, feel ill and dizzy. Are these possible symptoms of contaminated air?
   - ☐ Yes
   - ☐ No

10. To avoid contaminated air, I should have my cylinder filled only at reputable scuba air sources.
    - ☐ True
    - ☐ False

11. The two primary factors that influence how much nitrogen dissolves into my body tissues during a dive are _____ and _____.
    - ☐ a. depth, time
    - ☐ b. temperature, time
    - ☐ c. depth, temperature

12. If I exceed established depth and time limits while diving and then surface, bubbles can form in my body tissues, causing decompression sickness.
    - ☐ True
    - ☐ False

13. After a dive, a diver has numbness, tingling and weakness in the arms. Are these possible signs/symptoms of DCS?
    - ☐ Yes
    - ☐ No

14. Secondary factors thought to contribute to DCS include
    - ☐ a. age.
    - ☐ b. cold.
    - ☐ c. injuries.
    - ☐ d. poor fitness/high body fat.

15. A no stop dive means I can, _____ the dive, ascend directly to the surface without stopping if necessary (although I would normally plan a safety stop).
    - ☐ a. for the first half of
    - ☐ b. for the last half of
    - ☐ c. at any time during

16. If I am planning a dive to 12 metres/40 feet, my no stop limit will be _____ than my no stop limit for a dive to 10 metres/30 feet.
    - ☐ a. longer
    - ☐ b. shorter

17. Exceeding my computer or table's ascent rate may increase my risk of DCS.
    - ☐ True
    - ☐ False

18. On a repetitive dive, for a given depth my no stop limits will be _____ those of the first dive.
    - ☐ a. longer than
    - ☐ b. shorter than
    - ☐ c. the same as

19. I must use the same dive computer the entire day of diving, on all dives, and not share it with another diver.
    - ☐ True
    - ☐ False

20. During a dive with my dive computer, my buddy and I will turn the dive based on the first limit we reach: remaining no stop time or air supply turn point.
    - ☐ True
    - ☐ False

21. When diving with a computer, it is recommended that I
    - ☐ a. dive well within its limits.
    - ☐ b. follow the most conservative computer – mine or my buddy's.
    - ☐ c. start at the deepest point and progress shallower.
    - ☐ d. ascend slowly and make a safety stop.

22. During a dive, my dive computer fails, and I'm not using a backup. I should
    - ☐ a. continue the dive based on my buddy's computer.
    - ☐ b. ascend, make a safety stop and end the dive.
    - ☐ c. stay for the duration we planned before the dive.

23. One reason it is important to have environmentally friendly dive skills is to preserve the natural beauty for other divers.
    - ☐ True
    - ☐ False

Student Diver Statement: I've completed this Knowledge Review to the best of my ability and any questions I answered incorrectly or incompletely, I have had explained to me and I understand what I missed.

Name_____   Date_____

section

five

You can use the RDP Table or eRDPML to find minimum surface intervals. Like using an app, don't expect the times to exactly match your dive computer, but you will get a good approximation.

Planning a repetitive dive for a specific depth and time requires finding a minimum surface interval. This is determining how long to wait after the first dive to have the no stop time you want at the planned depth of the repetitive dive.

LEARNING OBJECTIVES

By the end of this section, I should be able to answer these questions:

1. Why would I need to find a minimum surface interval?

2. What are three ways I can find a minimum surface interval with a dive computer without using dive tables?

3. How can finding minimum surface intervals with the RDP Table and eRDPML help me plan them with dive computers?

Using Dive Computers and Tables II

Planning a Minimum Surface Interval

When making two or more dives, you commonly plan your dives by checking no stop times after your surface interval. You decide how long you want to dive and choose your maximum depth based on the no stop times, or you choose the depth you want and plan your time. When you can plan multilevel dives, you have more flexibility.

Sometimes, though, you want to make a repetitive dive to a specific depth for a specific time. Your objective may be very specific, and you need a minimum time to do it, such as photographing a wreck at 18 metres/60 feet. Or, when the dive site is flat (i.e., you can't ascend to a shallower depth to increase no stop time), you may simply want enough time to make the dive worth it.

Planning a repetitive dive for a specific depth and time requires *finding a minimum surface interval.* This is determining how long to wait after the first dive to have the no stop time you want at the planned depth of the repetitive dive.

Here's an example: You and your buddy are planning a repetitive dive to 15 metres/50 feet. The bottom will be relatively flat, so you can't plan a multilevel dive to increase your no stop time. Based on experience, you know that with a full cylinder, you can dive to that depth for about 50 minutes, ascend, make a safety stop and surface with 50 bar/500 psi reserve.

You and your buddy decide that you want at least 45 minutes of no stop time for a reasonably long dive within your air supply limit. Sticking to conservative dive practices, you also want your dive to be well within the no stop limits. You decide you want a surface interval that gives you a no stop time of *at least* 55 minutes at 15 metres/50 feet. To dive *well within* your dive computer or dive table limits, you also know that it's a good idea to plan your

surface interval to be longer than the absolute minimum.

There are three ways to find a minimum surface interval with a computer: wait and check, use the dive computer plan mode and use a tablet/smartphone app.

Wait and check. Just as it sounds, after your dive, scroll your no stop times and check the no stop time for your planned repetitive dive depth. If it's too short, you recheck every so often until you've been at the surface long enough to have the desired no stop time, plus some extra to stay well within the limits.

Although this method sounds imprecise, with experience you'll get a feel for about how long you have to wait. You'll notice that during a surface interval, your repetitive no stop times increase quickly at first, but the increase rate gradually slows as the interval gets longer.

Use the dive computer plan mode. Some higher-end dive computers have a sophisticated plan mode that allows you to enter a surface interval. The computer tells you what the no stop time will be after you've been up that long. If your computer has this feature, enter surface intervals (this may take a bit of trial and error) to find out how long you need to wait to have the desired no stop time, plus extra time so you're well within limits, at your planned depth.

See the manufacturer literature or your instructor for specifics on how to use this function with your computer, if it has it.

Use a tablet/smartphone app. In Section Four, you learned that you can get dive planning apps that calculate no stop times. Tec divers use dive planning apps that calculate no stop times, but recreational divers also use them to estimate minimum surface intervals. With such an app, you enter your first dive maximum depth and time, a surface interval and the desired second depth and time. If

223

the app shows that the second dive requires decompression stops, enter longer surface intervals until it shows the desired no stop time, plus a conservative margin, at the planned depth.

Your app probably won't exactly match your dive computer, but it will give you a good estimate. Be sure to scroll your computer's no stop times before diving to confirm you have the time you want.

Using Tables

You can also use the RDP Table or eRDPML to find minimum surface intervals with your computer. Again, don't expect the times to exactly match your dive computer, but you will get a good estimate, and scroll your computer's no stop times before diving. Also, if the first dive was a multilevel dive, you may not be able to use the RDP Table to get a good estimate because you have to use a single depth. The eRDPML is generally more useful, but you need to track your depth levels and times to do this.

The steps for finding a minimum surface interval are in the Instructions for Use included with the RDP Table and eRDPML. Your PADI Instructor can also help you.

Exercise 5-1

1. I would find a minimum surface interval when, after a dive, I want to know how long the _____ would be.
    - ☐ a. no stop time and depth for the next dive
    - ☐ b. time at the surface

2. One way to find a minimum surface interval with a computer is to periodically check the no stop times for the depth you want, between dives.
    - ☐ True   ☐ False

3. I can use the RDP Table or eRDPML to find the exact time my dive computer requires for a minimum surface interval.
    - ☐ True   ☐ False

    How did you?
    1. b. 2. True. 3. False. The RDP Table or eRDPML will give you a useful estimate of your computer's minimum surface interval, but it will probably not be exactly the same.

Flying After Diving and Altitude Diving

In Section Four, you learned that you need to keep the excess dissolved nitrogen in your body tissues within accepted limits. Failure to do so may allow the nitrogen to come out of solution and cause decompression sickness. The decompression models used in most dive computers and tables are based on surfacing from your dives and making your surface intervals at sea level.

Going to a higher altitude lowers the pressure around you at the surface. This means that dissolved nitrogen would come out of solution faster than at sea level. Going to altitude after diving is therefore a possible problem, because the lower pressure can increase the risk of DCS. If you will be flying after diving (or going to altitude by driving over a mountain pass, etc.), or diving at altitude (in a mountain lake), you follow special recommendations and procedures to account for the reduced pressure.

Flying after diving and altitude diving both involve altitude, but they differ and have different recommendations and procedures. When flying after diving (or ascending to altitude after diving), you start and end your dive at sea level (normal surface pressure), and then go to altitude (lower surface pressure). When altitude diving, you start and end your dive at altitude (lower surface pressure).

Flying After Diving Recommendations

Over the years, recommendations for flying after diving have changed. At this writing, the dive medical community's recommendations for flying after diving are:

For no stop dives:

- **Single dives (no repetitive dive)** – A minimum preflight surface interval of 12 hours is suggested.

- **Repetitive dives or multiday dives (diving every day for several days in a row)** – A minimum preflight surface interval of 18 hours is suggested.

Dives requiring emergency decompression stops:

- A minimum preflight surface interval greater than 18 hours is suggested.

These recommendations are based on a cabin altitude pressure range of 600-2400 metres/2000-8000 feet. While these guidelines represent the best estimate presently known for a conservative, safe surface interval before flying for the vast majority of divers, remember that no flying after diving recommendation can guarantee that decompression sickness will never occur. There always may be divers whose physiological makeups or special dive circumstances result in decompression sickness, even when following the recommendations.

As with other aspects of diving, you're responsible for your own dive safety and behavior. Flying after diving recommendations change as we learn more about how pressure changes affect the body, so follow the most current recommendations, which can be found in diver publications and websites including diversalertnetwork.org.

There are presently no recommendations for driving to altitude after diving, so the prudent practice is to be conservative. The longer the interval between diving and going to altitude, the lower the risk. In areas where driving to altitude is common, local divers may have a procedure they use. Some divers use the flying after diving recommendations for driving to altitude. While these practices appear to work for many divers, few (if any) have had formal testing. So, use them conservatively. If in doubt, take a longer surface interval before driving to altitude.

Altitude Diving

With most dive computers and dive tables (including the RDP Table and eRDPmL), you need to use altitude diving procedures if diving at an altitude of 300 metres/1000 feet or higher. Altitude diving procedures with dive computers may differ. Some automatically adjust, some have settings you use and others can't be used at altitude (see the manufacturer literature).

To use most tables (including the RDP Table and the eRDPmL) at altitude, you use a special table that converts your actual depth to a theoretical depth that adjusts for the pressure difference. If you're interested in altitude diving or will be diving at altitude locally, you can learn the procedures in the Altitude Adventure Dive in the Advanced Open Water Diver course, or PADI Altitude Diver course.

Going to a higher altitude lowers the pressure around you at the surface. This means that dissolved nitrogen would come out of solution faster than at sea level. This is a possible problem because the lower pressure can increase DCS risk.

Flying after diving and altitude diving have different recommendations and procedures. When flying after diving, you start and end your dive at sea level, and then go to altitude. When altitude diving, you start and end your dive at altitude.

1. Going to altitude after diving may be a problem because the
   - ☐ a. lower pressure can increase DCS risk.
   - ☐ b. higher pressure can increase DCS risk.
   - ☐ c. lower pressure can increase oxygen problems.
   - ☐ d. higher pressure can increase oxygen problems.

2. The difference between flying after diving and altitude diving is that when flying after diving, I go to altitude after a dive, and in altitude diving, I begin and end a dive at altitude.
   - ☐ True   ☐ False

3. My buddy and I have made two no stop dives a day for the last two days. Based on current recommendations, we should wait at least _____ after our last dive before flying.
   - ☐ a. 6 hours
   - ☐ b. 12 hours
   - ☐ c. 18 hours
   - ☐ d. 24 hours

4. Flying after diving recommendations may change over time, so I should check online and print sources to keep up with and follow the most current ones.
   - ☐ True   ☐ False

5. When diving at an altitude of _____ or higher, I need to use altitude diving procedures.
   - ☐ a. 150 metres/500 feet
   - ☐ b. 300 metres/1000 feet
   - ☐ c. 450 metres/1500 feet
   - ☐ d. 600 metres/2000 feet

How did you do?
1. a. 2. True. 3. c. 4. True. 5. b.

LEARNING OBJECTIVES

By the end of this section, I should be able to answer these questions:

1. Why are being cold and/or exerting myself strenuously issues with respect to decompression sickness risk?

2. What should I do if I am cold or exert myself strenuously on a dive?

Cold and/or Strenuous Dives

You've already learned that you need to avoid overexertion and hypothermia while diving. If you get cold or exercise a lot during a dive, you may end the dive with more dissolved nitrogen than calculated by your dive computer (or tables). This could increase your DCS risk.

If you are cold or exert yourself strenuously during a dive, be more conservative. Stay *well within* the no stop limits, being even more conservative than normal, having extra no stop dive time available throughout the dive. Some computers allow you to set them to be more conservative, though you usually have to do this before the dive. See your instructor or

the manufacturer literature on how to do this if possible with your unit.

With the RDP Table and the eRDPML, you plan cold/strenuous dives as though they are 4 metres/10 feet deeper than their actual depth. Safety stops are recommended at the end of all dives, but they're especially wise after a cold and/or strenuous dive.

Exercise 5-3

1. Cold and/or strenuous dives may be a problem with respect to DCS risk because
   - ☐ a. I may end the dives with more dissolved nitrogen than calculated by dive computer or tables.
   - ☐ b. it is easier to ascend too fast when I make a cold or strenuous dive.
   - ☐ c. cool water can shut down my computer.

2. If I'm cold or exert myself strenuously during a dive, I should
   - ☐ a. not make the safety stop.
   - ☐ b. be even more conservative.

3. Using the RDP Table or eRDPML, I should calculate a cold or strenuous dive as
   - ☐ a. 4 metres/10 feet shallower than the actual depth.
   - ☐ b. 4 metres/10 feet deeper than the actual depth.
   - ☐ c. having no surface interval.
   - ☐ d. requiring emergency decompression.

   How did you do?
   1. a. 2. b.   3. b.

◀ *If you get cold* or exercise a lot during a dive, you may end the dive with more dissolved nitrogen than calculated by your dive computer (or tables). This is could increase your DCS risk. In this case, stay *well within* the no stop limits, being even more conservative than normal.

By the end of this section, I should be able to answer these questions:

1. When do I need to make an emergency decompression stop?

2. How do I determine the depth(s) and time(s) of emergency decompression stop(s)?

3. What should I do if I surface from a dive without making a required emergency decompression stop?

Emergency Decompression Stops

In Section Four, you learned that if you exceed a no stop limit, you will have to make one or more *emergency decompression stops.* Unlike safety stops, emergency decompression stops are *required* so that you don't exceed accepted theoretical nitrogen levels. Safety stops *keep* you *well within* limits, whereas emergency decompression stops *return* you from *outside* limits.

In recreational diving, required emergency decompression stops are *emergency* situations only. They mean you either failed to monitor your dive computer (or timer and depth gauge), or something forced you to overstay your time at depth. Failure to monitor your instruments doesn't have to happen (it's your responsibility). Circumstances that keep you from starting your ascent are exceptionally rare.

In recreational diving, emergency decompression usually results in one required stop. More than one required decompression stop would be highly unlikely, but it could happen if a diver were to significantly exceed no stop limits.

section five

Emergency Decompression Stop Depths and Times

If you exceed your computer's no stop times, it will go into decompression mode. Decompression mode guides you by providing the depth of your emergency decompression stop and how long you have to stay there before you can ascend to the surface (or the next stop if there is more than one). Don't ascend above the stop depth. You may be slightly deeper, however.

Computers differ in how they display emergency decompression information. See the manufacturer literature for the details of yours. You can find the RDP Table and eRDPML emergency decompression procedures printed on each and in their Instructions for Use guides.

Missing a Required Decompression Stop

If you don't have enough air to complete an emergency decompression stop, stop as long as you can, but save enough air to surface and exit safely. This is an emergency, but *don't* run out of air underwater trying to make the stop.

If you didn't complete the entire emergency decompression stop (or accidentally skipped it altogether), after ascending, relax, breathe 100 percent emergency oxygen if available and monitor yourself for decompression sickness symptoms. Don't dive again for *at least* 24 hours. Many dive computers will go into an error mode and lock up, not allowing a dive for that long or longer.

1. If I go over a no stop limit, I
   - ☐ a. must surface at a very slow rate.
   - ☐ b. will have to make one or more emergency decompression stops.
2. The depths and times of emergency decompression stops are
   - ☐ a. given by my dive computer.
   - ☐ b. standardized as 6 metres/20 feet and 3 metres/10 feet for 3 minutes.
   - ☐ c. not important, as long as I make the stops.
3. If I surface without making an emergency decompression stop, I should get a fresh cylinder of air and then go back underwater to make the stop.
   - ☐ True   ☐ False

How did you do?
1. b. 2. a. 3. False. If you miss an emergency decompression stop, relax, breathe emergency oxygen and monitor yourself for DCS symptoms, and don't dive for at least 24 hours.

LEARNING OBJECTIVES

By the end of this section, I should be able to answer these questions:

1. What is meant by decompression illness?
2. What is the first aid for a diver with suspected decompression illness? What treatment is usually required?

First Aid and Treatment for Decompression Illness

Decompression Illness

Lung overexpansion injuries and decompression sickness can produce very similar signs and symptoms, even though they result from different causes. The first aid for both is the same, so you *don't* need to tell them apart. For simplicity in dealing with diver emergencies, therefore, the dive community uses the term decompression *illness* (DCI) for both lung overexpansion injuries and decompression sickness.

Helping a Diver with Suspected DCI

If a diver is suspected of having decompression illness, follow the steps you learned in Section Three:

- The diver should stop all diving.

- Check for breathing. Provide CPR as needed.

- Contact emergency medical care. Some areas have diver emergency services for consultation and to coordinate with local medical services.

- Keep the diver lying down and provide emergency oxygen.

- Monitor the diver and take steps to prevent shock.

- If the diver is unresponsive but breathing normally, lay the diver level, left side down, head supported, breathing oxygen.

- Continue this care until emergency medical personnel arrive.

Almost all cases of decompression illness require treatment in a recompression chamber. Recompression puts the diver under pressure, which helps the body absorb the gas bubbles present. The pressure is then lowered very slowly over many hours.

Don't delay first aid and getting the diver to treatment. The faster treatment begins, the lower the risk of permanent residual symptoms. The PADI Rescue Diver and Emergency Oxygen Provider courses, and the Emergency First Response Primary and Secondary Care courses, are recommended for learning more about managing diver emergencies.

If you exceed your computer's no stop times, it will go into decompression mode. Decompression mode guides you by providing the depth of your emergency decompression stop and how long you have to stay there before you can ascend to the surface (or the next stop if there is more than one). **1** stop depth, **2** deco mode indicator, **3** stop time indicator.

Exercise 5-5

1. The term "decompression illness"
   - ☐ a. is another term for DCS.
   - ☐ b. refers to lung overexpansion injuries.
   - ☐ c. includes both lung overexpansion injuries and DCS.

2. Treatment for most cases of DCI requires _____.
   - ☐ a. recompression in a chamber.
   - ☐ b. long sleep.
   - ☐ c. putting the diver back underwater.

How did you do?
1. c. 2. a.

A PRUDENT MEASURE

Statistically, the incidence of DCI is very, very low. If you follow accepted, conservative diving practices and stay within your limits, the risk of DCI is also very low.

But the risk is not zero. The cost of recompression can be significant, and may not be entirely covered by normal medical insurance. In most areas, you can get diver accident insurance very inexpensively. This insurance is *highly* recommended if available for your area. Diver accident insurance:

- May reduce treatment delays caused by questions over who will pay for the treatment.

- Provides coverage for expenses that regular medical insurance often doesn't cover, such as air ambulance and recompression.

Your PADI dive shop can recommend a dive accident insurance provider for your area.

It's your responsibility not only to dive safely, but to be prepared if something happens. Diver accident insurance is simply too affordable not to have.

PADI EMERGENCY OXYGEN PROVIDER COURSE

Most countries and territories allow laypeople to give emergency oxygen to a diver with suspected DCI. However, some require or recommend special (nonprofessional) training in emergency oxygen administration.

The PADI Emergency Oxygen Provider course gives you specific training in the handling and use of typical emergency oxygen systems used in diving emergencies. It qualifies you to give emergency oxygen to divers with suspected DCI (and patients in other emergency situations). You complete the PADI Emergency Oxygen Provider course as a step toward PADI Rescue Diver, and you can take it immediately. Ask your PADI dive shop about how to enroll.

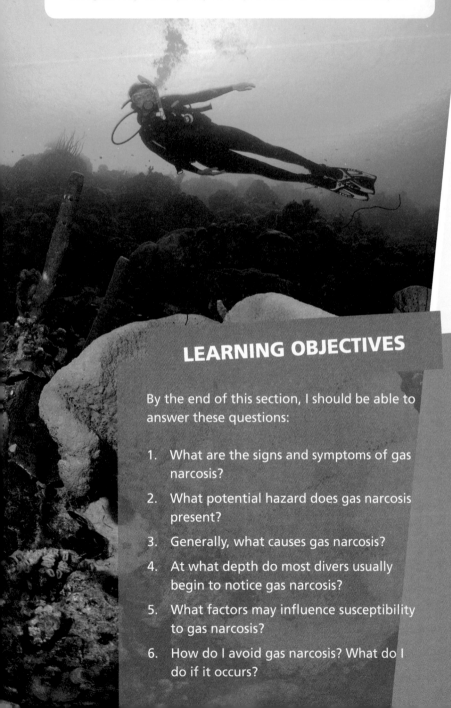

Breathing air or EANx, most divers begin to notice narcosis at approximately 30 metres/100 feet. Narcosis differs, however, from individual to individual and in the same diver from one dive to the next.

If you experience narcosis, immediately ascend to a shallower depth. Continue the dive at a shallower depth, or abort the dive. Narcosis generally fades quickly when you return to a shallower depth.

LEARNING OBJECTIVES

By the end of this section, I should be able to answer these questions:

1. What are the signs and symptoms of gas narcosis?

2. What potential hazard does gas narcosis present?

3. Generally, what causes gas narcosis?

4. At what depth do most divers usually begin to notice gas narcosis?

5. What factors may influence susceptibility to gas narcosis?

6. How do I avoid gas narcosis? What do I do if it occurs?

Being a Diver V

The Air You Breathe Continued – Gas Narcosis

Section Four discussed contaminated air, oxygen toxicity and decompression sickness. The fourth issue related to the component gases in air is *gas narcosis*.

Many gases, including oxygen and nitrogen, cause an intoxicating effect under pressure. This is called *gas narcosis*. Signs and symptoms may include:

- Feeling intoxicated (drunk or "high")
- Loss of coordination
- Slowed thinking
- Slowed reactions
- Inappropriate laughter
- Depression
- False sense of security
- Ignoring or disregard for safety
- Anxiety and/or panic (when under stress at depth)

Gas narcosis is not thought to be harmful itself. The hazard is that it impairs the good judgment, clear thinking and timely responses you need to avoid and manage problems underwater.

At one time, it was thought that narcosis was only caused by nitrogen, and it was common to call *gas* narcosis *nitrogen* narcosis. Today, it is known that oxygen is similarly narcotic (hence, EANx doesn't have a gas narcosis advantage). However, some gases – such as helium – are not narcotic, and tec divers breathe gas mixes with helium, which helps manage narcosis. This is beyond the scope of, and not necessary for, recreational diving.

Causes and Effects

Gas narcosis is thought to be caused by increased dissolved gases in body tissues slowing nerve impulses that travel in the brain and nervous system. It slows the communication between the brain and the body, and between different parts of the brain.

Breathing air (or EANx), most divers begin to notice narcosis at approximately 30 metres/100 feet. Narcosis differs, however, from individual to individual and in the same diver from one dive to the next. Being tired, dehydrated or generally fatigued may make narcosis noticeable shallower, and some prescription and over-the-counter drugs combine their effects with narcosis, making intoxication stronger (this is another reason why you don't use alcohol and certain drugs before diving).

Cool water, darkness and limited visibility seem to increase narcosis, though it may be that added stress simply makes the effects more noticeable. Diving experience seems to reduce narcosis – but physiologists think that you learn to compensate for it.

Avoiding and Managing Gas Narcosis

You avoid gas narcosis by not diving too deep. For most people, assuming no predisposing factors, gas narcosis isn't likely to be a concern diving as deep as 30 metres/100 feet (as a new PADI Open Water Diver, you're qualified to a maximum of 18 metres/60 feet). Recreational divers with further training and experience can qualify to dive as deep as 40 metres/130 feet (the maximum depth for recreational diving). One of the benefits of the PADI Deep Diver course is that you learn more about narcosis and are provided the opportunity to experience it under instructor supervision.

If you experience narcosis, immediately ascend to a shallower depth. Continue the dive at a shallower depth, or abort the dive. Narcosis generally fades quickly when you return to a shallower depth. If your buddy appears or acts "narked," guide your buddy to a shallower depth.

Exercise 5-6

1. Signs and symptoms of gas narcosis include (choose all that apply):
   ☐ a. discomfort in the ears and/or sinuses.
   ☐ b. loss of coordination.
   ☐ c. slowed thinking.
   ☐ d. ignoring or disregard for safety.

2. Gas narcosis is thought to be harmful itself.
   ☐ True
   ☐ False

3. Gas narcosis is thought to be caused by the increased amount of dissolved gases in body tissues slowing nerve impulses that travel in the brain and nervous system.
   ☐ True
   ☐ False

4. Most divers usually begin to notice gas narcosis at a depth of approximately _____.
   ☐ a. 18 metres/60 feet
   ☐ b. 30 metres/100 feet
   ☐ c. 40 metres/130 feet
   ☐ d. 50 metres/165 feet

5. Before a dive, I feel a bit tired. This may make narcosis
   ☐ a. noticeable at a shallower depth.
   ☐ b. unlikely within recreational depth limits.
   ☐ c. noticeable at a deeper depth.

6. If I am diving and begin to feel intoxicated, I should
   ☐ a. signal my buddy to stay close.
   ☐ b. stop my descent and go no deeper.
   ☐ c. breathe deeply until my head clears.
   ☐ d. signal my buddy to ascend to a shallower depth.

How did you do?
1. b, c, d. 2. False. Gas narcosis is not thought to be harmful itself. The hazard is that it impairs the good judgment, clear thinking and timely responses you need to avoid and manage problems underwater. 3. True. 4. b. 5. a. 6. d.

By the end of this section, I should be able to answer these questions:

1. What are five benefits of navigating underwater?

2. What four basic features does an underwater compass have? What is the purpose of each?

3. How should I hold a compass when navigating with it underwater?

4. How should I set a compass to navigate a straight line from one point to another? How should I set it to return along the same line (the reciprocal heading)?

5. How should I use an electronic compass to navigate?

The standard underwater compass has four basic features you use when navigating underwater: ❶ magnetic north needle, ❷ lubber line, ❸ bezel with index marks, and ❹ heading references.

1. It helps you plan your dive so you don't waste air trying to find the best parts of the dive site.

2. It allows you to avoid long surface swims by navigating to your ascent/exit point underwater.

3. It helps you take the shortest route to the boat or shore if you have a problem.

4. It lets you avoid certain areas if necessary, or stay within a certain area.

5. It reduces stress, because you know generally where you are at any point of the dive, and you can be less concerned about how far you are from your exit/ascent point, etc.

Finding Your Way

During your open water dives, you will learn and practice basic underwater navigation with a compass. Navigating underwater has at least five benefits:

Compass Features

In learning to use a compass, you'll either use a standard (analog) underwater compass, or an electronic compass (typically part of your dive computer). The standard underwater compass has four basic features you use when navigating underwater.

Magnetic north needle – This is a needle (or an arrow printed on a card) that can rotate so it always points to magnetic north (as long as the compass is level and not too close to something made of steel or iron). The north needle is the basis for compass navigation, because you know that it is always pointing in the same direction.

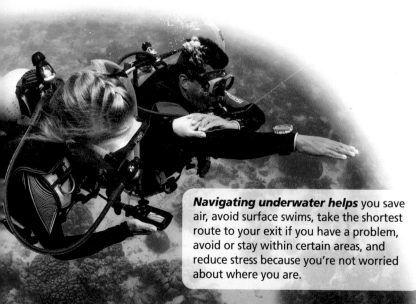

Navigating underwater helps you save air, avoid surface swims, take the shortest route to your exit if you have a problem, avoid or stay within certain areas, and reduce stress because you're not worried about where you are.

Compass navigation is simply determining direction relative to the north needle's known direction.

Lubber line – This is a straight line through the center of the compass face or along the side from the 6 o'clock to the 12 o'clock positions. The lubber line is always your direction of travel.

Bezel with index marks – The bezel rotates so you can align two, small parallel marks (index marks) over the north needle. This helps you maintain a straight line while swimming and navigating. Some compasses have two sets of index marks. The second set is 180° opposite the first. This lets you set a return (reciprocal) course without having to reset the compass.

Heading references – Most compasses have numbers to record your heading (your travel direction, measured in degrees from magnetic north). Some compasses have detailed markings (a mark every two degrees), whereas others may only have 0°, 90°, 180° and 270°. More detail gives you more precision; you may write down headings on your slate and in your dive log for reference when returning to and relocating a site.

Holding, Setting and Navigating with a Compass

Before discussing how to set your compass, let's look at how you hold it. Properly holding and positioning your compass is important for swimming in a straight line. If you don't hold your compass properly, you won't navigate accurately even if you set it correctly.

Hold your compass so it's relatively level (so the north needle can rotate) and so the lubber line is aligned with the centerline of your body. Wearing the compass on your wrist, hold the arm without the compass straight out. Hold it with your other hand near the elbow, putting the compass straight in front of you. With a console, hold the compass squarely in front of you with both hands.

With either method, lock your arms and look over the compass, not down on it. This allows you to watch where you're going while continuing to read it.

To set your compass and navigate a straight line from one point to another (typically, from where you are in a direction you want to go, or toward a known destination), follow these steps:

- Hold the compass as you just learned with the lubber line pointed in your desired travel direction.

- Let the north needle settle on magnetic north, then rotate the bezel until the index marks straddle the needle.

- Continuing to hold the compass properly, swim along the *lubber line* keeping the needle within the index marks. Remember that the lubber line is *always* your travel direction, regardless of which way the compass needle points.

- If you turn off course, the needle will drift outside the marks, cuing you to correct your direction. Don't move your arms. Turn your *body* to return to the correct course, then continue.

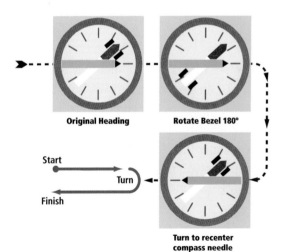

Original Heading **Rotate Bezel 180°**

Start
Turn
Finish

Turn to recenter compass needle

To set a reciprocal (return) heading, rotate the bezel to set the index marks 180 degrees from your original setting. Turn until the north needle is within the marks again; you will now be facing the way you came.

Typically, one buddy in the team navigates, while the other buddy(ies) maintains contact and watches the depth. Buddies continue to communicate as they do this, and not let themselves get so focused on navigation or depth that

Underwater navigation isn't difficult, but it is a skill you have to learn. Like many skills, you learn it faster with guidance followed by practice and application.

The PADI Underwater Navigator course builds upon your basic navigation skills. In the course, you learn to use natural navigation (navigating based on what you see) and compass navigation together, as well as patterns to return to your start point.

You also learn to find your way back to a spot so you can revisit favorite places or find something you dropped

You can enroll in the PADI Underwater Navigator course as a newly certified PADI Open Water Diver, and the first dive of the course credits (at your instructor's discretion) toward your PADI Advanced Open Water Diver certification.

they don't pay attention to each other.

To set a *reciprocal* (return) heading so you go back along the same line, rotate the bezel to set the index marks 180 degrees from your original setting. Turn until the north needle is within the marks again; you will then be facing the way you came. As mentioned, some compasses have two sets of index marks directly opposite each other. If yours does, don't move the bezel. Simply turn until the north needle is within the other (reciprocal) index marks.

Electronic Compass

Your dive computer may have an electronic compass built in, but not all computers do. Electronic compasses differ in how they show direction and how you read them. Check the manufacturer literature or ask your instructor for help for specifics if your computer is equipped with one.

With most electronic compasses, hold the compass as previously described and face your desired travel direction. The compass shows you the heading as a number (0 degrees to 359 degrees). Hold the compass squarely in front of you as you swim, keeping the same heading showing. If the number changes, you're turning off course. Stop and turn until you're back on your heading.

To set a reciprocal course, if your original heading is 179 degrees or less, add 180 degrees to find the reciprocal heading. For 180 degrees or more, subtract 180 degrees. This gives you the degree number for the return heading. Some electronic compasses have other functions for assisting with navigation.

Tip: "Round" degree headings (e.g., 160, 170, 180, etc.) are often close enough for general navigation in moderate to good visibility. This makes it easier to add or subtract 180° mentally. But use the precise heading for the most precise navigation, which you may need when looking for a specific dive site or when navigating in low visibility.

Exercise 5-7

1. Underwater navigation helps me save air and can help me get to an exit point the shortest way if I have a problem.
   ☐ True   ☐ False

2. The _____ is/are always my direction of travel when navigating with a compass.
   ☐ a. north needle
   ☐ b. lubber line
   ☐ c. bezel with index marks
   ☐ d. heading references

3. I should hold my compass so the _____ is/are aligned with the centerline of my body.
   ☐ a. north needle
   ☐ b. lubber line
   ☐ c. bezel with index marks
   ☐ d. heading references

4. As I swim while navigating with a compass, I should keep the _____ within the index marks.
   ☐ a. north needle
   ☐ b. lubber line
   ☐ c. bezel
   ☐ d. heading references

5. With most electronic compasses, to navigate in a straight line, I swim with the same degree heading showing.
   ☐ True   ☐ False

How did you do?
1. True. 2. b. 3. b. 4. a. 5. True

Continuing Your Adventure

It's important to consider how you grow as a diver after you're certified. People who plan and start their next steps while still in the PADI Open Water Diver course are more likely to continue as divers and get what they want out of diving. You also need to be aware of some responsibilities and limits you have as a certified diver.

Course Evaluation Questionnaire

One of the first things you may do after your certification as a PADI Open Water Diver is to fill out a Course Evaluation Questionnaire from a PADI Office. Completing this may be one of your first contributions to the dive community.

The questionnaire is a survey that allows PADI Offices to recognize outstanding performance by instructors, and to verify that your course included certain key training elements. It helps PADI maintain the quality of its diver education programs.

Please take a moment to answer the Course Evaluation Questionnaire when you're invited to do so. If you don't receive a questionnaire but would like to complete one, you can request one on padi.com/ceq/student/ceq-paper.htm.

Your Limits as an Open Water Diver

Throughout this course, you've learned about the limits recommended for you as a newly certified PADI Open Water Diver. Let's summarize some of them. You were trained to a maximum depth of 18 metres/60 feet (or the actual depth you reached, if shallower). With additional experience and training beyond the Open Water Diver course, the maximum depth for recreational diving is 40 metres/130 feet.

You're were also trained to dive in conditions as good as, or better than, those in which you trained, within the no stop limits of your dive computer or tables. You can enroll and participate in the PADI Advanced Open Water Diver course, Discover Local Diving program and many (but not all) PADI Specialty Diver courses to increase your skills and experience. Ultimately, it is your responsibility to set your limits for each dive based upon your assessment of your skills, comfort level and the dive conditions.

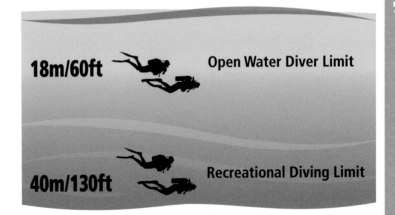

18m/60ft — Open Water Diver Limit

40m/130ft — Recreational Diving Limit

Staying Involved and Continuing Your Diver Education

Often, the biggest challenge new divers face is staying involved with diving after certification. You may already be thinking about this, and the dive community has found that three things consistently keep divers involved with diving:

1. Social settings that allow divers to meet other divers who become buddies.

2. Going different places to dive.

3. Setting training goals and continuing to dive by continuing their diver education.

These aren't surprising, because interacting with other divers, going diving and increasing your diving opportunities are the heart of the dive experience and lifestyle.

Meeting and making friends with people who dive.

Divers everywhere connect with each other routinely through local dive centers and resorts, and the internet. Here are some suggestions:

Meeting and making friends with people who dive is a great way to keep involved with diving. Stay connected with your PADI Dive Center and Resort, and online with ScubaEarth®.

- Stay connected with your PADI Dive Center or Resort; it's the social hub for divers in your area.

- Exchange emails and phone numbers with people you meet on dive trips and in different courses, including this course.

- Join your dive operation's club and attend social events. Participate with specialized dive groups that focus on your passion, like underwater photography or wreck diving. Clubs and events welcome new divers as enthusiastically as experienced ones – don't be intimidated because you're new to diving.

- Take part in group dive travel.

- Meet new divers and make new friends at ScubaEarth®.

- You can also meet new divers at other social sites like Facebook and Google+.

- Attend events like dive shows and underwater film festivals.

- Bring your nondiving friends to your dive operator and get them diving, too.

Going different places to go diving.
As a new diver, you may not be comfortable planning dive trips yourself. You don't have to. Your PADI Dive Center or Resort likely organizes local and distant guided dive outings and trips. Beyond this, virtually all dive clubs and many online social groups host dive outings in which you can participate, and often, your local PADI Dive Center or Resort is part of hosting or promoting them as well.

With experience, you may want to start planning more individualized diving (for you and a spouse or a couple of friends who are certified divers, etc.). Your dive operator can help you arrange this type of outing as well.

SCUBAEARTH

THE SOCIAL SITE FOR DIVERS: SCUBAEARTH®

Want to make new diver friends and get hooked up with your local PADI Dive Center or Resort? You don't even have to get out of your chair – log on to scubaearth.com and join diving's top, fastest-growing social website. ScubaEarth® is your online home for meeting other divers and professionals from around the world, getting the latest scoop on dive site conditions and sharing information.

Join ScubaEarth® for free and start interacting with divers near and far today. It's a great first step toward staying active as a diver after you complete the PADI Open Water Diver course.

Continuing your diver education. This keeps you involved with diving, because it opens new opportunities for growth as a diver, lets you gain experience under supervision, and lets you try out specialized equipment that may interest you. It increases your qualifications, making it possible to participate in new environments and/or activities. Set goals about what you want to accomplish as a diver. If you think you'd like to be an instructor, it's not too early to start on that path. Having training goals makes each course a step toward what you want to accomplish as you increase your dive opportunities.

Most of your continued training is primarily guided open water diving, and many courses take only a couple of days to complete. You can begin all PADI core courses, and a growing number of other PADI programs and specialty diver courses, online at any time with PADI eLearning. Your PADI dive shop or Instructor may offer courses in connection with dive travel and social events, so they're also opportunities to visit new places and meet people who want to dive with you.

If you have not done so already, invest in your own gear. Besides social interactions, dive outings and diver education, it has also been found that divers who invest in a BCD, regulator and instruments package, and/or an

exposure suit, tend to be more active as divers. There are at least three reasons why:

- Having your own equipment is part of the fun of diving, because it's the gear you prefer, adjusted and configured the way you like it.

- Divers who have their own equipment (beyond mask, fins and snorkel) dive more often, at least partly because it's more convenient and more enjoyable to use your own stuff.

- Having different types of gear opens more diving to you. For example, in climates with wide seasonal water temperature changes, divers who have both wet suits and dry suits have the longest dive seasons. Ask the pros at your PADI Dive Center and Resort for their expert guidance.

The PADI System of diver education is a systemized approach to learn more as a diver, but more broadly, it helps you to continue to enjoy diving. It does this by addressing your interests and by giving a clear path to reach your training goals, so that each course you take doesn't stand alone, but is a step toward what you want to accomplish. This is one of the main "secrets" of growing as a diver and enjoying diving, with social interaction and dive outings integrated. The PADI System is flexible to meet your interests, while providing the structure you need for wide ranging, valid training that helps you become the diver you want to be.

section five

Divers who have their own equipment (beyond mask, fins and snorkel) dive more often, at least partly because it's more convenient and more enjoyable to use your own gear.

Continuing your diver education keeps you involved with diving, because it opens new opportunities for growth as a diver, lets you gain experience under supervision, and lets you try out specialized equipment that may interest you.

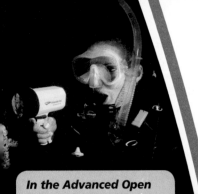

Refer to the PADI Continuing Education Flowchart (see Page 248) for a graphic view of your training options and paths. Ask your PADI Instructor, Dive Center or Resort about the schedules for the courses that interest you. Visit padi.com regularly for updates and additions to the PADI System.

PADI Advanced Open Water Diver. The PADI Advanced Open Water Diver is typically a two-day (usually over a weekend or on holiday) course that develops your open water skills, and it's intended for newly certified PADI Open Water Divers. It includes an introduction to deep diving, more advanced underwater navigation and three Adventure Dives that you and your instructor choose together.

Adventure Dives let you try out different underwater activities including underwater photography, night diving, wreck diving, search and recovery, altitude diving, boat diving, drift diving, dry suit diving, fish identification and more. Adventure Dives can credit toward the related specialty course.

In the Advanced Open Water Diver course, you try out different underwater activities. Adventure Dives credit toward the related specialty course.

After earning your Advanced Open Water Diver certification, you qualify to begin the PADI Rescue Diver course.

PADI Rescue Diver course. As you learned in Sections Three and Four, the PADI Rescue Diver course builds on the emergency prevention and management skills you master in the PADI Open Water Diver course. You practice adapting rescue techniques to your personal characteristics, and learn to coordinate with other divers working together to handle problems. Although the subject is serious, many divers name the PADI Rescue Diver course as one of the most rewarding challenges on their training goal path.

PADI Specialty Diver Courses and Master Scuba Diver. PADI Specialty Diver courses qualify you in the same activities covered by the Adventure Dives, and many more. Most have two to four dives; you can complete most of them in a couple of days.

The certifications you earn in specialties like PADI Enriched Air Diver and Cavern Diver are required, for safety reasons, by the dive community to participate in those activities.

The certifications you earn in specialties like PADI Enriched Air Diver and Cavern Diver are required, for safety reasons, by the dive community to participate in those activities. Certification in other specialties, like Digital Underwater Photographer, is not required for participation, but these courses allow you to get up to speed enjoying such activities more quickly.

Earn five PADI Specialty Diver certifications, the PADI Advanced Open Water Diver certification and the PADI Rescue Diver certification, and have 50 dives logged, to qualify as a PADI Master Scuba Diver – the highest nonprofessional rating in recreational diving.

ReActivate. As you learned earlier, if you are away from diving for a while, the ReActivate program is available to refresh your knowledge and skills under instructor guidance.

The ReActivate program is available to refresh your knowledge and skills.

Emergency First Response Courses. Sections Three and Four mentioned the Emergency First Response Primary and Secondary Care courses. These aren't specifically diver courses, but CPR and first aid training that follows the same protocols used (at a lay level) by emergency medical personnel. These are good skills to have, and you need them for Rescue Diver.

PADI Rebreather Diver. PADI Rebreather Diver teaches you to use Type R (recreational) rebreathers – scuba equipment that recycles your breathing gas – for recreational, no stop diving. This differs from the conventional open-circuit scuba you learn as a beginning diver.

Rebreather diving is growing in popularity, especially among underwater photographers and nature enthusiasts. Rebreathers are very quiet (you can get closer to fish than with open-circuit scuba and its bubbles) and offer longer dives than conventional scuba, but there are important considerations in using them. You need to complete the PADI Enriched Air Diver course before enrolling in PADI Rebreather Diver (you breathe enriched air with a rebreather).

Going Pro. A surprising number of new divers know *immediately* that they want to become dive professionals, going perhaps all the way to PADI Open Water Scuba Instructor. If you're one of them, see your dive shop or instructor about the PADI Divemaster course (you qualify to begin the course as a PADI Rescue Diver with 40 logged

dives and Emergency First Response training) and the PADI Instructor Development Course and Examination.

This discussion just barely touches on everything the PADI System offers. For more detail, ask your PADI Dive Center or Resort, and visit padi.com.

▶ To view the entire selection of courses available to you, see the PADI Continuing Education Flowchart on page 248. ◀

Exercise 5-8

1. The Course Evaluation Questionnaire helps to maintain the quality of PADI courses and to recognize instructors for outstanding performance.
   ☐ True   ☐ False

2. As a new PADI Open Water Diver, I was trained to a maximum depth of _____ (or the actual depth I reached, if shallower).
   ☐ a. 10 metres/30 feet
   ☐ b. 12 metres/40 feet
   ☐ c. 15 metres/50 feet
   ☐ d. 18 metres/60 feet

3. Generally, the purpose of the PADI System of diver education is to help me continue to enjoy diving.
   ☐ True   ☐ False

How did you do?
1. True. 2. d. 3. True

section five

PADI Rebreather Diver teaches you to use Type R (recreational) rebreathers – scuba equipment that recycles your breathing gas – for recreational, no stop diving.

A surprising number of new divers know immediately that they want to become professionals, perhaps going all the way to PADI Open Water Scuba Instructor. If you're one of them, see your dive operator or instructor about becoming a PADI Professional.

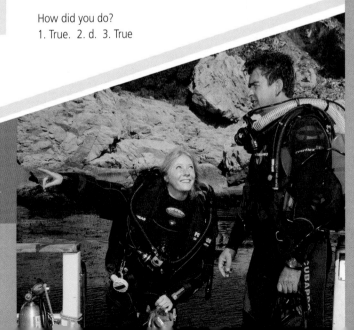

It's very rare to actually need to remove and replace your scuba kit underwater, but you practice this skill for situations such as needing to untangle yourself. Remove it from your left arm first, then stand it on your raised right knee. When you replace it, start with your right arm.

Your Skills as a Diver V

Let's look at more skills you'll learn during this course. Your instructor may demonstrate a method that differs from what you learn here.

Remove and Replace the Scuba Kit Underwater

It's very rare to actually need to remove and replace your scuba kit underwater, but you practice this skill for situations such as needing to untangle yourself. You may also choose to do this to adjust your equipment. The following describes a common technique, but your instructor may show you others.

- This is one of the few skills in which it may be important to be negatively buoyant, so you could kneel on the bottom if necessary.

- In open water, if possible, do this on insensitive bottom away from fragile aquatic life. If dealing with entanglement or another safety situation, however, you probably have no choice about where you do it.

- With a weight-integrated BCD with a small or moderate amount of weight, or using a BCD without integrated weights, completely deflate your BCD and kneel on the bottom with your left knee down and your right knee up. If you have a lot of weight (while wearing a dry suit, for example), you may want enough air in the BCD so that it is not too negative to handle once you remove it.

- Remove the BCD starting with your *left* arm, so the regulator stays in your mouth.

- Keep the kit upright and do not let go of it. Stand it on your right knee. You may keep your right arm partially through the harness for control.

- To keep stable on the bottom with weight-integrated BCDs, keep the unit close and positioned so that you don't float away from it. Keeping it on your knee is one effective way to do this.

- Start with the right arm when you put it back on, so the regulator stays in your mouth.

- Before fastening the straps, check to be sure you won't trap any hoses or accessories.

Remove and Replace Weight System Underwater

The main reasons for removing and replacing your weight system underwater are to make trim adjustments, to remove weight you can retrieve later, to replace a dislodged weight pouch or to untwist a weight belt.

- This is the other skill in which it often helps to be negatively buoyant (again, on insensitive bottom), though it may not be necessary, depending upon your weight system and the amount of weight you're wearing.

- Deflate your BCD and kneel.

- Remove the weight pocket and rest it on your knee. If using a weight belt, release it and pull it from behind your back with the buckle (left side) free, and drape it over your knee. Resting the weight on your knee helps you keep your balance.

- Your instructor will show you the technique(s) suited to your kit.

Descents and Ascents Without Reference

In open water, you may have to descend and/or ascend without anything you can see or touch for reference. To practice these in confined water, you may have to focus on your buddy(ies) and dive computer and ignore what you see around you.

- When descending, watch your computer and control your descent rate with your BCD.

- Stay close to your buddy.

- Equalize regularly as you descend.

- Control your buoyancy. Slow descents and ascents are easier to control.

- When ascending, watch your computer and be sure you ascend within its ascent rate.

- When you ascend, make a safety stop by hovering in midwater at 5 metres/15 feet. Practice this about half way to the surface in confined water.

- If you need to navigate while descending and/or ascending, one buddy navigates while the other controls the depth and the descent/ascent rate.

Minidive

Minidives let you practice an actual dive's steps, from beginning to end, much as you would in open water, under instructor supervision.

Minidives include:

- Dive planning, including SPG pressures and time for ending the dives

- Predive safety checks

  - Use the PADI Skill Practice and Dive Planning Slate for dive planning and the predive safety check

- Entry

- Five point descents

- Neutral buoyancy practice

- Practicing skills with your buddy(ies)

- Air supply awareness and management

- Ending the dives based on SPG pressure or time

- Five point ascents

- Exits from water

To make minidives more realistic, your instructor will assign certain areas as "sensitive bottom," or use objects (such as weights or toys) to simulate fragile organisms. Avoid contact with these just as you would on an open water dive.

During the dive, your instructor will indicate (verbally, with signals or written on a slate) simulated emergencies or skills to practice without prior notice. Follow the procedures for these you've learned, and as briefed by your instructor. Respond to simulated out of air with an alternate air source ascent. Do not make a Controlled Emergency Swimming Ascent. Your instructor may have specific instructions about what skills to practice, and when – listen closely to these directions and follow them with your buddy.

Depending upon time and logistics, your instructor may include some games or other dive objectives. These may include buoyancy challenges, playing "catch" with toys, taking pictures, etc. Such activities are fun and teach you to enjoy what you're doing while applying your scuba skills, paying attention to your air supply and other limits, and maintaining buddy contact – just like when open water diving.

When you reach the planned time or someone in your buddy team reaches a turn point, make a five point ascent. Stop at about half way to the surface, establish neutral buoyancy, and practice a safety stop. Finish your ascent after the stop. At the surface, establish positive buoyancy and exit the water as you planned.

The main reason for removing and replacing your weight system underwater is to make trim adjustments, to remove weight you can retrieve later, to replace a dislodged weight pouch or to untwist a weight belt.

Confined Water Dive Five

- ☐ Briefing
- ☐ Equipment assembly, dive planning, gearing up and pre-dive safety check
- ☐ Entry
- ☐ Weight and trim check and adjustment
- ☐ Five point descent without reference
- ☐ Remove and replace scuba kit underwater
- ☐ Remove and replace weight system underwater
- ☐ Minidive
- ☐ Dive planning, entry
- ☐ Weight check and neutral buoyancy practice
- ☐ Avoiding simulated sensitive zone or objects
- ☐ Simulated emergencies, skill practice, games/objectives
- ☐ Five point ascent without reference
- ☐ Exit
- ☐ Debrief

Note: Your instructor *may modify this to some extent to meet class and logistical requirements.*

To practice descents and ascents without a reference in confined water, you may have to focus on your buddy(ies) and dive computer and ignore what you see around you.

Open Water Dive Three

- ☐ Briefing and dive planning
- ☐ Assemble, put on and adjust equipment
- ☐ Predive safety check
- ☐ Entry
- ☐ Weight and trim check, adjustment
- ☐ Controlled five point descent with visual reference
- ☐ Buoyancy control – establish neutral buoyancy with oral BCD inflation and hover
- ☐ Remove, replace and clear mask
- ☐ Underwater exploration
- ☐ Exit
- ☐ Debrief and log dive
- ☐ Post dive equipment care

Note: Your instructor *may modify this to some extent to meet class and logistical requirements.*

Open Water Dive Four

- ☐ Briefing and dive planning
- ☐ Assemble, put on and adjust equipment
- ☐ Predive safety check
- ☐ Entry
- ☐ Weight and trim check, adjustment
- ☐ Five point free descent without reference
- ☐ Underwater exploration
- ☐ Ascent with safety stop
- ☐ Exit
- ☐ Debrief and log dive
- ☐ Post dive equipment care

Note: Your instructor *may modify this to some extent to meet class and logistical requirements.*

Knowledge Review Five

Some questions may have more than one correct answer.
Choose all that apply.

1. My buddy and I have just finished a dive to 15 metres/50 feet for 60 minutes. We want to return to the same site and depth and stay another 60 minutes. We can _____ to see about how long we have to remain at the surface to have enough no stop time.
   - ☐ a. wait and check our no stop times on our computers periodically
   - ☐ b. use the dive computer plan mode, if our computers have them,
   - ☐ c. use a dive planning app
   - ☐ d. check the RDP Table or eRDPmL

2. Going to altitude after diving may be a problem because
   - ☐ a. dive computers read too deep at altitude.
   - ☐ b. oxygen toxicity problems result from the thinner air.
   - ☐ c. most decompression models are based on surfacing at sea level.

3. I've just finished a single no stop dive with my buddy. We have not been diving in the past several days, and this is the only dive we make. Based on current recommendations, the minimum surface interval before we fly is
   - ☐ a. 6 hours.
   - ☐ b. 12 hours.
   - ☐ c. 18 hours.
   - ☐ d. 24 hours.

4. I need to use special altitude diving procedures when diving at an altitude greater than
   - ☐ a. 150 metres/500 feet.
   - ☐ b. 300 metres/1000 feet.
   - ☐ c. 600 metres/2000 feet.
   - ☐ d. 3000 metres/10,000 feet.

5. If I am cold or exercise a lot during a dive, I may surface with more nitrogen than calculated by my dive computer or dive tables.
   - ☐ True
   - ☐ False

6. At the end of a dive, my dive buddy's foot gets tangled in an abandoned fishing net. It takes five minutes to get free, but that delays our ascent making us exceed our no stop limit. This means that before we surface, we will have to make a(n) _____ stop to return our nitrogen level from outside the accepted limits.
   - ☐ a. safety
   - ☐ b. emergency decompression

7. On a dive boat, after coming aboard two divers discover they accidentally surfaced without making an emergency decompression stop. They should _____, and not dive for at least 24 hours.
   - ☐ a. re-enter the water and make the stops
   - ☐ b. exercise and drink fluids
   - ☐ c. relax, breathe oxygen and check themselves for DCS symptoms

8. In an emergency decompression situation, I find I won't have enough air to complete all the required stop time. I should
   - ☐ a. stay at the stop until out of air, then make a Controlled Emergency Swimming Ascent.
   - ☐ b. surface immediately and not make the stop at all.
   - ☐ c. stop as long as I can, but save enough air to surface and exit safely.

9. To help a diver with suspected decompression illness, I should
   - ☐ a. monitor the diver's breathing and provide CPR as necessary.
   - ☐ b. contact emergency medical care.
   - ☐ c. have the diver sit or stand as much as possible.
   - ☐ d. provide emergency oxygen.

10. Nearly all cases of decompression illness require treatment
    - ☐ a. in the water.
    - ☐ b. in a recompression chamber.
    - ☐ c. with bubble-dissolving drugs.

11. During a dive, I feel I'm having trouble thinking clearly. I should
    - ☐ a. carefully continue.
    - ☐ b. signal my buddy and ascend to a shallower depth.

12. On a standard underwater compass, the magnetic north needle
    - ☐ a. points to magnetic north.
    - ☐ b. indicates my travel direction.
    - ☐ c. points south on a reciprocal course.
    - ☐ d. is absent.

13. My buddy and I want to travel in a straight line using a compass, I should point the _____ in our desired travel direction, then rotate the _____ until the _____ is/are over the _____.
    - ☐ a. lubber line, magnetic north needle, heading references
    - ☐ b. magnetic north needle, bezel, index marks, lubber line
    - ☐ c. heading references, bezel, lubber line, magnetic north needle
    - ☐ d. lubber line, bezel, index marks, magnetic north needle

14. As a PADI Open Water Diver, I have been trained to a maximum depth of _____ (or the actual depth I reached, if shallower).
    - ☐ a. 12 metres/40 feet
    - ☐ b. 18 metres/60 feet
    - ☐ c. 24 metres/80 feet
    - ☐ d. 30 metres/100 feet

Student Diver Statement: I've completed this Knowledge Review to the best of my ability and any questions I answered incorrectly or incompletely, I have had explained to me and I understand what I missed.

Name_____ Date_____

index

index

Continue Your
ADVENTURE
Today!

Course Director

▲

Master Instructor

▲

IDC Staff Instructor

▲

Master Scuba Diver Trainer

▲

Specialty Instructor

▲

Open Water Scuba Instructor
———
Assistant Instructor

Emergency First Response® Instructor Trainer

▲

Emergency First Response® Instructor

▲

Emergency First Response® Provider

Master Scuba Diver™

▲

Rescue Diver ▶ **Divemaster** ▶

Advanced Open Water Diver
———
Adventure Diver
▼Eligible Specialty

ReActivate®

DIVER SPECIALTIES

Advanced Rebreather Diver	Ice Diver
	Search and Recovery Diver
Cavern Diver	Semiclosed Rebreather - Dolphin/Atlantis
Deep Diver▼	Wreck Diver▼

Open Water Diver
———
Scuba Diver
*Eligible Specialty

DIVER SPECIALTIES

Altitude Diver	Diver Propulsion Vehicle Diver	Rebreather Diver
AWARE - Fish Identification	Drift Diver	Sidemount
AWARE Shark Conservation	Dry Suit Diver	Underwater Naturalist
Boat Diver	Enriched Air Diver	Underwater Navigator
Digital Underwater Photographer	Equipment Specialist*	Underwater Photographer
	Multilevel Diver	Underwater Videographer
	Night Diver	
	Peak Performance Buoyancy	

Seal Team
———
Bubblemaker
———
Discover Scuba Diving
———
Skin Diver

NON-DIVER SPECIALTIES

AWARE - Coral Reef Conservation
Project AWARE Specialist
Emergency Oxygen Provider
Digital Underwater Photographer
(for Snorkelers)

Discover Snorkeling